Divergent Trends in Indian Fiction in English

Divergent Trends in

Indian Fiction in English

Edited by

K.K. Khurana

Prestige

an international publishing house

Published by
Prestige Books
3/28, East Patel Nagar
New Delhi 110 008
Ph. 9818755529
Email: prestigebooks@gmail.com
Website: www.asiabookclub.com
ISBN: 81-7551-180-X

Printed at Chaman Offset Press, New Delhi 110 002

Contents

Preface

The present book *Divergent Trends in Indian Fiction in English* has emerged from the papers presented at the two-day U.G.C.-sponsored National Seminar organized by P.G. Department of English, D.A.V College, Ambala City. More than twenty articles have been selected for this publication based on the diverse trends shown in various ways—from homo-eroticism to identity crisis, from quest for identity to colonial consciousness, as also on other subjects including caste-related issues and gender problems, feminism and commitment problems, their decisive understanding and their preaching from the pulpit, the portrayal of their sentiments attached to the sacred Ganga and, above all, the wit and humour in Indian life and Indian fiction in English. All these articles give a multi-dimensional view of the Indian writing in English.

The book has been divided into eight sections. The first section deals with trend-defying novels and homo-eroticism in the Indian fiction in English. The second section deals with new themes and perspectives, the third with identity crisis or quest for identity. The fourth section discusses feminism and issues related to women. The fifth section deals with the relationship of literature and sociology, detachment and commitment. The sixth section offers papers related to gender, caste and colour. This is followed by a section that deals with broader themes in various novels. The last section deals with the future of the novel in India and elsewhere. The collection on the whole is fairly representative of the major trends in Indian writing in English.

The proliferation of novel in Indian English manifests itself multifariously encompassing almost every aspect of Indian social life. In the last one hundred years or so, this staggering branch of literature has blossomed like a fragrant flower and has become golden gate for the world to see India through. This literary explosion or renaissance has not been quite evolutionary but, in recent years, it has caused a boom in the realm of Indian fiction writing. Fruitful discussions, perceptive inquiries and valuable critical comments have been offered to accredit it with a more elevated stature than what it enjoyed earlier.

I cannot close these prefatory remarks without thanking those who helped me in the preparation of the present project. I wish to place on record my gratefulness for the valuable suggestions, continuous help and cooperation of our worthy Principal Shri J.S. Nain who has been a guiding star right from the initial hiccups of organizing the seminar and later tabulating the articles in the form of a book. This gesture of his will certainly help in promoting a spirit of research among the aspiring scholars and improve their academic acumen.

Among my many obligations, I want especially to mention my indebtedness to Dr. S.K. Sharma, Chairman, Department of English, KUK; Dr. R.K. Srivastava, Professor Emeritus and Director, Institute of Languages, Bundelkhand; Dr. Manjit Inder Singh, Chairman, Department of English, Panjabi University, Patiala; Dr. M.K. Bhatnagar, Chairman, Department of English, M.D.U., Rohtak; Dr. S.K. Bhatia, Director, Academic Staff College, GNDU, Amritsar; Dr. Gurupdesh Singh, Department of English, GNDU, Amritsar; Dr. Kumkum Bajaj, Director, Correspondence Courses, Panjabi University, Patiala, Dr. R.K. Dhawan, University of Delhi, and above all Shri D.R. Gupta, Director, DAV College Managing Committee, New Delhi.

My faculty colleagues, in particular, Professors Salit Dosaj, Sangeeta Behl, D.P. Sharma, Reema Rattan, Jyoti Sekri, Himani Sharma and Sonika Sethi have been constant sources of encouragement and they with their analytical and decisive approach, genuine and passionate flair, rational judgement and ready wit, kept the spark of compiling this book burning alive. I owe my sincere gratitude to all contributors, without whose generous help this book could not have seen the light of the day. I am also thankful to my publishers, Prestige Books, New Delhi, for producing this book elegantly and expeditiously.

My special thanks are due to my wife Asha Khurana, lecturer in English, MDSD Girls College, Ambala City. I appreciate her critical reading of this book for she took great pains in editing some of the articles and suggesting significant improvements in raising the level of the volume. I am also indebted to my learned father Shri M.L. Khurana and devoted mother Smt. Mohan Kumari and my loving children Prerna and Harshit for their unfailing support and cooperation. My friend Dr. R.K. Dhawan of Delhi University deserves my special thanks for his help, encouragement and support during the preparation of this book. Last but not the least, I owe thanks to all my friends and well-wishers who extended their moral support while I was at work on this book.

K.K. KHURANA

Head, Department of English
D.A.V. College, Ambala City
31 March 2006

Introduction: Divergent Trends in Indian Fiction in English

K.K. KHURANA

Indian fiction in English has emerged as a separate entity for the study of the rapid change and development in social, economic political and psychological facets of Indian society. "To judge rightly an author," wrote Samuel Johnson once, "we must transport ourselves to his time and examine what were the wants of his contemporaries and what were his means of supplying them." In the case of Indian novelists in English, it is not difficult for us to comprehend their view of life.

The seminal idea of the book is to examine divergent trends in Indian fiction in order to provide new perspectives on the various aspects of this genre. More than a century old Indian novel in English has faithfully recorded the challenges and confrontation of values and the process of transition and transformation going on in the Indian society. In particular, a large number of novels have been written underlining the essential dignity of man in the changing scenario and there is a strong ideational affinity of these works with the best in world literature. This creative output is of a sublime nature which can be favourably compared with the best creative work in the Western hemisphere. Hence this particular phenomenon needs to be critically investigated and evaluated.

In the century-old modern Indian novel in English, the novelists have looked to our past, imbibed its rich experience and looked ahead to the future of this genre in the 21st century. The literary stature of Indian novel in English has steadily grown with each successive work of fiction. Indisputably, it has achieved worldwide recognition as a significant genre. It has been read with deep interest and has elicited wide critical acclaim both at the national and international level. The novels of the 1930s reflected the progressive philosophy of the writers. They were vocal about injustice, cruelty and exploitation that the masses faced. Mulk Raj Anand's *Untouchable* (1935), *Coolie* (1936) and *Two Leaves and a Bud* (1938) took the creative imagination from historical romances to social realism and Gandhian idealism. G.V. Desani's *All about H. Hatterr* (1948) took it further to the psychological probings into individual personality.

The Fifties was a period of socially conscious novels such as Kamala Markandaya's *Nectar in a Sieve* (1954), K.A. Abbas's *Inquilab* (1955) and R.K. Narayan's *The Guide* (1958) which were imbued with didactic rumblings in the agonized psyche of the characters. Nayantara Sahgal's *A Time to be Happy* (1958) traced the development of nationalist movement and the contrast offered by the old devoted nationalists with young pragmatic mercenaries.

The Sixties showed the development of psychological novels which highlighted the Indian identity under the onslaught of the cultural influences of the west, while Manohar Malgonkar's *A Bend in the Ganges* (1964) was an attempt on the terrorist movement in India. Bhabani Bhattacharya's *Shadow from Ladakh* (1966) and R.K. Narayan's *The Vendor of Sweets* (1967) gave a perspective analysis of the historical process of social changes in India after Independence. Arun Joshi's *The Foreigner* (1968), on the other hand, rendered the alienation of Indian expatriates in the quagmire of inter-cultural flux.

The Seventies was a decade of the novelists' protest against the political tyranny and autocratic tendencies. An attempt was made to portray and project the scenario which was trying to stifle democracy and curb freedom. Political consciousness of the people was awakened by referring to the period of Emergency. The fictionalized world of the period was given due prominence so that the same sort of happenings may not take place again. A new lease of life with renewed pledges is promised through the fictional projection of the futuristic vision vis-à-vis socio-politico-economic situation in modern India.

The nineteen eighties was a fruitful period with Salman Rushdie getting the Booker Award for *Midnight's Children* and Vikram Seth stirring the Indian mind with the publication of *A Suitable Boy*. Alongside the richness, variety and abundance of ideas in the work of the old stalwarts, there existed a plethora of works by younger novelists illuminating the milky way of Indian fiction in English. It was an epoch-making and trend-setting era for Indian novel in English opening new vistas and showing possibilities of new avenues for fiction-writing.

The decade of the Nineties was the harbinger of more profitable business to the Western publishers and it gave a special niche to Vikram Seth, Shobha De, Amitav Ghosh, Upamanyu Chatterjee and they made quick bucks. The Western readers suffering from the angst of depression and melancholia needing some kind of diversion have turned to Indian novel in English for getting spiritual solace. Salman Rushdie's *Midnight's Children* and *Shame*, Shashi Tharoor's *The Great Indian Novel*, Rohinton Mistry's *Such a Long Journey* and Balraj Khanna's *A Nation of Fools* highlighted their divine propensities. Mistry was a runner up for Booker Award in 1991. Githa Hariharan too hit the buzzer with her novel *The Thousand Faces of Night*. Amitav Ghosh won acclaim for both his fiction and non-fiction.

A careful analysis of Vikram Seth's *The Golden Gate*, Rushdie's *Midnight's Children*, *Shame* and *The Satanic Verses*, Upamanyu Chatterjee's *The English August*, Amitav Ghosh's *The Circle of Reason* and *The Shadow Lines*, I. Allan Sealey's *Trotter-Nama*, Shashi Tharoor's *The Great Indian Novel*, P. Ranga Rao's *The Fowl Filcher* and *The Drunk Tantra*, Balraj Khanna's *A Nation of Fools* give us a variegated overview of religion, politics, history and mythology, feminism, family and man-woman relationship. More recently, the emphasis has shifted to mocking at our age-old saints and prophets, our martyrs and politicians, Gandhi and Nehru, our religion and the sacred sacrament of marriage.

Feminism has grown from Kamala Markandaya, Anita Desai, R.P. Jhabvala and Nayantara Sahgal to pave way for Shobha De, Shashi Deshpande, Nina Sibal, Anees Jung, Raji Narsimhan,

Bharati Mukherjee and others. These newer female voices have highlighted the interior landscape of the emancipated woman's sensibility and her psychological pragmatism.

This changing scenario in Indian fiction in English has witnessed change in tone, temperament and thought-content as a result of the novelist's newly acquired conviction and maturity. Modern woman has now acquired substance and an unconventional character and has paved way for a new dimension of the Indian novel in English. The novelists of today have begun to delineate the psychology of the characters and the complex environs which has greatly affected them. International marriages which were frowned upon earlier, have gained greater acceptance and have transformed the Indian young women, who are now falling unabashedly in love with foreigners. Their oddities and uniquenesses, vagaries and vanity, faith and fickleness still need to be rendered artistically in the changing scenario of Indian society.

Let us look at some of the recent novels and analyze their technique and themes in order to have a clear picture of the divergence and multiplicity of meaning in them. One of the most significant areas in this respect is the autobiographical novel. Many writers have portrayed their life through fictional mode. Some popular works in this area are Kamala Das's *My Story*, Amrita Pritam's *The Revenue Stamp* and the recently published Vikram Seth's *Two Lives*.

Many Indian novelists have based their fiction on the raw material of history. This is true in the case of novels like Shashi Tharoor's *The Great Indian Novel*, Chaman Nahal's *Azadi*, Khushwant Singh's *Train to Pakistan* and *Delhi*. Again, Salman Rushdie mingled history and fiction in his newly-released novel *Shalimar the Clown*. Set in the age of hyperbole and bloodshed, Rushdie's new work is inspired by Indian mythology, Los Angeles fakery and Hindu culture. The author follows the political assassination of ambassador Maximilian Ophuls, his killer and his daughter. The book details the transformation of a young Muslim boy from shy teenager to Islamic terrorist guided by a radical mullah. Says Rushdie: "One of my good fortunes as a writer is to have access to a lot of traditions—and not just inside western culture, high or low."

There is yet another category of novels with a focus on a particular city, viz. Mistry's *Such a Long Journey*, Anita Desai's *Baumgartner's Bombay* and Nayantara Sahgal's *A Situation in New Delhi*. In Suketu Mehta's first book *Maximum City: Bombay Lost & Found*, the city has finally found its restless chronicler. Mehta says: "I am happy in transit. My home can be any global city but it has to be a city." Mehta was 14 when he left Bombay. Twenty-one years later, he returned to Mumbai. The Bombay of his childhood was beautiful. But that was in the past. Mehta succeeds in recreating the city of Bombay. It's the city of dreams, the city of vice and the city run rife with the underworld. Mehta's keen eye tracks the life of a hit man, an encounter specialist, the neuroses in tinsel town and the poignancy in a cross-dresser's profession. Mehta shows readers the visceral Mumbai that lurked somewhere in the heart of the bustling megapolis. When he moved to New York, Mehta writes that he "missed Bombay like an organ of my body." On return visits, he finds "the terrain is littered with memory mines."

Yet another area of Indian fiction is growing interest in women's psychological and social issues. Many women writers like Manju Kapur, Anita Nair and Namita Gokhale have produced such fiction. A significant writer in this respect is Rupa Bajwa who has made a mark in the history of Indian fiction. Not only has her debut book *Sari Shop* been published in the U.K. but it has been longlisted for the prestigious Orange Prize as well. Moving out of Amritsar, Bajwa wanted to satisfy her creative urges. She travelled from one part of the country to another, trying to write and "carve out a space where there was none." The story of Ramchand, an employee at a sari shop in old Amritsar, started off as a short story, which stayed with her long after she was done. When she realized that there was no way she could forget it, she got down to writing it. And before she knew it, she had a novel in her hand. "I had no technical knowledge about the novel form but was sure-footed about my writing. Once the novel was done, I sent it to some friends, who in turn sent it to an agent. Till then, I didn't even know there was anything called a literary agent!" says the 27-year-old young author, who has been leading a nomadic life so far, eking out a living just enough to sustain herself.

Indian women settled abroad have depicted their diasporic experience in their novels. Women writers of Indian origin like Chitra Banerjee Divakaruni, Anita Rau Badami, Shauna Singh Baldwin and Meera Syal have published new fiction. Meera Syal's famous novel *Anita and Me* has been made into a successful film. Similarly Chitra Divakaruni's novel *The Mistress of Spices* has been made into a film by Gurinder Chadha.

The divergent trend in Indian fiction is best illustrated in the recently-published novel by Vikas Swarup whose novel *Q and A* has introduced a fresh theme to the wide-ranging terrain of Indian literature. A senior Indian diplomat, currently posted in the Ministry of External Affairs, Vikas Swarup is said to have sold his debut novel in over fifteen countries worldwide and has even won a film contract. The plot of *Q and A* lends itself to adaptation for the big screen. An eighteen-year-old waiter is nabbed by the Mumbai police. He has just finished reading the fifteenth episode of *Who Will Win a Billion?* and the Indian producers and the overseas associates are pulling everything they can. Published by Doubleday, the novel makes a rich contribution to the growing corpus of Indian English fiction.

There are a host of young novelists like Anurag Mathur, Samit Basu, Siddharth Shanghvi, Sarnath Banerjee and Chetan Bhagat who have introduced absolutely new themes in Indian fiction. Chetan Bhagat arrived on the literary scene with his *Five Point Someone* and then duly followed it with yet another bestseller, the novel *One Night @ the Call Centre*. The plot revolves around five friends working in a call centre and it is obvious that the writer spins his yarn with a definite audience in mind. The story of the call centre has sold more than 200,000 copies; the readers' curiosity to explore new themes has been duly satisfied. Samit Basu's *The Manticore Secret* is a fantasy-based work, a genre many Indian English authors like to dabble in. Basu is a novelist of fantasy and his novel takes us away from day-to-day life. New themes have been dealt with by other writers. Rana Dasgupta's *Tokyo Cancelled*, released recently, has done fairly well in the market. It employs an unusual style of storytelling and is about thirteen strangers stranded at an airport, waiting to board the flight to Tokyo. Thrown together by circumstances, they share and swap stories. Each story constitutes the different chapters of the novel.

An attempt is made in this book to look at our past in order to assess our present and also to make appraisal of our future through literary pointers. The creative impulse of Indian novelists in English is exotic here and there but is essentially native in spirit. Passing through different stages of rejuvenation in about a hundred years, it has come to stand in comparison with the best of world class literature and is ever fit to influence and inspire the outlook and attitude of the writers from other lands.

The book aims at providing a comprehensive as well as critical view of the achievements of the recent and not-so-recent Indian novelists in English and their irresistible urge to write on the local as well as universal issues. It will highlight the felt experience and humanistic vision of the young as well as old novelists.

Divergent Trends in Indian Fiction in English

S.K. SHARMA

I would like to begin with the good tidings that Indian fiction in English has come of age. The Indian novel in English is no longer a poor cousin of the British novel. It has happily survived the prophecies of doom which have been made about the novel form from time to time. The latest epitaph on the novel has come from the well-known practising novelist—V.S. Naipaul. In a recent interview, Naipaul made a gloomy forecast about the novel saying that the readers are no longer interested in imagined histories of imagined people, for they like to read real histories of real people. Let us allay Naipaul's fears with the re-assurance that the Indian novel in English is alive and kicking. It is no longer the tiny tot that lisped in native numbers and played around the front-door pyol or the village mango groves. It has new learnt many word-games and acquired a western accent and a taste for foreign travel. What is more, it sometimes talks of areas of "darkness" and "a million mutinies" like Naipaul himself. But I am sure that these are passing aberrations in the life of a nation or literature and do not suggest any real crisis of identity in the Indian fiction in English.

The recent proliferation and fecundity of the storytellers compels attention but forbids a full view in one glance. At least I lack the scholarship and stamina to look at the whole range. I shall therefore try to sample some broad trends and tendencies which add up to my view of the Indian novel in English. Obviously, these are small observations on a large subject.

The phrase "divergent trends" suggests suspension or cessation of sameness; it suggests variety, departure, and difference. It also suggests continuity, for divergence is only a special relationship with tradition. The story of Indian fiction is the story of continuity and change. That is why we have not outgrown the habit of referring back to the famous triumvirate of R.K. Narayan, Raja Rao and Mulk Raj Anand. In Raja Rao we have a rare blend of the philosophical novelist, a novelist of the Indian Diaspora, a Historical and Gandhian novelist. If the novel became an act of metaphysical inquiry for Raja Rao, of social inquiry for Anand, it became a comic experience for R.K. Narayan. If Raja Rao and Anand were innovators who experimented with language in order to express the spirit that was their own in a language that was not their own, R.K. Narayan moulded language down to its barest form in the service of irony as an instrument of moral vision—a vision that is truly Indian. Their methods may vary but they share the Indianness of voice and vision. Their fiction carries the unmistakably Indian flavour because their sensibility has been nourished on the nectar of Indian rivers, the colour of India's fairs and festivals, the love of her myths and legends, the wisdom of her scriptures and the natural piety of her people. They wrote about India, her people, their problems, doubts and dilemmas. The 'big three' did not exhaust the possibilities of the novel, but they were the pioneers who explored the fertile field of Indian fiction in English and mapped out the immense possibilities. Succeeding novelists followed their lead and carried the baton of tradition forward. So the most obvious trend in Indian fiction in English is its India-centric character. Even when the novelist chose foreign locales and characters (Raja Rao, Anand, Kamala Markandaya, Arun Joshi), the controlling consciousness has nearly always been Indian. As a result, the Indian fiction in English abounds in authentic images of India. The outsider's view of India tends to be archaic and exotic. The colonial viewfinder, in particular, is too narrow to embrace the vastness and variety of India. A certain lack of sympathy, involvement and insight becomes evident in the fictions, which tend to dismiss India as a "mystery" or "a muddle." If the colonial sensibility suffers from self-righteousness, some Indian novelists indulge in mawkish self-pity in a bid to showcase India for the foreign market. Novels like *Nectar in a Sieve* utilize human misery for the purposes of art so insistently that they fail to distil the nectar of Indian life. However, there is no dearth of satisfying pictures of the rural scene in India. Mulk Raj Anand's portrait of rural Punjab does not gloss over reality and yet fills the reader not with disgust or depression but with manliness and hearty zest for life. Likewise, Raja Rao's Kanthapura is full of poverty, ignorance, superstition, disease and corruption, but in the midst of these afflictions, the novelist does not forget to locate the hope, faith, idealism, sacrifice and the resilience that make life bearable. Generally speaking, if the Western view of India has relied on clichés like "heat and dust," the native imagination has found more appropriate images to capture the authentic flavour of Indian life. Thus Raja Rao's India as a Varanasi washed by the eternal Ganges of time, Anand's India as an ode to suffering and inequality, and R.K. Narayan's Malgudi (a microcosm of India) as a land of slow change and endless leisure have been widely accepted. Likewise, Bhabani Bhattacharya's "music" (*Music for Mohini*), Sudhin Ghose's "matra" (*The Flame of the Forest*), Arun Joshi's "labyrinth" (*The Last Labyrinth*) are apt metaphors for the Indian ethos.

I would next like to draw your attention to an important fictional trend that is characterized by an exploration of the relationship between history and fiction. Although no novel is completely devoid of the historical sense—the presentness of the past—a historical novel picks us a race, milieu and moment as its setting, and uses "history in narrative" and "history as narrative" in varying degrees. The Indian historical novels have been largely concerned with the freedom movement and the partition of the country. If Raja Rao's *Kanthapura* is a classic illustration of the former category, Khushwant Singh's *Train to Pakistan*, Manohar Malgonkar's *A Bend in the Ganges* and Chaman Nahal's *Azadi* are the well-known examples of the large body of fiction written on the theme of partition. In a recent publication *Indira Gandhi and the Emergency as Viewed in the Indian Novel*, O.P. Mathur has examined the fictional treatment of a dark chapter in the history of Indian democracy. The novels discussed by Mathur include Salman Rushdie's *Midnight's Chil-*

dren, Raj Gill's *The Torch Bearers*, Nayantara Sahgal's *Rich Like us*, Manohar Malgonkar's *The Garland Keepers*, O.V. Vijayan's *The Saga of Dharampur* and Rohinton Mistry's *A Fine Balance*. It was, however, the media-hype generated around Salman Rushdie and the magic realism of his modern fairy tales that forced attention to the history-fiction nexus in the Indian novel in English. Novels like John Fowles's *The French Lieutenant's Woman* and Salman Rushdie's *Midnight's Children* have been called "historiographic metafiction"[1] by Linda Hutcheon. The term is self-explanatory as applied to these novels because they are "both intensely self-reflexive and yet paradoxically also lay claim to historical events and personages."[2]

An outstanding example of historiographic metafiction is Shashi Tharoor's *The Great Indian Novel* in which the novelist comments on the nature of history, the nature of fiction and the history-fiction interface become a part of the narrative. Tharoor, the novelist, takes on the historian's mantle. The historian's job is to convey what exactly happened in the past. A difficult business indeed, because the past is seldom simple and a slight rearrangement of facts or a shift in perspective can yield a different history. The novelist's job is far more difficult, because he has not only to flesh out the dry bones of history, but also to verify what was, what could have been and what should have been. In other words, he has to re-interpret history in the moral framework of his tale. The slightest failure of nerve can have farcical consequences leading to a trivialization of history or fiction or both. Let us see how Tharoor negotiates some of these problems. *The Great Indian Novel* is a roman a clef that casts all the key-players in the freedom struggle and the post-Independence politics. The novel repeatedly claims to be a factual record, a history, but it is a history mediated through the story of the *Mahabharata*. Mythical characters are incongruously transported through time to the contemporary setting and each mythical hero is given the identity of a political hero or villain. The narrator, V.V.ji, is a modern incarnation of Ved Vyas, the legendary chronicler of the *Mahabharata*. The coupling of myth and history provides a duplex vision that enables Tharoor to juxtapose the mythical and the mundane. However, the marriage of myth and history, like any other marriage, involves problems and compromise. The mythical correspondence is not always apt. Every historical event may not have a mythical parallel. Moreover, the anachronism of time and sequence makes some manipulation of myth inevitable. Tharoor tries to solve these problems through the use of dreams and fantasy. The novel is replete with interesting asides on and send ups of modern writers on India like Rudyard Kipling, E.M. Forster, Paul Scot, Rajaji and Nirad Chaudhuri. Chapter headings like "The Duel with the Crown," "A Raj Quartet," "Midnight's Parents," "The Far-Power Villain," "Passages Through India," "The Bungle Book—OR, the Reign of Error" and "The Rigged Ved" reflect a comic muse whose light-hearted irreverence spares nothing. One wonders whether V.V.ji's last lapse into verse—his "iambic tribute to the tetrameter" (393)—is a requirement of the epic convention or an impish genuflection "at the golden gate of contemporary taste." (393) This is followed by the Krishna-Arjun dialogue in a sonnet sequence reminiscent of but far superior to Vikram Seth's inane sonnet sequence *The Golden Gate*.

Tharoor's penchant for poetry, puns, parody and pastiche might suggest that he suffers from Rushdie-pox, but the originality of his conception and style dispels that impression. Still Tharoor's conception has a handicap. The thrill of seeing ancient personages in modern costumes and contexts doesn't last long. One begins to feel that the job has gone too far. The caricature of some mythical and historical characters is likely to ruffle the sensibility of many. Tharoor is, however, saved by his humility. He never pretends to be bigger than his story or his subject, India. This basic narrative Dharma disciplines his metaphors, dreams and digressions. As a result, his style is never in excess of the demands of the narrative. The novel carries the stamp of intelligence, insight and a commitment to the country that it portrays. It is a Paean to India: "India is forever." (245) Tharoor paints India through the ages on a vast canvas in a wide variety of colours. This is Bharat Darshan, indeed, for Tharoor can talk about history, religion, philosophy and politics with the same verve that characterizes his observations on Kama Sutra, Taj Mahal, Akashvaani, cricket, computers and what have you! The description of various events from the movement for freedom, the carnage that followed the partition to the excesses committed during emergency is backed up by an impressive analytical ability. While describing "the Hastinapur Massacre" (Jallianwala Bagh Massacre), Tharoor brings out the agony and absurdity of Col. Rudyard's (Gen. Dyer's) action which was "no act of insane frenzy but a conscious, deliberate imposition of colonial will." (81) But Tharoor passes the final verdict without recourse to emotion, with the objectivity of a historian: "It was not, Ganapathi, don't get me wrong, it was not as if the British were going around every day of the week shooting Indians in enclosed gardens. Nor was Rudyard particularly evil in himself, his was merely the evil of the unimaginative, the cruelty of the literal-minded, the brutality of the direct. And because he was not evil in himself, he came to symbolize the evil of the system on whose behalf, and in whose defence, he was acting." (81-82) V.V.ji's witty interactions with his silent scribe, Ganapathi, introduce tonal variations and make for a richness of perspective. V.V.ji is full of jokes which laugh at the poverty of Indian diplomacy and some leader's utter lack of understanding of foreign relations: "he thought foreign relations were what you acquired if you married abroad." (47) Again: "They say it [Indian diplomacy] is like the love-making of an Indian elephant: it is conducted on a very high level, accompanied by much following, and the results are not known for three years." (268)

Leaving aside the humour, many of V.V.ji's observations are hard to question: "nationalization only means transferring functioning and successful institutions from the hands of competent capitalists to those of bumbling bureaucrats." (346) Again, look at V.V.ji's view of bureaucracy: "Bureaucracy is Ganapathi, simultaneously the most crippling of Indian diseases and the highest of art-forms." (398) The whole of Chapter 46 is a metafictional essay on the concept of "the end" in a story, on philosophy and its relationship with the story. The chapter ends with the question: "How much may one select, interpret and arrange the facts of the living past before truth is jeopardized by inaccuracy?" (164) The "selection" and "arrangement" of facts is a form of plotting which turns history into a verbal artefact indistinguishable from fiction. The question clearly implies an awareness of the overlapping boundaries of history and fiction. The epic saga of India could not have been told without such narrative sophistication. Let me end this section with a selection of opinions about Tharoor's novel from the Penguin blurb: "Perhaps the first work of fiction written by an Indian in recent years," says Khushwant Singh. "A classic," says *The Hindu.* "A real tour de force only an Indian could write," says *The Financial Express. The Indian Express* recommends: "Every sane Indian should buy a copy of this book."

Let us now look at the trail-blazers among women novelists. A substantial contribution to Indian fiction in English has come from women. Women are born storytellers. Their fiction can be the expression of a different way of looking at the world with a female pair of eyes. The work of novelists like Kamala Markandaya, Anita Desai, Nayantara Sahgal and Shashi Deshpande has been widely noticed and acclaimed. But the recent emergence of women writers like Shobha De, Manju Kapur, Kusum Sawhney and Arundhati Roy forces one to consider whether our best-selling or prize-winning authors are really our best. Here, I have space only for a quick look at Shobha De. Well, she has an impressive record as a journalist and exponent of Hinglish. One must admire her column "Politically Incorrect." Her urbane wit and sharp tongue give a piercing directness to her prose. Her observations carry the mark of a cultured sensibility that is delicately distressed at any violation of the norm. But as a novelist, unfortunately, she allows her moral sensibility to be swamped by commercial considerations or a weakness for sensation. Her realism is confined to the sexy and the sordid details and as such lacks the strength of a comprehensive moral vision.

From *Socialite Evenings* (1989) to *Second Thoughts* (1996), De's kitschy novels talk about strange obsessions, starry nights and small betrayals of the urban elite. She assumes the mantle of the unofficial chronicler (or voyeur?) of the swinger set that has suddenly become visible in the wake of globalization. However, Shobha De's sleazy tales of social climbers and hangers-on stand the Indian ethos on its head.

De's India is a far cry from the land of the *Gita* or Gandhi. The Indian virtues of contentment, simplicity, and self-denial are now dead and buried with the past. Conspicuous consumption, indulgence and ostentation are the buzz-words now. India, accordingly, appears in her novels as a consumer's paradise. It is a sexual utopia where everybody is committed to the pleasure principle in life. Her characters—models, film stars, socialites, businessmen, politicians, pimps and prostitutes—either make money or love. And they do it in the oddest of places: they make love in elevators and aeroplanes, on sea-beaches, dining tables, office tables, and of course on the old-fashioned beds. Their love takes bizarre forms and fantasies as do their violent hatred and self-disgust so that kinky sex, infidelity, incest, rape and murder are everyday events. De presents this decline and fall not with moral anguish or insight, but with cheap thrills. In spite of the grim realism of her snapshots, De's decadent society is confined to a small (though powerful) segment of urban India. De seizes upon ambition, sensual indulgence and irresponsible action as the symptoms of a society sick with crass materialism divorced from ethical norms. Crudity of cupidity is her favourite theme. But she seldom goes beyond journalistic documentation and makes no attempt at social or moral probing. Her characters live "below the level of belief," to use T.S. Eliot's words, and are fit neither for comedy nor tragedy.

One wonders how an author so devoid of moral purpose, so divorced from the social mainstream, so completely cut off from the mythical past could be worthy of serious consideration? And yet bulky books and papers have been written trying to establish Shobha De as a great writer, and a leading feminist. One can only say that feminism will be ill-served if it adopts Shobha De's bed-hopping nymphets and nymphos as role models in India. These bold and beautiful women are qualified to be home-breakers, not home-makers. The female protagonists of Shobha De are autonomous, not complete; they maybe educated but they are not intelligent; they are free, not fulfilled. The female counterparts of Kingsley Amis's Jim Dixon (*Lucky Jim*) and John Braine's Joe Hampton (*Room at the Top*) may have a right to exist and even make it to the top, but they will ever remain a far cry from the Indian ideal of womanhood.

And finally, let's mark a trend in Indian fiction in English that is full of wonderful possibilities: the growing popularity of Indian fiction in translation. A good translation can extend the frontiers of regional fiction and enrich the Indian fiction in English. How many of us had heard of Jnanpeeth award-winning Kannada novelist U.R. Anantha Murthy before his work was translated into English? His novel *Samskara*, published in 1965, was made into an award-winning film in 1970. But it was only after A.K. Ramanujan's translation of the novel in 1976 that Anantha Murthy came into limelight and won international acclaim. Sahitya Akademi has introduced many regional novelists to a wider audience through translation. Last April, Penguin India launched the first set of books in Indian languages in New Delhi. It was for the first time that Penguin had published in a language other than English. Another first in Indian publishing was the launching of Namita Gokhale's new novel *Shakuntala: The Play of Memory* (*Shakuntala: Smriti Jaal*), simultaneously in English and Hindi. This is a happy development which not only underscores the growing recognition of good literature in regional languages but also of the fact that Indian literatures in English and regional languages can grow together. In a multilingual, multicultural society like ours, it is not possible to enjoy the history and literature of a linguistic group other than our own. One way to understand India is to read the literatures of her vast and varied regions. With a view to painting a wide picture of India for all, Macmillan India has launched the series "Modern Indian Novels in Translation." I would like to share with you my appreciation of a novel entitled *Vasaveswaram*[4] (1966, Trans. 1988) by Krithika. Krithika is the pen name of the well-known Tamil writer Mathuram Bhoothalingam.

Vasaveswaram is a *sthala-purana*. A strong sense of place comes out of the novel. It is firmly located in a community and a sensibility that is uniquely Indian. The locale is a village bordering the state of Kerala in the 1930s. The village is named Vasaveswaram after Lord Vasaveswara whose temple stands as a proud pillar of tradition in a stratified society. But despite the caste differences, the villagers belong to a shared community of custom, belief and practice strengthened by religious discourses, fairs, festivals and community feasts. Under the benevolent leadership of a widely respected old Brahmin landlord, Periya Petta, they live together as the children of tradition until it is challenged by Picchandi, a young college-educated Brahmin enthused by the Communist ideology. The socialist rebellion gains momentum, but is eventually crushed beneath the weight of tradition: "The petty trouble that disturbed Vasaveswaram vanished like dew drops before the sun." (134) However, the emergence and collapse of the challenge to the established order gives the novelist the chance to test the strength and weakness of tradition. The strength is evident in the villagers's sense of community. "Our People! Our people! There can't be others elsewhere like these," reflects Subbukutty Sastry, the Harikatha man. The possessive pronoun "our" is proudly applied even to the fruits and foodstuffs produced in the village: "The banana varieties of Vasaveswaram were as well known as its sthala-purana. Its kuzhivazhai, matti, poovam, kadali, palaiyam, kodan were all quite tasty. Of these, matti was believed to be of a superior quality. 'Our Matti,' the villagers would say, referring to it with special pride." (10) The sense of plenty, peace and togetherness depends on a delicate equilibrium between morality and corruption. Petty envies and intrigues do exist. Evils like dowry, ignorance, ostentation and superstition have been sanctified by tradition. The individual can be anytime sacrificed for the sake of the herd instinct. The worst victims are women. Their speech has been muted by custom; their private space has been swallowed by society. Their dreams and desires, even their love and dust are governed by a strict social code. Even as women submit to the love-code of Vasaveswaram, Krithika raises the question: "In lives such as theirs, where everything was bound by tradition, can love alone take wing?" (21)

Krithika highlights the plight of a wife in a joint family where her freedom is cramped under the watching eye of an antiquated mother-in-law or a widowed sister-in-law: "Never a day when she could speak her heart to him. No chance of venting her anger or her heart's longings. She could never spontaneously pour out her feelings, she always had to rein them in, ever afraid that Meenakka might hear." (54) No textbook feminist schooled in the West could portray such an experience. Only an Indian writer can do it. Only a woman writer can do it. And Krithika does it with aplomb. Her originality as a feminist is evident in her insight into man-woman relationship. She examines every aspect of Rohini's relationship with her husband, Chandrashekhar Aiyer. Rohini gasps in a loveless marriage like a caged bird. She longs for her husband's attention. He is indifferent to her beauty and her being because he is too busy with his crops and cattle to think of her longings. He invokes the false gods of self-esteem and male-authority and ruins his marital happiness. Ironically, instead of admiring his wife's beauty, he fears it as the source of her "arrogance" and her desire to "control" him. Actually, it is he who tries to control her and her sexuality. He carries his notions of self-importance even to his bed and expects her to submit to his will. The novel makes it clear that instead of playing power-politics, husbands should win over their wives through caring and sharing. Krithika's androgynous imagination can also sympathize with the male point of view. She would like women to understand their men and live in tune with them. Denial of emotional support by the wife can destroy the husband's confidence and manhood. The failure of the Vicchu-Subbaiya relationship brings misery to both. Krithika studies the libidinal drives of men and women and shows how they can be clogged by female insensitivity as surely as by male egotism and pride.

The novelist pokes fun at the stupid sexual mores of the inhabitants of Vasaveswaram. There is Muthu, who made love to his wife every night, but superstitiously abstained from dalliance on days of important business. Subbukutty Sastri preaches chastity and control, but after every discourse, he seeks his mistress like a secret debauchee. The erotic poetry of his tale of Indra's love throws the whole village into a frenzy of passion. And yet they pretend to shun passion in public. The gap between pretence and practice is wider in the case of Dr. Sunda who swears in the name of the sacred tradition only to seduce other people's wives. However, the novelist executes scenes of betrayal and seduction with remarkable reticence, the emphasis always falling on psychological discovery rather than on sexual titillation. Krithika's interest in her people covers their habits of dress, speech, work, worship, gossip, eating and mating. The short sentences, the crisp dialogues are a measure of the novelist's control over her material and medium. And above all, her similes seem to grow from the village soil itself:

> The sky reddens like kumkum. (76)
> Her words burst out like crackers. (31)
> His ready laughter was like cowries being rattled in a metal pot. (32)
> His face lit up . . . like a stiff ghee wick in a kindled lamp. (10)

Thus *Vasaveswaram* is a "live narrative" with beautiful sights and insights. A brief comparison with Arundhati Roy's *The God of Small Things* would be revealing. Krithka's novel is set in Vasaveswaram, a village near Kerala. Roy's Ayemenen is also located in Kerala. But if the people of Vasaveswaram are related with one another, the people of Ayemenen are alienated. If Krithika emphasizes the beauty and bounty of her village, Roy's eye settles on ugliness, dirt, decay, vomit and excreta. Krithika exercises a delicate restraint in her treatment of love and sex. On the other hand, there is neither refinement nor restraint in Roy's blow-by-blow account of adultery, incest and kinky sex. And finally, if Krithika's style has a natural economy and ease, Roy's verbal jugglery is often unnecessary, inappropriate and annoying. To use the words of C.D. Narasimhaiah, Roy's "*atyukti* verbal excess offends against *auchitya*, propriety, authenticity."

The lines are well drawn. It is for the future novelists to make their choice. I am sure they will go for *sukti* and authenticity. In this choice, they will be guided by tradition and the illuminating torch of criticism. The Indian fiction in English has not let us down. Let us hope the Indian critic also will not let us down. The Indian critics (academics) have been very large-hearted in the past. They have shown undue reverence to everything in print. But if we can admire a Raja Rao and a Shobha De with the same gusto, it betrays a lack of discrimination, an abdication of the critical responsibility of separating grain from the husk. Let our critics rise to the occasion and lay down sound criteria of taste and judgement to preserve and propagate the best that has been known and thought. Among other criteria of judgement, Indianness still remains a valid touchstone. Let it not be the Indianness that is cosmetic or confused, but a shaping joy that transmutes the very spirit of man.

NOTES

1. Qtd. A.N. Jak, "Historiographic Metafiction and Chaman Nahal's *Azadi*: An Appraisal," *Akademi Awarded Novels in English*, ed. Mithilesh K. Pandey (New Delhi: Sarup, 2003), p. 110.
2. Loc. cit.
3. Shashi Tharoor, *The Great Indian Novel* (Penguin, 1989).
4. Krithika, *Vasaveswaram*, trans. T. Sriraman (Macmillan India, 1998).
5. Arundhati Roy, *The God of Small Things* (New Delhi: IndiaInk, 1997).
6. C.D. Narasimhaiah, *The Swan and the Eagle* (New Delhi: Vision Books, 1968, revised ed. 1999), p. 254.

Homoeroticism in Indian Fiction in English

SARIKA GOYAL

Fiction relies on imagination, which is moulded in the frames of reality and vice-versa. A writer is known for picking up things from the socio-cultural milieu. The small unnoticeable matters are thought upon, elaborated and then presented in a new light with the free play of imagination. Robert Brecht recognises that artistic decisions reflect fundamental moral choices of the authors.[1] Almost all the writers, native or west, feel an urge to voice various realities prevalent in the society. In a fast changing modern world, the ancient norms are no longer observed and many new trends are emerging which are hitherto silenced. These silenced voices have been expressed in the works of modern fiction by some Indian authors also, many of them belong to upper middle class or the elite sections of the society.

The writers of generation X and Y are witnessing a cultural change under the impact of westernization or, to be more precise, globalization. There are many new trends discernible in this scenario that are not only socio-political but also related to one's personal feelings and experiences, issues related to community living and ethnicity, new challenges faced within the country and the Diaspora. A writer records his observations of the society and presents them before his readers with an aim to mould their opinions successfully He puts all his energies to this singular task and wraps his material with powerful imagery culled from the faculty of imagination to create an illusion of reality. "In the grammar of a language or literature of a society, the expressions not valid till yesterday may find an easy acceptance today: a wrong thing as and which in vogue among the masses becomes a right thing."[2] The problem is that most of people feel an urge to come out of their private zones to thrust their ideologies on like-minded persons to seek self-realization not only of mind but also that of body and emotions and the postmodern markets of today provide multimedia technologies which easily serve this purpose.

Homoeroticism comes out of repressed desires or certain inhibitions on the part of the individual. Frustration, oppression by adults and discontent etcetera move people towards these tendencies. As a result, they show a liberal behaviour which is "a defence against deeply embedded conflicts between the erotic instincts and the imperatives of a culture that denies it."[3] Many critics have commented upon these tendencies in young children, on the verge of teens,. where unhappiness and an egocentric attitude turns them inward in an effort to gratify their needs. The other possible outcome is aggression and violence. But man has an instinct to relate pleasurably with others for tenderness and intimacy and forms these kinds of associations.

Taking an Indian perspective of the situation, in earlier times, there existed a relation of care, compassion and fellow-feeling between the people of the same sex. A young maiden often addresses her friend as:

> If he is not dear to you,
> My sakhi,
> Why does your face bloom
> Like lotus touched by rays of sun?
> Only his name was spoken![4]

Thus, a friend shared many secrets, provided consolation and offered advice but now the very definition of 'friend' has changed. Sadomasochistic desires have appeared in the place of love and care. Most of the young students are exposed to this kind of atmosphere in dormitories that begins with abuse but ends with similar feelings in a few and makes them acquire a pathological character. The society is against all this as is evident from the response to sadistic desires portrayed on celluloid in a few Indian movies.

Michel Foucault takes repression of these feelings as 'being silenced' by the social and religious institutions in an exercise of domination and power. Carrette, while throwing light on him, studies other Foucaldian critics saying that being silent and being silenced are different things. Homosexuals were silent and therefore free because to confess is to be controlled and moreover they were guardians of truth.[5] He also studies a positive silence in avant-garde literature of Sade, Artaud and Roussel.

In the Indian social scene, homoeroticism is based on lust and desire in most of the cases and causes humiliation to gays and lesbians who have chosen this life deliberately. Shobha De, in her prose piece "Of Friends, Gaily" finds them more compassionate and trustworthy as compared to others.[6] She even feels more secure in their company whereas society at large avoids any contact with them.

As far as presentation of these issues in literature is concerned, two modern authors can be taken up here. The first is Rohinton Mistry who entered the hall of fame with the publication of his first collection of short-stories entitled *Tales from Firozsha Baag*[7] and thereafter was nominated for the prestigious Booker Prize for his novels *Such a Long Journey*[8] and *A Fine Balance*. He is a Parsi and a Bombayite and, therefore, presents ethnic issues in the socio-political milieu of Mumbai where a Hindu extremist party dominates. He studied in St. Xaviers, Mumbai, and seems to have closely observed the life of young boys there. He presents the character of Jehangir Bulsara in one of his short stories who displays homoerotic desire at the sight of some athletes because his normal relation with a girl is thwarted by his mother. The story named "Exercisers" shows the dominating attitude of the mother over her grown-up son. She does not like the girl Behroje and takes her son to one Bhagwan Baba as if the religious saint will keep away the infatuation and the so-called evil design of the girl. She ruins their love and her son has to pay for it by transferring his feelings to the strong masculine athletes who come to the Hanging Gardens for their routine practice as they were unable to pay the fees of a gym and used swings of little children during twilight hours. He used to admire them while hiding himself behind a bush and tried to hide his teenage lust, illicit relation and cowardly attitude before a dominating mother. She exercised such a powerful authority that once when he couldn't reach home as per the deadline of 8 p.m. set by her, he had to wait outside for the whole night.

Jennifer Takhar studies this deteriorating effect of the mother in her essay where repressed feelings of a boy get transformed into homosexuality. She also says that, according to Freud, "homosexual urges in boys create the preconditioning of their eventual recognition of heterosexuality."[9] She also studies the parental pressure on children forcing them to go against their desires in Mistry's novel *Such a Long Journey* and his reaction against this visibly moral attitude of Indians.

In another story in the same collection, *The Collectors*, he traces the same behaviour in school children. Here again the name of the boy is Jehangir who is initiated into the habit of collecting stamps by a neighbour Dr. Mody whose own son Pesi was a delinquent child. The boy in order to influence his guide, who had shown him a rare stamp of a Spanish lady besides giving him a few others, gets trapped in the designs of another lusty boy Eric. Eric himself wants to be satisfied and as a result offers him stamps stolen from two street-vendors who sit outside their school. At the detection of their stealth, Eric is expelled and Jehangir loses the trust of Dr. Mody and the stamp collection is eaten by moths within a few years.

The first story depicts the trend to be a result of the oppression by parents whereas the second one presents it as the misadventures of youthful boys and the subsequent demand due to the pleasure derived out of it. Mistry may also be afraid of it because if such trends persist in the boys of Parsi community, the population of which is already declining rapidly, it will prove a threat to the society. He, no doubt, takes on himself the duty to tell others about his community and its peculiarities being a sort of last witness but shows a sympathetic concern for their would-be spouses.

Another writer Upamanyu Chatterjee, the author of the widely-acclaimed novel *The English August* presents lesbian trends in his second novel *The Last Burden*. He is a writer of extraordinary merit and lucid prose. The novel is the story of Jamun, who has parents besides his brother, sister-in-law and two nephews in the family. He pays a visit to his home when his mother falls seriously ill. He listens to the grumbling of his father against Joyce, his daughter-in-law, and receives the burden of a secret lying with his mother which she lessens only before her death. It is the secret of having a mad brother Belu and tense relations with the husband throughout life.

Joyce feels irritated by her abusive father-in-law, who all the time keeps on falsely accusing her of having illicit relations with his other unmarried son or by her cowardly husband who goes to the house of her friend, Rani. Her husband Burfi is unable to bridge the gap between his father and his wife. One day irritated over Joyce's burning of his father's possessions, he remembers how his wife was getting angry when they got late for going to Rani's house as he had recently returned from the hospital after attending to his serious mother. He muses: "At which I retorted that I would not chaperone her for dinner to her bloated, lesbian ex-beau, except that Rani's not ex. We bickered at that incendiary level for a while. Joyce then set fire to some of my stuff, and is now swanning off for Rani's house, never to return, which should mean Sunday."[10]

He was aware that any kind of chat with his wife ends with her going to her soulmate Rani with his Doom packed into her armpit and creating a bad impression of her in-laws before her relatives and friends.

When their mother dies Rani's visits to their home increase, she was now not only a chaperone for Doom but also used to lie on the bed as if she was in her own home. Whatever was the reason of her visit, Jamun didn't like her especially when she came at the death in tight jeans with spectacles over her eyes. She was searching for a silver rattle that she had given to Doom and which his mother Urmila had kept in trunk after taking it from her grandson.

Jamun had illicit relations with his maid Kasibai and his neighbours often thought that he doesn't even spare her son Vaman to which he sometimes responded: "Well, in a family, the most hideous things can happen without the wider world knowing—without even other members of family catching on, and if the incident—the misadventure—has been adequately distanced by time . . . then it doesn't even remain grisly." (284) This opinion was modelled after hearing Kuki's family history. The incident related to Kuki's family in the last chapter supports this lusty trend and appears an instance of the cheap behaviour. Thus, the author depicts lesbian attitude of Joyce, shown even after she becomes the mother of two children, as an outcome of the desire to live in an atmosphere of peace and compassion whereas that of Kuki's grandfather is base.

In short, the novelists offer the modern conceptions of these issues whereas Ruth Vanita studies similar relationships, at the time of the Vedas, which were not for personal gratification but for the benefit of the community at large. She studies some ancient texts which tell us about the birth of sage Bhagiratha, "possessing extraordinary capabilities, influential in bringing the heavenly Ganges to the earth, as a result of union of two mothers. She says that this "love between co-widows is embedded in kinship and conduces to the welfare of the patrilineal family and the community . . . and occurs with divine blessing."[11] The parents do share feelings of each other in such a relationship.

Though it must be understood that the basis of these relations is mostly an emotional need than a physical one but those who choose this path of their own free will also enjoy life and are more creative. In the words of a famous French critic, "But there is no invention possible, whether it be philosophical or poetic, without the presence in the inventive subject of an abundance of the other, of the diverse persons—detached, persons—thought, peoples born of the unconscious, and in each desert, suddenly animated, a springing forth of self . . . our fellow creatures, our fears."[12] In the end I will only say that society must provide conducive environment to people instead of criticizing them.

NOTES

1. Robert Brecht, *Thinkers of the 20th Century*, ed. Elizabeth Devine, Michael Held, James Vinson, and George Walsh (New Delhi: Himalayan, 1987).
2. Motilal Jotwani, *Of Grass and Roots* (New Delhi: Sampark, 1987), p. 19.
3. Qtd. Ted Clark, *The Oppression of Youth* (New York: Harper Colophon, 1975), p. 98.
4. Qtd. K.S. Srinivasan, *The Ethos of Indian Literature* (Delhi: Chanakya, 1985), p. 79.
5. Jeremy R. Carrette, *Foucault and Religion* (London: Routledge, 2000), p. 34.
6. Shobha De, *Shooting from the Hip* (New Delhi: UBSPD, 1994).
7. Rohinton Mistry, *Tales from Firozshah Baag (*London: Faber and Faber, 1987).
8. Rohinton Mistry, *Such a Long Journey* (London: Faber and Faber, 1991).
9. Jennifer Takhar, "Mother and Son: Oedipus Wrecks in Rohinton Mistry." *Postcoloniul* Web.org.20sep2004.
10. Upamanyu Chatterjee, *The Last Burden* (New Delhi: Viking, 1993), p. 84.
11. Ruth Vanita, "Female-Female Love and Miraculous Birth in Hindu Texts," *Manushi*, Jan.-Feb. 2005, p. 22.
12. Helene Cixous, "Sorties," *Modern Criticism and Theory*, ed. David Lodge (New York: Longman, 1992).

Of Divergences and Trends and Trend-Defying Novels of Raj Kamal Jha

SWARAJ RAJ

My aim in this paper is to discuss the genre blurring fiction of Raj Kamal Jha in order to lay bare the inadequacy of thinking literary history in terms of literary trends and movements. However, before I talk about Raj Kamal Jha's two novels *The Blue Bedspread* (1999) and *If You are Afraid of Heights* (2003) and try to attempt a notional fit of these two remarkable texts in the putative "emergent trends" in the Indian fiction in English, I wish to interrogate the very ideas of divergences and trends because to me these twin ideas are not innocent of heterogamous reduction of autonomy and uniqueness of those literary texts which are assumed to be the hypostasis of the trends to which they belong or they follow.

The word 'divergent' comes from to 'diverge' which, as the *Cambridge International Dictionary of English* describes, is "to follow a different direction, or to be or become different." Hence the word 'divergent' is clearly haunted by the presence of a centre—in the present case, the spectral presence being that body of mainstream writing from whose all-subsuming centrality certain recalcitrant streams diverge tangentially in different directions but the céntre remains intact, immutably monolithic. The presence of a centre not only means absence of difference; it also means denying destabilizing, destructuring arid decontextualizing impulse of a literary text; and it also means constructing hierarchies and binaries of centre and margin. In his *Writing and Difference*, Derrida first quotes Maurice Merleau-Ponty: "My own words take me by surprise and teach me what I think."[1] And then Derrida himself writes: "It is because writing is *inaugural,* in the fresh sense of that word, that is dangerous and anguishing.

It does not know where it is going."[1] Each writing being inaugural in the sense of its possibilities of the unanticipable which happens to be the very condition of writing, each literary text ceaselessly destabilizes any context, any centre. Looked at from this Derridean point of view, there can be no divergences in the absence of any centre. There can only be rhizomatic proliferation of texts in a network of inter-textual connections. Emerging trends point to the future, the future which, as Derrida writes in *Of Grammatology* (1976), "can only be anticipated in the form of an absolute danger. It is that which breaks absolutely with the constructed normality and can be proclaimed, *presented,* as a sort of monstrosity."[2] Hence, the very idea of future (emerging) trends is alien to Derridean thought.

Besides this, the word "trend", because of its association with fashion is quite problematic. It is as if a literary trend is a fashion, a transient fad dictated by a trendsetter and the authors who follow the dominant trend are trendy. Let us also not forget the role of the publishing industry and the academy in setting up trends. However, in our anxiety to rein in the aleatory chaos of history to within manageable limits, we do tend to oversimplify, bracket out differences, think of trends and historical epochs in terms of linear unities. This is a problem which bedevils literary historiography. However, this fitting of bewilderingly rich and variegated panoply of Indian English fiction into certain dominant trends is actually what we come across when we read surveys of Indian writing in English. In the concluding chapter of their *Indian English Literature 1980-2000: A Critical Survey* (2001), M.K. Naik and Shyamala A. Narayan write: "Where does Indian English literature stand today? The answer is, at the moment, it does not stand anywhere in particular, for the simple reason that it is sitting pretty. Things have never been so propitious for the Indian English writer. Time was when, with a few exceptions, he was not fully sure of himself, and of the reception of his work. Then came Rushdie and the hearts of 'Midnight's children's children' were filled with new hopes. An age began, when 'Every morning brought a. noble chance. And every chance brought out a noble night.'"[3]

In a similar vein almost, Richard Cronin writes about a paradigm shift in the post-Rushdie period:

> With *Midnight's Children,* Rushdie established what has remained since 1981 the most distinctive pattern for the Indian novel: the family chronicle that is also a history of the nation, a distorted autobiography that embodies in equally distorted form the political life of India . . . as Rushdie puts it, an 'imaginary country', a country that could never have existed 'except by the effort of a phenomenal collective will except in a dream we all agreed to dream.'[4]

Blaise Clarke, Bharati Mukherjee's husband, in his *New York Times* article also talked about Rushdie's *Midnight's Children*, redrawing the literary map of India. And once the trendsetter is named and the leading pattern is established, all the confusing pieces of the jigsaw puzzle fall into their places and the puzzle thus unscrambled looks very trimly symmetrical. Eviscerated of all their differential heterogeneity, all kinds of literary works can now be accommodated within the rubric of the trend, their 'dangerous and anguishing' undecidability becomes very comfortably containable within the easily definable limits of the trend. For example, after Rushdie, all kinds of novelists like Shashi Tharoor, Allan Sealy, Boman Desai, Rohinton Mistry, Amitav Ghosh, Nayantara Sahgal and David Davidar are assumed to follow the trend set by Rushdie. If Rushdie's success is understood to have spawned a trend, Arundhati Roy's success in 1997 becomes another trendsetter. Then we have Jhumpa Lahiri's success becoming a trendsetter for diasporic writing. Thus we have a plethora of trends with their undifferentiated homogeneity.

However, each literary text with its irrepressible intransigence overruns all the limits assigned to it. Tending to breach all the boundaries, it asserts its uniqueness in its difference from others. In which trend can we accommodate Raj Kamal Jha's disjointed, rambling, phantasmagoric, miasmic fictions about paraphiliacs—paedophiles, paederastic fathers and their traumatized children, all living in a dying surreal city and inhabiting the twilight zone between dreams and reality, self-conscious fictions narrated sometimes in lyrical-poetical prose and sometimes with the deadpan accuracy and vapidity of journalese by unreliable narrators with failing memories, fictions in which different incidents do not cohere with each other through causal connections but seem to follow the 'butterfly effect' of 'chaos theory', and that too hinted at vaguely, obliquely, insinuated with images which resist interpretation? Before we attempt an answer to this question, let us discuss Jha's novels.

Delhi-based journalist Raj Kamal Jha's first novel *The Blue Bedspread* appeared in 1999 and though it did not prove to be a runaway success, it did excite a lot of controversy and for certain obvious reasons. Jha, on the basis of three short stories had reportedly sold the world rights of his first novel to Picador for an astronomical sum of £160,000. The 'memory novel', written in the form of a confessional, shocked the readers with its unconventional narrative style, its elliptical prose and its subject matter; it is about incest, domestic violence, and child abuse—all taboo subjects, shrouded in silence and always kept under wraps. Jha lifts the veil of secrecy from these subjects and lays bare the dysfunctional aspects of the middle-class Indian family, which has always been touted as the custodian and purveyor of all the fabled moral values of our society.

The unnamed middle-aged narrator of *The Blue Bedspread*, with almost Prufrockian consciousness of his growing age, is a man without moorings, just a name in a city of 12 million names, which happens to be Calcutta:

> I could begin with my name but forget it, why waste time, it doesn't matter in this city of twelve million names. I could begin with the way I look but what do I say, I am not a young man any more, I wear glasses, my stomach droops over the belt over my trousers.[5]

On receiving a phone call from a police officer that his sister had died in childbirth, he brings his dead sister's baby girl home and while the baby sleeps on a blue bedspread in the next room, he writes stories for her which will provide her an account of her family history:

> Something you will see or hear will remind you of something, missing in your heart, perhaps a hole, the blood rushing through it, and then like a machine which rumbles for a second just before it goes click, just before it begins to hum and move, you will stop and ask: 'Who am I?' They will then give you these stories. (2-3)

The presence of the child spurs the narrator to exhume his own buried past, to come to terms with his own history, his relationship with his sister, their not-so-lucky childhood, their childhood 'theatre of pleasure and fear' on their blue bedspread, the scars on his psyche; in short he promises the child: "I will tell you happy stories and I will tell you sad stories. And remember, my child, your truth lies somewhere in between." (6) This hesitancy, this tentativeness whose markers are 'perhaps', 'maybe', and the 'truth', that lies 'somewhere in between', and the narrative's self-conscious references to its authorship are the dominant motifs of the entire narration. The narrator often shies away from being forthright. He tells the child:

> We shall visit all these places, I shall hold your hand, open all those rooms that need to be opened, word by word, sentence by sentence. I will keep some rooms closed until we are more ready, open others just a chink so that you take a peek. And at times, without opening a door at all, we shall imagine what lies inside. Like the murder, the screaming, a red handkerchief floating down, just as in the movies. (6)

Since memory is the device for remembering and recasting personal history, the fallibility of memory keeps all the stories open-ended. The fallibility of memory can also be an act of intentionally and tendentiously forgetting that which is very painful. The narrator is aware of the role subjectivity plays in recasting history. He says: "At a different time, maybe, at a different place, I would have told you other stories." (47) While narrating the story of his sister's unfulfilled marriage, he pauses and asks:

> How should we end the story? We could have her go down to get him the second drink, hear the crackle as it hits the ice in the steel glass, climb the stairs again and listen to him to talk about the school, the child she couldn't give him. . . . Or we could end it like this. (137)

And the result of all this hesitancy and self-reflexivity is that we have a novel which is a series of brief chapters divided into five sections—Father, Mother, Sister, Visitors and Brother. There is no plot linking all the stories together in a chain of cause and effect. There are many loose ends, which don't seem to belong and don't fit in. All the stories are strung together by a predominantly lugubrious mood spread over the entire narrative like one long unending night. This elegiac mood is the outcome of the sadness, which forms the kernel of the narrator's psyche. All the relationships in the novel are marred by guilt and trauma associated with transgressions of normative moral interdictions. The narrator lost his mother in early childhood. The father is a paederast who, in a drunken state, molests the narrator when the latter is a school-going kid. Out of sheer perversity he hides his daughter's sanitary napkins and she is forced to borrow her brother's handkerchief. He unleashes mindless violence upon her. He traumatizes both the children with his brutality. Bereft of love and conviviality which binds families together, the two feel trapped in this cage of a house like 'dead insects trapped in the plexiglass cover' of the sodium vapour lamp just outside the window of their room on the second floor. Their loneliness drives them to seek solace in each other's company. The blue bedspread becomes their home, their 'ninety square feet of fabric sky' on which they discover the forbidden pleasures of incest. Pleasure, fear, pain and guilt intermingle in this daily theatre played on the blue bedspread. The narrator tells the child: "But I needed to tell you this little story, my child, so that when you have to pull your blanket over your head, remember that with a little bit of imagination, you can always find some love trapped in some fear." (110)

His sister runs away when she grows up, for a man she obviously loves. For several years, he misses her and then reconciles to her absence:

> And then, slowly, like sunrise on a winter's day, it dawned on me, cold and clear, that perhaps my sister had to run away for me to carry on. Because, in a way, it was essential that one of us should leave never to return. It saved both of us the discomfort and the

> pain of sitting together as adults and talking about everything except those nights on the blue bedspread, that July night on the bedspread, moments that were key to your survival and yet better left untouched, and. unsaid! (62-63)

In Jha's second novel *If You are Afraid of Heights* an eleven-twelve year old girl's dead body is found lying at the bottom of a canal twenty-five feet deep. To reach the canal one has to take a 'service lane'. Not a road, not even a dirt track; the 'service lane' is 'half-mud half-slush' marked in several places by black pools of water. The 'service lane' is: 'the neighbourhood's most neglected stretch, choked with garbage furtively packed in plastic bags or newspaper wraps, tossed from windows on either side which are opened only for this purpose and remain closed for the rest of the time. No one wants to see the service lane, even acknowledge its presence.

As we have already seen, Jha himself takes the forgotten service lane of the human mind to unravel the hidden monsters of the deep. Both his novels transgress many novelistic conventions to reveal the transgressive nature of these monsters. In the second novel too, he broaches taboo subjects in his fragmentary and magical-realist manner. All the characters in this dystopic novel carry wounds in their hearts. His prose is sparse, lyrical, elliptical and encoded and the images elusive but some of which keep recurring in an obsessional way help to link the three segments of the book. The omniscient narrator rides on the back of a crow and that allows him not only the bird's eye view but the perspective of a voyeur too.

The first section 'Of Heights' is about a poor post office clerk ironically named Amir whose job is to write letters for those who cannot write. After a freak tram accident he lands mysteriously in Rima's house—whose name is a mirror reflection of Amir's—in Paradise Park, a high-rise building and perhaps the most expensive area of the city. Amir recuperates in her house and though she nurses him and an injured crow whose beak has been sawed off by someone, she herself has many holes in her heart:

> However, watching Rima closely in Paradise Park has made Amir aware of her true nature: that she has holes in her heart she needs to fill every day, be it someone like him, a stranger hurt in an accident, or a crow . . . with its beak sawn off, holes he can never plumb the depths of. (109)

Rima moves with Amir to his house of poverty but troubled by the cries of a weeping child, she leaves Amir never to come back.

In the second section 'You are Afraid', Mala, a newspaper reporter, goes to a distant village to investigate the death of an eleven-year old girl whose dead body was fished out of a canal. The post mortem report suggests that she was sexually assaulted and then killed before being thrown into the canal. While investigating this case Mala grapples with her own troubled past. There are vague suggestions that she herself had been subjected to sexual abuse when she was about eleven or twelve. In the hotel where she stays she meets her doppelganger Alam—his name being the mirror reflection of Mala's:

> She looks at him, carefully, he reminds her of all the men she has met this morning, in the town and in her dreams. . . . It's as if right through the day, Alam has been forming himself, bit by bit, picking up features, this from there, that from there, adding some of his own like the ears, small and flared, his height, a few inches taller than hers, his walk, slow. Or maybe he's not ready, fully formed yet, for Mala expects him to change any moment. (215-16)

He helps her in many odd ways and takes her once again to the exact site where the body of the dead girl was found. But even the second visit proves futile; the 'jigsaw seems to grow and grow'. She comes back with more questions than answers.

In the last section 'If,' a girl in a red dress stands at her balcony and watches a crow circling over the city. She is shocked by growing number of unconnected suicides in her neighbourhood. She is worried about her parents too. But the voyeuristic omniscient narrator who rides on the back of a crow, who can hide anywhere and seek anything—the Champion of Hide and Seek—squeezes under her bed one night claiming to be her friend, stalks her parents as a detective at her bidding, takes photographs of her father, makes notes of her mother's activities, listens to their private conversations and allays the girl's tears about her parents' suicide.

The three segments of the narrative are sought to be threaded together with some recurring images: dolls, red dress, trams, brass Buddha, the crying child, incessant rain and many others. The loose ends, however, still remain a reminder of the spooky, spectral quality of the narrative, which disturbs the reader with, to borrow the suggestive title of Bataile's?? book, its 'visions of excess'. The reader is once again overwhelmed and troubled by the eerie melancholy that pervades the narrative and is left with more questions than answers.

Jha's two texts *The Blue Bedspread* and *If You are Afraid of Heights* are the names of the problems which defy easy explanations and settled solutions. Their indeterminacy defies us to subsume them under any trends. And this brings me to my original question: in which trend can we accommodate Raj Kamal Jha's novels? Are they postmodernist texts? Are they magical-realist texts? Are they impressionistic texts? Are they novels at all, in any conceivable sense of the term? The answer to these questions is both Yes and No. They are all these but are much more than these terms would have us imagine. These terms and the trends they connote are like nets we cast over the play of difference in plural to master differences and to control them. Derrida's notions of 'supplementarity' and 'ghastliness' of the text militate against the poverty of literary historiography which arrests differences to render them manageable as trends. Raj Kamal Jha's novels are a testimony to the inadequacy of thinking literary history in terms of trends—both divergent and emerging or emergent.

NOTES

1. Jacques Derrida, *Writing and Difference,* trans. Alan Bass (London: Routledge and Kegan Paul, 1978), p. 11.
2. Jacques Derrida, *Of Grammatology,* trans. Gayatri Chakravorty Spivak (Baltimore: Johns Hopkins University Press, 1976), p. 4.

3. M.K. Naik and Shyamala A. Narayan, *Indian English Literature 1980-2000: A Critical Survey* (New Delhi: Pencraft International, 2001), p. 247.
4. Richard Cronin, "India," *The Oxford Guide to Contemporary World Literature*, ed. John Sturrock (New York: Oxford University Press, 1996), p. 215.
5. Raj Kamal Jha, *The Blue Bedspread* (London: Picador, 1999; rpt. 2000), p. 1.
6. Raj Kamal Jha, *If You are Afraid of Heights* (London: Picador, 2003), p. 137.

Indian English Novel: A Historical Perspective and Problems

RAVI BHUSHAN

Indian writing in English is about 150 years old. It was Raja Ram Mohun Roy (1774-1833) who first wrote in English. Introduced in the mid-nineteenth century, the English language in India has become a powerful medium of expression and a cementing force.

K.S. Ramamurti in his book *Rise of the Indian Novel in English* traces the origin of the Indian novel to the general socio economic changes, political awareness, spread of education, the gradual emancipation of women and similar other causes. With Bankim Chandra Chatterjee's *Rajmohan's Wife*, significant for its stark realism, the first novel in English was published in 1864. Since then the Indian novel in English has grown enormously in many directions.

Of late, the importance of Indian English fiction has been well recognised. Many Indian English novels have demonstrated the feasibility of Indians writing English fiction. Though the great hurdle, in the form of the unique intricacies of social life and the untranslatable nuances of conversational speech, the creative Indian English novelists have overcome this insurmountable hurdle. Many good novels and short stories have appeared either as translations or as original works. The present century stands testimony to the fruitful developments in the field of fiction in English by Indian writers.

The marvellous Toru Dutt, besides her many poems and her French novel, wrote in her teens an English novel *Bianca or The Young Spanish Maiden*. It was a remarkable performance for a girl to whom English was utterly an alien language.

Romesh Chander Dutt's *The Lake of Palms: A Story of Indian Domestic Life* and *The Slave Girl of Agra: An Indian Historical Romance* (1909) are great novels on Indian sensibility in Mughal times. Another Bengali novelist S.K. Ghosh wrote *1001 Indian Nights* (1905) and *The Price of Destiny* 1909.

Among prominent South Indian writers, B.R. Rajan Iyer wrote *Vasudeva Sastri*, a great work in English fictionin the Fieldingian burlesque style. T. Ramakrishna, another South Indian novelist, wrote *Padmini* (1909) and *The Dive for Death* (1911). Former is a historical romance of the 16th century and latter a work on superstitions practised in South India. J.C. Durai, A. Subramanyam and Panchapakesha Ayyar are other writers worth mentioning.

The only writers from the Punjab who have attempted English fiction are Miss Sorabji for *Love and Life behind the Purdah, Sunbabies* and *Between the Twilights*. She talks of love and life behind Purdah, of sensibilities of Indian womanhood, but inevitably they leave behind a feeling of gloom. Sir Joginder Singh the Ex-member for Education and Health in the Governor General's Executive Council wrote *Nur Jahan* and *Nasrin*.

K.S. Venkataramani, one of the distinguished Indian English novelists of post-World War era wrote *Paper Boats*, *On the Sand Dunes*, *Kandan, the Patriot* and *Murugan, the Tiller*. Like Tagore, Venkataramani is a poet to the core but his skill at using the novel form as the most suitable channel for communication is unparallelled. Shankar Ram, another Indian English novelist, penned *The Children of the Kaveri* (1927), *Creatures All* (1938) and *Love of Dust*.

Mulk Raj Anand, who wrote in the Thirties, is known for *Across the Black Waters*, *Coolie*, *Two Leaves and a Bud*, *Untouchable*, *The Village* and *The Big Heart*. As a delineator of Indian social life, Anand's sympathies are with the masses, the downtrodden. Another Indian English novelist of present day India is D.F. Karaka. *Just Flesh* and *There Lay the City* are his two novels.

Raja Rao, one of the widely admired post-World War Indian English novelists, is greatly influenced by Joyce, Gertrude Stein and T.S. Eliot. *Kanthapura* by Raja Rao resembles great Indian epics, the *Ramayana* and the *Mahabharata*. The evocation of nightfall in *Kanthapura* is as vibrant with nervous potency as the evocation of evening in T.S. Eliot's "Lovesong of J. Alfred Prufrock." R.K. Narayan, S. Nagarajan, Dewan Sharar and A.S.P. Ayyar are other important novelists of this era.

The frustration brought about by the partition of our country germinated two types of perceptions in the writers. Some were melancholic and others were dreaming of new values and new vistas. After Independence, the Indian English writer of fiction was more self-confident than ever before. There was a sudden widening of the horizons and a deeper interest in the history of our people and country. A peculiar conflict of Ideologies rages in the minds of post-Independence novelists. This phase of novelists seems to stand between two worlds—one dead and other yet to be born.

Though post-Independence Indian English novelists are large in number, substantive work has been done in this regard. Sudhin Ghose with his three books *And Gazelles Leaping*, *Cradle of the Clouds* and *Vermilion Boat* seems to be closer to life than anything that has come from India since Tagore. Bhabani Bhattacharya is another prominent novelist of this era whose *Music for Mohini* and *So many Hungers* have been translated into many European languages.

Ruskin Bond needs no introduction *The Room on the Roof* is a remarkable work by him. The other prominent novelists of this era are: Dilip Kumar Roy (*The Ipward Spiral*), Khushwant Singh (*Train to Pakistan*), Venu Chitale (*In Transit*), M.V. Rama Sarma (*The Stream*), Santha Ram Rau (*Remember the House*) and K.A. Abbas (*Inquilab* and *Tomorrow is Ours*).

Among the women novelists, Anita Desai, Kamala Markandaya, R.P. Jhabvala and Shakuntala Shrinagesh are most important.

Nationalist Movements and political developments in any country affect its literature; for example, *A Tale of Two Cities*, *War and Peace* and *A Farewell to Arms*. The political scene of the 20s, 30s and 40s found a place in the Indian English novels.

Venkataramani's *Murugan, the Tiller* and *Kandan the Patriot* advocate the nationalist spirit. The former advocates Gandhian economics and the latter is an exponent of Gandhian politics. Raja Rao's *Kanthapura* deals with the life of a village that is strongly influenced by the national spirit. Venu Chitale's *In Transit* and K.A. Abbas's *Inquilab* have the theme of the struggle for independence. Kamala Markandaya's *Some Inner Fury* and Balachandra Rajan's *Dark Dancer* exploit the nationalist theme only for its sensational and melodramatic values. Khushwant Singh's *I Shall Not Hear the Nightingale* is another such novel on this theme.

Mulk Raj Anand's *The Private Life of an Indian Prince* and Malgonkar's *The Princes* deal with the problems of the princely states during the national struggle. They present a picture of the Maharajas most of whom indulged in carnal pleasures.

The Indian English novelists have exploited Gandhi's image and presence. Besides the great "trio" Anand, Narayan and Raja Rao, other novelists too have looked at the national leader in different ways. Such novels on Gandhiji can be divided into four groups.

(i) Novels in which Gandhi appears as a character. *Waiting for the Mahatma* (Narayan), *Chronicles of Kedaram* (Nagarajan), *Untouchable* and *The Sword and the Sickle* (Anand)

(ii) Novels in which Gandhiji is a driving force. *Kanthapura* (Raja Rao) and *Kandan the Patriot* (Venkataramani)

(iii) Novels in which Gandhi's followers appear. *The Vendor of Sweets* (Narayan), *A Time to be Happy* (Nayantara Sahgal)

(iv) Novels based on Gandhian Ideals. *Shadow from Ladakh* (Bhattacharya), *Azadi* (Chaman Nahal)

Novelists in India have not lacked the spirit of social criticism. Anand's *Coolie* and *Untouchable* are two powerful examples of social protest. T.S. Pillai in his *Two Measures of Rice* highlights the possibilities of a class war if the justice to the peasants is denied. Hunger and despair, caused by industry and modern technology, are aptly depicted by Kamala Markandaya in her *Nectar in a Sieve*.

From time immemorial the saffron robed sanyasin has been a part of the Indian life. Novelists have tried to expose the bogus sanyasins. *The Guide* by Narayan is a good example. Again, in Bhattacharya's *He who Rides a Tiger*, pretence of a bogus sanyasin is exposed. Many other novels dealing with the ascetics are *Inner Door* by Nergis Dalal, *A Silence of Desire* by Markandaya and *All abort H. Hatterr* by G.V. Desani.

Isolation, Alienation, Divided self, Schizophrenia and other related concepts have been explored in world literature. The sense of isolation, in the 60s, 70s and 80s became a strong recurrent motif in Indian novel in English. The restless and rootless lives of innumerable immigrants have been aptly depicted in Markandaya's *The Nowhere Man*, Dilip Hiro's *A Triangular View*, Murari's *The Marriage*, Anita Desai's *Bye-Bye Blackbird* and Jamila and Reginold Massey's *The Immigrant*. The different kinds of alienation portrayed in Anita Desai's *Cry, the Peacock* and *Voices in the City* remind us of the Biblical idiom "a cry in the wilderness."

One of the most difficult problems which the Indian writers faced was the problem of language. The Indian writer in English must evolve a language flexible and varied enough to suit different fictitious characters drawn from most varied professions and strata of society to create the impression of verisimilitude and authenticity. Mulk Raj Anand has tried to solve the problem by Indianisation of English words, by literal translation into English of Indian expressions and proverbs. Raja Rao has more successfully solved this problem. He does not write 'Babu' English, but successfully transmutes into English, the idiom, the rhythm and tone of the natural speech of his characters. R.K. Narayan writes admirably lucid English, perfectly adapted to communicate Indian sensibility. The Indian novelist in English must evolve an Indian English, before he can achieve any significant success. Indian English as defined by V.K. Gokak is the language whose body is correct English usage but whose soul is Indian in colour, thought and imagery.

Another problem faced by Indian novelist in English is that of creating an Indian consciousness. Novels in English are likely to command a market not only in India but all over the English-speaking world. Hence he must project an image of India and her culture, authentic and national in character, rather than distorted, narrow and regional.

Another problem for the Indian novelist in English is that of expression of western impact on Indian culture. The Indian novelist faces problem in giving artistic expression to the effect of economic changes and Industrialisation on the community, the class structure, the old relations among occupations and profession and above all in family ties. Cultural contact and cultural change must be faithfully expressed by the Indian English novelist.

The fact that the novel in English has an all-India character and is likely to be read even beyond national borders, becomes a serious artistic fault. The regional customs, rites and ceremonies are to be made an integral part of story and they should be justified by their context. Explanatory details are, therefore, unavoidable, but they must be carefully and skilfully woven into the fabric of the total design.

Today, the themes of the Indian English novel are many and varied, viz.; portrayal of poverty, hunger and disease; portrayal of widespread social evils and tensions; examination of the survivals of the past; inter social relations, the Indian national movement and struggle for freedom, partition of India and the conflict between tradition and modernity etc.

The younger novelists display an increasing inwardness in their themes. The theme of loneliness and rootlessness, the exploration of the psyche and the inner man have been dealt with by Anita Desai in *Cry, the Peacock* and *Voices in the City* and by Arun Joshi in *The Foreigner*.

The Indian novel continues to change and grow, and adapt itself to the changing Indian environment. Social, political, technological and industrial changes have brought corresponding changes in its substance. However, in the field of characterisation, the Indian novelist in English has not been quite so successful. His characters continue to be stereotypes. The problem of creating 'round' three-dimensional figures has not been successfully tackled so far. Many Indian novelists have failed to create adequately individualised characters.

Leaning of Indian English novelists towards didacticism and allegory is a great obstacle in their success as novelists of international repute.

Though many Indian English writers have used the latest narrative techniques like the stream of consciousness and flashback, they cannot stand comparison with European giants like Kafka and Joyce. Again, mentally abnormal characters have not so far found their way into Indian fiction as in *The Sound and the Fury* by Faulkner.

Of course, India with its long hoary tradition of myth, religion and literature and its present life with all its social, political, linguistic and religious diversity will always provide material for future novelists. The Indian novelist even today is sometimes carried away by the lure of creating the image of romantic and glamorous India, the India of Rajas and Maharajas, and of mystic saints and sadhus who can achieve miracles. Thus Mulk Raj Anand in his *Private Life of a Prince* and Malgonkar in his *The Princes* portray the splendours of royal life and Kamala Markandaya in her *Possession* presents a weird picture of mysterious India. There is an urgent need for Indian novelist in English to safeguard himself against the tendency to distort reality. He has to be sensitive to the development in the technique of fiction of the experimental kind. Juxtaposition of tradition with modernity and myth with reality is the need of the hour.

Identity Crisis of Arun Joshi's Protagonists

ADARSH KHANNA

According to *The Oxford English Dictionary*, identity in an individual context refers to "the sameness of a person or thing at all times or all circumstances; the condition or fact that a person or thing is itself and not something else."[1] Personal identity has three basic components: "a sense of personal distinctiveness," "a sense of personal continuity" and "a sense of personal autonomy."[2] A person comes to develop a strong sense of his or her identity if (a) he or she sees himself or herself as different from other people, indeed distinctive and unique, (b) if he strives to be self-consistent displaying continuity in his attitudes, beliefs and actions and (c) if he has the ability to act in an "autonomous" way, making his own independent decisions. He will feel his identity to be threatened if he is faced with a situation not salutary to any one of the essential components of his sense of identity.

Erikson identifies eight developmental stages: early infancy, later infancy, early childhood, middle childhood, puberty and adolescence, early adulthood, middle adulthood, late adulthood[3] in which the identity is crystallized. Each stage leads the person through a new conflict or crisis which has to be resolved satisfactorily for successful transition to the next stage. Even if one has resolved the crises during various stages, it does not mean that identity has been constructed once for all. There are plenty of disequilibrating events in the course of life to engender identity crisis. Erikson observes that a sense of identity "is never gained or maintained once and for all. Like a good conscience, it is constantly lost and regained."[4]

Identity crisis in general refers to psychological stress or anxiety about the sense of identity. A person undergoes this psychologically distressing experience when he feels that his personal identity is being spoiled or threatened. It entails in particular a sense of disjuncture from what one has hitherto assumed oneself to be one's 'real identity.' In short, identity crisis means the feeling of the loss of a sense of personal identity or depersonalization. Two types of experiences generally represent threats to personal sameness (i) violations of self-expectations and (ii) changes in the self, in whole or in part. A person, who pretends to an identity that he does not have or dissembles an identity that is fundamental to him, often becomes neurotic, even schizophrenic. This feeling of split personality is both painful and troublesome. Having lost the sense of personal identity, such a man feels alienated and lonely and makes frantic efforts to seek, organize and affirm his sense of identity. His affiliation with the group of his choice, his acceptance and recognition as a person in a career-role in society, his commitment to definite values and beliefs in life will produce feelings of belonging and security resulting in regaining and reaffirmation of his lost identity.

Arun Joshi is undoubtedly a great psychological novelist, for he withdraws from outer reality and delves deep into inner recesses of human heart, "exploring human pains and predicaments, sense and sensibility."[5] He is passionately concerned with "crisis of self and a quest for fulfilment."[6] All his protagonists whether it is Sindi of *The Foreigner*, Billy Biswas of *The Strange Case of Billy Biswas* and Som Bhaskar of *The Last Labyrinth* face an existentialist dilemma. According to R.S. Pathak, "Joshi's novels read like the spiritual odyssey of the twentieth century man who has lost his spiritual moorings."[7] His fiction reinforces an increasing awareness of man's rootlessness and the consequent feelings of anxiety and alienation that afflict him.

Arun Joshi's first novel *The Foreigner* deals with the story of an orphaned young man Sindi Oberoi who loses his parents in an air-crash and is brought up by an uncle in Kenya. He receives his education in East Africa, London and America. Devoid of paternal love, familial bonds and cultural roots, Sindi grows up as a rootless young man with a built-in fissure in his personality. Dislocated as he is, his only feeling of himself is of an alien as he says: "My foreignness lay within me and I could not leave myself behind wherever I went."[8] The little sense of security, which he has when his uncle is alive, is totally shattered after his death. His experiences of living in Kenya, London and Boston further deepen his feeling of insecurity. He feels restless in Kenya and even contemplates suicide. He immigrates to London but there also he finds his life dull and meaningless. He invariably holds discussion with a Catholic priest to find a clue to the mystery of his existence. In the absence of a firm sense of identity, he tries to define it by developing intimacy with two young women Anna and Kathy. Their company and friendship enlivens his personality for sometime. He experiences pleasure and pain which make him acutely conscious of the fact that "all love . . . was illusion and all pain sprang from this illusion." (170) He realizes that self-involvement is the root cause of his emotional problems and by adopting an attitude of detachment, he can better meet the challenges of life.

Despite the death-struggle of his soul to practise detachment, Sindi gets involved with a beautiful and benign American girl June. His involvement with her is very baffling for it does not resolve his predicament. He is all the time afraid of possessing her and in turn getting possessed by her. Even June discerns something strange about him as she says: "I have a feeling you'd be a foreigner anywhere." (33) The individual whose being is insecure cannot have complete union with anyone. For this reason, he does not respond favourably to June's proposal and tells her frankly, "Marriage would not help June. We are alone, both you and I." But when June leaves him, he feels miserable and insecure. The emptiness that surrounds him leaves him dazed. Sindi is sad to think that he has wasted twenty-five years "in the search of peace," (92) what he has got in return is a bankrupt soul and "no amount of plundering can enrich it again." (140)

Babu's suicide gives Sindi a jolt in his life. He wishes that instead of Babu, he should have died for he has nothing to lose. He begins to hate himself more and more. He comes to believe that his total preoccupation with self in pursuit of detachment has resulted in the death of his friend and his sweetheart. After June's death, he realizes that detachment consists in right action and not inaction. He finally decides to come to India hoping that it will provide him "a place to anchor on this lonely planet." (76) But here he is faced with a different problem. While in Britain and America, Sindi is Kenya-born Indian, in India he is treated as an outsider. He fails to establish any bond with the people of India. Thus his last attempt to strike his roots in India ends in dismal failure. Drifting aimlessly from country to country Sindi fails to affiliate himself to any country, culture or community as "his alienation is of the soul and not of geography."[9]

In *The Strange Case of Billy Biswas*, Arun Joshi has carried "his exploration of the consciousness of helpless, rootless people a stage further and has revealed to our gaze to new gas chambers of self-forged misery."[10] Billy's identity crisis is different from and deeper than that of Sindi. Despite his conventional roots, high social status and a secure job, Billy feels estranged from the upper crust of Indian society and craves for the primordial. He is a man "with extraordinary obsessions."[11] He opts to study anthropology and not engineering for which his parents sent him to America. He prefers to stay in Harlem, an abode of American aboriginals, instead of Manhattan. Billy at times does such crazy things which betray a streak of primitivism in him. At a music party in Gorge's apartment, Billy all of a sudden starts playing on a drum at a feverish pitch which holds everybody by its "mesmeric pull." (21)

After his return to his native land, Billy does not feel at home. He begins to feel that his roots are elsewhere. He tells Romi, "I was not where I belonged." (181) In order to cure his obsession for the primitive, Billy marries Meena Chatterjee and tries to settle down in life. He is blessed with a son. But these bonds do not help him get rid of his visions. Something goes on corroding him and brings him to the verge of despair. Though he is son of a Supreme Court judge, lecturer in anthropology at Delhi University and husband of Meena, yet his identity is a question mark for him. He withdraws from his parents, wife, friends and relatives. He fails to identify himself with sham values of the upper strata of the society and a sense of hollowness haunts him. No one has any idea of what is going on in the "dark, inscrutable, unsmiling eyes of Billy Biswas." (99)

During his anthropological expeditions to the Saal forest, Billy gets an opportunity to taste pleasures of primitive life and he feels that he himself was a tribal. This experience is in fact crystallization of the one he had had at an impressionable age of fourteen at Bhubaneswar. In Maikala hills, all that Billy has been confusedly driving towards is brought into sharp focus. The great moment of self-fulfilment comes in his life when he meets Bilasia, a tribal beauty. He finds in her the very essence of that primitive force which had called him night after night, year after year. Quite irresistibly and naturally, Billy gets drawn to Bilasia and finds himself becoming part of her world. Having discovered his roots and moorings among the tribals of Saal forest, Billy settles down to a primitive way of life. When Romi meets Billy after a gap of ten years, he finds him totally tribalised. He relishes their food, speaks their language, and shares their beliefs and superstitions. All that he wants is mahua, feasting, dancing and love-making. The tribals adore him as a prince and he becomes the healer who can cure dying children and ward off tigers.

Billy has absolutely no desire to return to the civilized world. Rather when the civilized world comes to claim him, Billy resists and prefers death and disaster to going back to that materialistic and meaningless existence. He pays the price of his life to save and preserve his real identity as a tribal. What the civilized world could take back was not Billy—the engineer, the anthropologist but ashes of Billy Bhaiya—the mythical king of the tribals.

In *The Last Labyrinth*, Arun Joshi explores Som Bhaskar's mind which is perplexed by the questions about life, existence and reality. The contradictory impulses of intellect and intuition, doubt and faith, scepticism and blind submission pull him in opposite directions with the result that he suffers from the crisis of consciousness. His every experience and every relationship, much to his dismay, deepens his sense of inadequacy and he continues to wander through the maze of existence. Blessed with almost everything of the world—an extraordinary wife, two children, name, fame and fortune—he suffers from "an undefinable hunger, a restlessness, a Hamlet-like incertitude, an inherent sickness."[12] The mysterious voices that he hears and the strange visions that he sees make him gloomy and insomniac. Sleeping pills, tranquillisers and hot baths fail to soothe his tortured mind and his frayed nerves. His psyche is affected deep down by his heredity. His mother's blind faith in Krishna and his father's scientific and analytical outlook baffle him. The dichotomy in the outlook and beliefs of his parents affect the harmony and balance of his personality. His scepticism aggravates his predicament as he says, "If I believed in God I could pray. . . . But that's out."[13] Leela Sabnis, Michigan-trained psychologist analyses him and tells him, "You are a neurotic." (80) His dialogue with Leela Sabnis regarding faith and intuition proves to be futile.

Som Bhaskar finds some strange mysterious attraction in Anuradha—the pock-marked woman and is irresistibly drawn towards her. He utters, "I wanted her body and soul, every bit of her." (33) Gifted with a special vision, Anuradha finds Bhaskar a victim of deep-seated scepticism and overwhelming rationalism. Though Som is fascinated by the obsolete world of Anuradha and Aftab yet he does not share their faith in the invisible and the mysterious. His two selves do not cohere and he is in great agony. He becomes a stranger to his wife and children, neglects his companies and feels himself becoming vulnerable to melancholy. He finds his existence meaningless and his life, "a labyrinth within the labyrinths." (29) He even meets Gargi, the deaf-mute daughter of a Sufi pir to get rid of his restlessness. She suggests to him to believe in God but Som requires evidence for that also. He badly needs the healing touch of faith but his scientific temperament and outlook obstruct this leap of faith. Bhaskar knows what ails him, what afflicts him, for he exclaims, "If discontent is my trademark, trust is *Gita's*." (63)

Bhaskar's "nagging, enervating doubts" (53) finally bring him to the brink of insanity. His emotional and spiritual distress begins to assume alarming proportions. He cries out "Anuradha if there is a God . . . tell Him, tell this God to have mercy upon me." (223) Like his father Bhaskar does not want to die of melancholy which seems to be getting better of him. There is sincere and continuous effort on his part to find satisfactory answers to his inexplicable questions. He is like Abhimanyu in the *Mahabharata* who is not able to come out of the chakravyuha. Som continues to languish in the chakravyuha of life and death, reality and illusion, doubt and faith.

Thus we see that all the three protagonists of Joshi suffer from existential anguish, feeling of alienation, estrangement from the self and lack of belongingness. Sindi remains a drifter all his life. He finds all shores alien to his soul. He remains an uprooted young man who fails to get rid of his foreignness which is intrinsic. In the case of Som Bhaskar, there is tortured awareness of his conflict. Having entered the mysterious labyrinths of life, he tries to come out of them by logic and reasoning but fails to find a way out. He prefers to cry and wail than to trust and follow anyone blindly. Billy alone is able to resolve his crisis by liberating himself from the clutches of fake civilization. Listening to the call of his inner self, he goes to live with the tribals and succeeds in finding his roots there. By leading the life for which his soul had been craving, Billy attains self-fulfilment and his instinctive and real self blossoms into one whole.

NOTES

1. *The Oxford English Dictionary* (Britain: Oxford University Press, 1961), vol. V, p. 19.
2. M.J. Apter, "Human Action and the Theory of Psychological Reversals," G. Underwood and R. Stevens, ed., *Aspects of Consciousness*, Vol. 1: *Psychological Issues* (London: Academic Press, 1979).
3. Erik H. Erikson, "Identity and the Life Cycle: Selected Papers," *Psychological Issues*, 1 (1959).
4. *Ibid.*, p.57.
5. Pramod Kumar Singh, *Major Indo-English Novelists and Novels* (Jaipur: Sublime Publications), p. 102.

6. Hari Mohan Prasad, *Arun Joshi* (Liverpool: Lucas, 1985), p. 46.
7. R.S. Pathak, "Human Predicament and Meaninglessness in Arun Joshi's Novels," *The Fictional World of Arun Joshi*, ed. R.K. Dhawan (New Delhi: Classical, 1986), p. 109.
8. Arun Joshi, *The Foreigner* (New Delhi: Hind Pocket, 1968), p. 61.
9. Arun Joshi, "Introduction," *The Foreigner*.
10. K.R.S. Iyengar, *Indian Writing in English* (New Delhi: Sterling), p. 514.
11. Arun Joshi, *The Strange Case of Billy Biswas* (New Delhi: Orient Paperbacks, 1986), p. 7.
12. Hari Mohan Prasad, p. 86.
13. Arun Joshi, *The Last Labyrinth* (New Delhi: Orient Paperbacks, 1981), p. 10.

Quest for Identity in Ruth Prawer Jhabvala's *Three Continents*

SUSHIL KANSAL

As an expatriate writer, Ruth Prawer Jhabvala occupies a unique and a somewhat confusing position in Indian fiction in English. While some of the critics tend to classify her as an 'insider', others vehemently claim her to be an 'outsider'. This controversy notwithstanding, Jhabvala, with her dozen novels and half-a-dozen collections of short stories, holds an envious position among the women novelists of Indian fiction in English.

Jhabvala was born in 1927 in the German city of Cologne, being the daughter of a Polish Jewish lawyer named Marcus Prawer and his wife, Leonora Cohn Prawer. The Nazi movement forced the family to migrate to England in 1939. In 1951, she married an Indian architect and came to India. She remained in India for 24 long years and has since 1975 made the United States as her abode.

Ruth Jhabvala has been the recipient of a number of major awards and prizes. In 1975, her novel *Heat and Dust* won Britain's prestigious Booker Prize. The following year, she received John Simon Guggenham Memorial Fellowship. Three years later, in 1979, she was awarded the Neil Gunn International Fellowship, and in 1986 she was given the Mac Arthur Foundation Award. Jhabvala's screenplays for the Ismail Merchant James Ivory film of E.M. Forster's novel *A Room with a View* won an Academy Award in 1987. She has also won an Oscar Award for her film script play adaptation for the Merchant Ivory film of E.M. Forster's novel *Howard's End.*

Jhabvala's twelve novels can be neatly divided into three groups. The first group includes the "Indian" novels where her focus is on Indian families and the inherent Indianness. In the second phase, her focus is on social intercourse vis-à-vis East-West encounter with special reference to the European attitudes to India. *Heat and Dust* was published during this phase in 1975 after which she took residence in New York. The four novels published after 1975 may safely be labelled as the European novels. These novels include *In Search of Love and Beauty*, *Three Continents*, *Poet and Dancer* and *Shards of Memory*. They form the third and final phase of her writing. The concern here is to probe the Bohemian European psyche with Indian characters remaining at the periphery. The theme of spirituality forms the axis around which these novels revolve. The present paper will focus on her novel *Three Continents* and try to explore how subtly the theme of quest for identity has been handled by Jhabvala.

As suggested by the very title *Three Continents*, the action of the novel spans over the three continents: America, Europe (Britain) and Asia (India)—thereby achieving an epic-like width. The main characters in the novel are inspired by the dream of an international life. They, therefore, wish to start a *Sixth World Movement*[1] ensuring peace and happiness for the whole mankind. The new sage, a minor Indian prince with the title of Rawul, leads this movement, which offers 'a religion for a world which has outgrown religion,'[2] a doctrine of universal brotherhood which will dissolve the boundaries between nations and continents and lead, in time, to world unity. He appears in the United States, accompanied by Rani, his glamorous consort, and Crishi, their adopted son. The trio wins the confidence of the nineteen-year-old American twins Harriet and Michael Wishwell and tries to lay their hands on the property of the twins. The action of the novel begins in the American continent. Michael Wishwell, brother of Harriet Wishwell, acts as the leader of the group. He invites many of his friends from different parts of the world to discuss the new ideas and put them into practice, if possible. They formally inaugurate their programme by hoisting a flag in the garden near the imposing ancient building called 'Propinquity'. The twins accompany the three foreigners first to London and then to India. In India, we see the true colours of this movement when we see it as purely political. The reader sees these events through the eyes of the narrator, Harriet, who is so besotted by her sexual bond to Crishi that she does not comprehend the many facts to the discredit of this man, of the Rani, and to a lesser extent of the Rawul, that gradually come to her knowledge.

Michael and Harriet Wishwell are American twins residing in the Hudson River Valley, which is in the heart of America. Their parents being divorced, they mostly lived with their 'grandparents in the various embassies to which grandfather was posted.' (11) Harriet Wishwell (Michael's sister) is the narrator of the novel who feels that it was due to -the spending of some crucial years in the middle East and then farther East that "we got our restlessness or dissatisfaction with what was supposed to be our heritage that is, America." (11) It is due to this feeling of restlessness that Michael once again travels back to the Orient 'sometimes in Kathmandu and sometimes in Goa, and then he turned up in Bodh Gaya, and then Gangtok, and back in Kathmandu.' (11) In fact, this sense of dissatisfaction and boredom had already given rise to many serious and weighty questions in the minds of the young Wishwells.

Quest for 'something' becomes evident from the very first line of the novel when it suggests the search of the twins for something better; when the narrator says: 'Michael, my twin brother, and I always wanted something other—better—than we had.' (11) And it is Michael Wishwell's search for Love and Beauty, his expectation 'of Beauty, Truth and Justice' (383) that brings him into contact with the Rawul's movement and leads to the introduction of the Rawul and his followers into Propinquity—the twins' family home in the Hudson River Valley. Michael is a 'Wishwell'—full of hope; but about to discover at the cost of his life the difficulties of putting 'all the ideals' into practice. Before his involvement with the movement, Michael's first decision has been (like Bellow's Henderson, like James himself and a number of his protagonists) to flee across America in search of wisdom, to thwart the apparently enslaving propinquities of family and society in favour of freedom which, as Michael's case reveals, can become an almost pathological loneliness and isolation. When Michael meets the trio—Crishi, Rani and the Rawul—on his second visit to India, he is literally swept off his feet. He feels that he has found a leader, a guru, a spiritual healer in the Rawul, whose seventh World Movement (later Transcendental Internationalism) would certainly liberate him, free him from all worldly desires and help him achieve salvation. Totally mesmerized by the Rawul and his movement, Michael invites him and his entourage to America, to Propinquity, their home. So utterly desperate is the young Michael to cling on to something, to someone, that he feels that he has finally found 'Om, the real thing'. He tells Harriet that the Rawul, Rani and Crishi 'operated on the highest level possible'. For once Harriet does not agree with her brother. For one reason, neither of them was the type to join a leader or a movement without testing the whole thing: "For us, believing was something you had to do for yourself—find for yourself and not be influenced by anything or anyone outside. Perhaps it was quest for truth, though we never called it that." (22) The twins have between them an expression coined for all that is phony—they call it '*Neti*': "When something didn't come up to our standard, it was *neti:* not right, not Om, not Tao, not the real thing; phony." (22)

Michael, like a tragic hero, falls prey to the falsities of the Rawul, the Rani and Crishi, chiefly because of his own vulnerability. The twins and the other followers of the Rawul seek to transcend their own egos. Whereas the religious devotees give up the rational and humanitarian values ,which dictate that every human being is to be respected as a unique individual and *that* suffering is to be relieved by such material means as the scientific medicine—Michael, who has an affluent background and good lineage, becomes ready material for the vultures of spirituality. Michael's search for spirituality is actually the search for his own identity. Michael has had occasion to' travel to the Middle East and Far East for holidays with a grandfather who held ambassadorial assignments. But even though they have "what people would say was pretty good," the twins Michael and Harriet Wishwell are yearning for something more. They suffer from the ills of a materialistic society; a broken home, divorced parents seeking in vain more satisfying relationships in numerous philandering. They both drop out of college eventually but it is Michael who does so first and sets out in quest of an emotional sustenance or "the real thing." He resists the usual abodes of "hippies"—Kathmandu, Gangtok, Bodh Gaya and Goa. But it is in Delhi that he encounters the dubious Crishi in a seedy hotel they are both occupying, very near a Hindu temple. Crishi is wicked from the start but Michael is blind to it.

The reason of Crishi's interest in Michael is for his family's wealth, connections, and heritage. When the novel starts we see that Michael has no interest in his family's heritage unlike Mark of *In Search of Love and Beauty* who spends much of his time and money attempting to recover his paternal American heritage. We see that Propinquity (meaning "nearness in place or in blood relationship"), the title of a section of the novel and the name of the Wishwell home, suggests that heritage is important. This house is in one of the heartlands of America and not only is a private inheritance but also a symbol of the whole of the patriarchal American cultural heritage.

In *Three Continents,* Jhabvala tries to show that it is the family which is the basis of all the happiness and thus any quest for identity finds its true destination within the familial happiness. The reason for Michael and Harriet's succumbing to the movement is not only their materialistic ennui but also the bankruptcy of familial happiness and the rootless kind of life that they lead. Harriet's parents are divorced. Her father Manton, who is now having an affair, with. Barbara, young enough to be his daughter, lives outside Propinquity. Lindsay, her mother, who does live in Propinquity, shares a homosexual relationship with her female friend Jean. It is then clear that the children have never had an occasion to feel familial joys and the kind of healthy relationships that are offered in normal families. So it is their rootlessness, which serves as the cause of their quest for identity. Their quest for spiritualism is actually the search for their family, their heritage. According to Henry Summerfleld: "In *Three Continents,* revulsion from a society of easy divorce, frequent changes of partner, and rootless children becomes as important a theme as falling into the hands of false teachers."[3] As Peter Ackroyd comments, the experience of the characters suggest, "that to be without a "home" is to be without a moral sense also."[4] Manton Wishwell, the feather-headed father of them, and Barbara, his glamorous girlfriend eventually turn with relief to the joys of marriage and parenthood. Even Manton's divorced wife finds solace with a lesbian lover. She attends her ex-husband's wedding when he marries Barbara and takes pleasure in the couple's baby. Manton feels strongly about the family, and, as Barbara puts it, hates 'everyone not caring and letting everything go and fall apart. It's taken him till now to realize that it's more important than anything—the family, and everything that's been built up; holding it all together . . . that we should all be together. Hold together.' (229)

The charisma and magical spell of the movement breaks but not before Harriet has married Crishi. Slowly but surely, it now dawns upon her, that she has been tricked, cheated and taken for a ride. The reality of the trio is so nauseating, so overwhelming, so sinister, but at the same time so powerful that Harriet cannot do anything.

It turns out that Rani is not the Rawul's wife, nor Crishi his adopted son. Theirs was a chance meeting and what brought them together were their common interests in drug peddling, smuggling and stealing of antiques. The Rawul, who is "the owner of a small kingdom, called the Kingdom of Dhoka in some obscure corner of India, managed to send rare paintings to England and America, which were in turn handled by Rani (her real name is Renee) and Crishi, who eventually turns out to be Rani's lover.

The action of the novel moves from America to England. To escape the police and to protect Crishi especially, the whole group moves to London. Here, Harriet has more bitter truths in store for her. The Rawul has a second wife, *Bari Rani* and three daughters. Rani is already married and her ex-husband Rupert runs an art gallery where surreptitious deals are made with the connivance of Crishi. Thus, Rupert too is an accomplice. Harriet finds it extremely difficult to adjust under these horrifying circumstances. Her life in London is not what she had expected: "My married life really started in London and it wasn't what I had expected." (157) Michael too starts distancing from the organization. Although there are sufficient hints in the novel to suggest that Michael had been sharing a physical relationship with Crishi, their bond seems to loosen a bit. Michael understands as much as Harriet does but is yet not ready to give in.

Harriet, with the thoughts of achieving absolute destination, keeps on comforting Michael and feels that their ultimate journey to the kingdom of Dhoka would certainly be more productive and. fruitful. She is desperate to achieve "our real destination: that is, to Dhoka, to the Rawul's kingdom, the source and fountainhead of our movement, where everything would be refreshed and restored." (266) She feels it to be 'a sort of absolute destination from which there was no looking back.' (266) Thus, in a heat of hope of getting to their destination, their identity, the twins accompany the entourage to New Delhi where darker passages await them.

It is back in India and upon meeting regularly with his step grandmother Sonya, and watching the true colours of the Rawul and the movement, that the Maya or illusion begins to disappear from Michael's eyes. His feeling is both true and tragic. His situation at that moment is of 'Christ among the moneychangers.' (332) His is a case of classic dilemma. He cannot go back to America, 'not to Lindsay and Manton and everything else you've always run away from. All that damn neti'. (334) The Rawul and his group do best to cajole him not because they were afraid but because they might lose them and thereby the whole of Propinquity, the paternal property and the hard cash. Both Michael and Harriet are trapped. Michael urges Harriet to leave then and there: 'Sonya's right. Tom's right. We should go.' He is completely broken inside and his entire spiritual quest and the quest for Truth, Beauty and Justice seems to be leading him nowhere. He does not mince words to confess that there's been a mistake: "It's like you think and think and think—about what you want and don't want; about what you're going to do and not going to do; and all the time something quite different is preparing inside you, so suddenly you know not what you want to do but you have to." (334)

Harriet's position is no better. Having found a husband, even if he is a smuggler, a swindler and a highly organized criminal, she is ready to cling on to him for she still believes that wherever there is Crishi there is always hope. Having no other choice, Michael decides to leave and Harriet decides to stay. Harriet's decision to stay has been variously interpreted by critics. Most of them feel that this is due to her sexual enslavement by the cunning Crishi. This, however, is not the case. Since childhood, Harriet has always looked upon Michael for all kinds of emotional support. Now after her marriage to Crishi, she cannot think beyond him. So, she still feels that Crishi will not fail her. Harriet, even after knowing the truth about Crishi, decides to live with him. Crishi, realizing that Michael can prove to be the biggest irritant in his scheme of things, gets him murdered in cold blood, instructing Rani to return to London and await his orders. Harriet is constantly kept under the impression that Michael has been wounded in a scuffle and is now convalescing at Dhoka. In fact, Crishi is so thorough that he even manages to have Michael cremated before Harriet and her step grandmother can realize that Michael is dead. Eventually, on reaching Dhoka, all Harriet's dreams are dashed to the ground. Her first impression of the place suggests that she has encountered a sort of anti-climax to all the grand ideas she had formed:

> I had often thought of this palace, of which I had heard a great deal, but it turned out entirely different from my conception. From a distance, that is, when we first came in through the gates, it looked imposing and intact, but as we drew nearer, I could see that it was entirely derelict . . . rain had poured through and rotted the floors . . . and everywhere it was the same, complete and utter ruin, emptiness and desolation. (377)

Crishi has such an influence on Harriet that even when Harriet knows Michael has been murdered, she goes along with Crishi's plans to present his death as suicide. The unfeeling Crishi makes her write a fake suicide note in the name of Michael and when she does so, she tries to feel like what Michael would have felt if he had committed suicide and had also left a suicide note:

> I, Michael, was going away because there was nothing in this world that was good enough for me; that I had tried everything and had looked in every direction and there was just absolutely nothing that came up to my expectations—that is, of Beauty, Truth, and Justice—then you feel cheated by everything that falls short of them; and everything here—that is, here in this world does fall short of them. It is all neti, neti, and neti. (383)

When Michael dies, we see that though he too is taken in by Crishi and the movement, yet he has the strength to admit that his commitment to the movement was misguided. His search for identity in the movement comes to its end when he realizes his mistake. He is prepared to go back to his family, his roots and he is prepared to change his mind about donating his inheritance and that is why he is killed. But, what about Harriet? With Harriet's dreams shattered, she has hardly any options left. Going back to Propinquity is obviously out of question. Revolt is impossible against Crishi because after Michael it is only he whom Harriet has so completely loved. And after the death of Michael, she has no other option but just to go on with Crishi, who loves her only for her estate. Harriet's search also ends with Crishi, as she is totally dependent on him for her physical needs.

For the Rawul, heritage is important. The Rawul particularly values the heritage that Michael opens up to him: "What he especially values in using our house as his headquarters was that it placed him right at the heart of American society." (45) That is, it gave him a sense of belonging and thus effectively opened a significant door for the Rawul's movement. And the Rawul makes much of his own heritage: "he had a kingdom—a very small but very ancient one: the kingdom of Dhoka." (12-13) The kingdom may never have been of anything but minor importance, but the Rawul emphasizes that it is an ancient one, that his kingdom has a long heritage. Yet we know too well that the Rawul is no longer sanctioned to use the title Rawul. Thus to a degree the Rawul has lost his heritage, his identity; he is a displaced and dispossessed person, in search of his identity, which makes the heritage he can claim and perhaps inherit from Michael and Harriet all the more appealing. Rawul is also in search of power and popularity which is possible only after getting the property of the twins.

Much more significant is Crishi and Rani's lack of any clear heritage. We don't discover the full details of their backgrounds for some time—because neither has a family heritage of which her or she can boast. They both have ambiguous backgrounds. Only after the journalist Anna Sultan has written her article about the Rawul's movement does Harriet find about Rani's background and learn the "truth" or at least a more convincing version of Crishi's background. Both are of mixed parentage: "The Rani's mother, part French and part German, had married an Afghan," (138), while Crishi's mother, who we are told now lives in Hong Kong with a Chinese wrestler, is "partly Assamese, partly English—grew up in Calcutta and still has such a sweet Calcutta accent." (188) She isn't sure who Crishi's father is. Both have no identity or heritage. The Rawul, Renee and Crishi claim to be a family. But far from being a "family," then, this trio strikes a blow at the very structure of the family. These are the people—clearly caring nothing about family or propinquity—who invade Propinquity.

According to Feroza Jusawalla, "In *Three Continents,* though Jhabvala firmly locates herself as the outsider looking inside with possibly bitter and hostile memories of India, we see her firmly the 'in-law' bound India not by 'propinquity' but only by ties of marriage signified and personified by the fact that we think of her as Mrs. Jhabvala, the daughter-in-law who never became part of family."[5] This symbol becomes an image as it falls outside the purview of simply being a 'textual signifier'[6] and becomes an overriding image of the representations of Indians is shocking and outrageous. India and Indians are allegorically represented as 'Dhoka', literally translated as deceit, fraud or 'Dhoka' as a verb meaning to dupe. It seems that Jhabvala, the outsider, looking back on India sees it (the country) entirely as a 'dupe'—a deceitful dhoka! She depicts that reality, the image all of India and all that India stands for religiosity, spiritualism etc.

is a fraud, a deception and that through India one cannot know the Absolute, not yet at least. The twins who are in search of Absolute or identity fail to get it through spiritualism.

We see that the novel ends on a note of despair and dejection. It is the first of Jhabvala's novels which does not symbolize any sort of hope in the end. In *A New Dominion*, Raymond returns to his mother, Lee to the ashram and Miss Charlotte back to England, suggesting that all these characters have found their own footholds. In *In Search of Love and Beauty,* Leo is on a path of self-realization when he drives through the snow in search of Stephanie; in *Three Continents,* Jhabvala's tragic vision surfaces itself and continues up to her last published novel *Shards of Memory* through *Poet and Dancer.* Aruna Chakravarty is right when she says: "A central concern in all Ruth Prawer Jhabvala's writing after 1975, then, is the vulnerability and helplessness of western youth in the face of a stronger personality."[7] Such youth become preys to dominating personalities as they are on a quest for identity and not finding their own self, succumb to charlatans and gurus.

Thus, *Three Continents* is once again about the reaffirmation of the fact that family is the basic constituent of society; this alone can provide happiness and peace. Henry Summerfield is nearer the truth when he affirms: "Harriet and Michael, belonging to the class of wealthy young Americans from broken homes, are engaged in a rebellion against the modern rootlessness that has undermined their family's long tradition of public service. . . . Harriet and Michael turn their backs on a tradition of family loyalty combined with patriotism and public service—a tradition rooted in a vision of an organic society of which stable families are the constituent cells." (86)

Search for identity starts from within the family and also ends at the family. It begins as a direct consequence of living and being brought up in an unhappy family. Michael's search for Truth, Beauty and Justice, which actually is a quest for his own identity ends with his physical death. On the other hand, Harriet's desperate need to make a home renders her mentally paralyzed in the hands of the empiric Crishi. Nonetheless, she is still able to understand the sinister designs under which Crishi operates. The shocking revelation that Michael was got killed by Crishi and her eventual succumbing to Crishi's pressure in writing a suicide note on behalf of Michael helps her understand the *modus operandi* of the world she is living in. Thus, her quest for identity ends in a kind of mental abortion—she becomes an individual with a fractured vision, and not able to find a foothold, slides from pegs of sanity. It might not, therefore, be wrong to conclude that in *Three Continents,* quest for identity ends on a note of whimper. And maybe, deep inside the mind of Harriet, the quest still continues.

NOTES

1. In the earlier John Murray and Morrow editions of the novel, the Rawul's movement is known as the Fourth World Movement.
2. Ruth Prawer Jhabvala, *Three Continents*, pp. 184-85.
3. Henry Summerfield, "Religion becomes Political: Ruth Prawer Jhabvala's Tenth Novel," *Passages to Ruth Prawer Jhabvala*, ed. Ralph J. Crane (New Delhi: Sterling, 1991), p. 80.
4. Review of *Three Continents*, *New York Times Book Review*, 23 August 1987, pp. 3, 13.
5. Feroza Jusawalla, "On *Three Continents*: The 'Inside' the 'Outside'," *Passages to Ruth Prawer Jhabvala*, ed. Ralph J. Crane, p. 87.
6. Jacques Derrida, 'Of Grammatology,' *Critical Theory since 1965*, ed. Hazard Adams and Leroy Searle (Tallahassee: Florida State Universal Press, 1986), p. 104.
7. Aruna Chakravarty, *Ruth Prawer Jhabvala: A Study in Empathy and Exile (*New Delhi: B.R., 1998), p. 260.

From Detachment to Commitment in Arun Joshi's *The Foreigner*: Reflections from *The Gita*

ALKA SHARMA

The Gita has profoundly influenced not only Oriental but Occidental cultures as well. It remains a predominant force, an inspiration to braver and nobler living in the present-day existential world. Its deep holistic and religious significance has seeped to the literature of various languages too. Arun Joshi's *The Foreigner* may correspond to many contemporary existential novels, yet on a closer scrutiny it may be seen that the *Gita's* philosophy of action has been delicately interwoven in the sensitive handling of the plot and the psychological delineation of the protagonist's approach towards life and its problems.

Arun Joshi stands almost alone among the Indian English novelists who are preoccupied with modern man's predicament. Joshi has renounced the larger world in favour of man and has engaged himself in a search for the essence of life. He tries to understand the labyrinth of life. Shyam Asnani says that Joshi's skill lies "in his ability to describe experience in a human voice so that the texture of the experience comes through, and his ability to convey the philosophical moral complexities of human life without losing the life itself."[1]

The most besetting problem that man faces today is the problem of meaninglessness. Man fails to perceive any purpose in life and the relevance of his existence in a hostile world. Jean-Paul Sartre says, "Man can count on no one but himself, he is alone."[2] Man is shocked to find that he is no longer the master of his destiny and that there are forces which threaten his life and all its joys and hopes. The absence of meaningful relations is the greatest curse of this age. As Erich Fromm says: "The danger of the past was that men became slaves. The danger of the future is that men may become robots, who will destroy their world and themselves because they cannot stand . . . a meaningless life.'"[3]

The works of Arun Joshi read like the spiritual odyssey of the twentieth century man who has lost his spiritual moorings. The novelist has tried to project through his experiences the crisis of the urbanized and highly industrialised modern civilization along with its dehumanizing impact on the individual who is ever eager to find out and reaffirm the value of meaningful relatedness in life. Every human relationship seems to be casual, objective and functional. Heir to two different sets of customs and torn asunder by the dual code of behaviour, Joshi's characters live on ad hoc basis in no man's land of values. Their quest for props is doomed to end in a perception of the futility of human life. But the novels of Arun Joshi are not entirely critiques of alienation. Joshi uses alienation as a means to lead his characters to community.

The protagonist in *The Foreigner* (1968) is "an existential character rootless, restless and luckless in a bad and absurd world.'"[4] He finds himself in the predicament of a 'foreigner,' a man who does not belong anywhere. This sense of rootlessness springs from his cumulative life experience, which moulds not only his personality but also his vision of life. The protagonist, Sindi Oberoi, presents the dilemma of insecurity and anomic, which has become a stigma for today's youth. In the novel, Arun Joshi explores the individual's anguished consciousness of being isolated from the whole apparatus of social conventions and moral values, and his attempt to understand and face with dignity the "abominable absurdity of the world."[5]

Sindi's parentage and early life made him an ideal foreigner. Born of an English mother and an Indian father in Kenya, Sindi was orphaned at the tender age of four and was brought up by an uncle, with whose death sometime later he lost his anchor forever. Sindi describes his whole life as being "alone in darkness." When Mr. Khemka wants to know how his parents' death took place, his reply has a sting: "For the hundredth time I related the story of those strangers whose only reality was a couple of wrinkled and cracked photographs." (11)

Denied of love, nourishment and cultural roots, he grows with a built-in fissure in his personality and becomes a wandering alien. Against this background of emotional rootlessness, the various incidents of Sindi's life which took him from Nairobi where he was born, to London where he studied, to a night club in Soho where he worked as a dishwasher, to Scotland where he worked at a small village library and discussed religion, god and mysticism with a Catholic priest, to Boston where he studied for six years and met June and Babu and to Delhi where he ultimately settled down, failed to establish in him a sense of meaningful existence with the world. He remained an outsider wherever he went. R.S. Singh says that his dilemma is socio-psychological: "His alienation is not so much geographical or physical, as spiritual as it is born out of the crisis of conscience. He could not, therefore, develop any emotional attachment to any place, person or thing."[6]

Sindi's background and infertile relationship with Anne and Kathy generate an attitude of deliberate inaction in him. These relationships instead of integrating him with society, freeze him emotionally and morally. His words and behaviour created the same impression in all those with whom he came into contact. Very early in her acquaintance with Sindi, June remarked:

> There is something strange about you, you know. Something distant. I'd guess that when people are with you they don't feel like they are with a human being. Maybe it's an Indian characteristic, but I have a feeling you'd be a foreigner everywhere." (30)

Sindi is trapped in his own loneliness, which is accentuated by his withdrawal from the society around him. He reflects on the absurdity of existence:

> I wondered in what way, if any, did I belong to the world that roared beneath my apartment window. Somebody has begotten me without a purpose, . . . perhaps I felt like that because I was a foreigner in America. But then, what difference would it have made if I had lived in Kenya, or India or any other place for that matter? It

> seemed to me that I would still be a foreigner. My foreignness lay within me and I couldn't leave myself behind wherever I went. (61)

After his affairs with Anna and Kathy, frustrated Sindi withdraws himself into a small village in Scotland where after a series of discussions with a Catholic priest, just as the samvad between Lord Krishna and Arjuna, a revelation dawns upon him: "All love, whether of things, persons or oneself, was illusion, and all pain sprang from this illusion. Love begot greed and attachment, and it led to possession." (171) This revelation infused Sindi with a new understanding making him realize that "you can love without attachment, without desire. You can love without attachment to objects of your love." (171) This revelation by Catholic priest represents the philosophy of detachment in the *Gita* that one can remain detached while getting involved.

For Sindi, impermanence of life makes every social institution an illusion and every endeavour a futile exercise. Consequently, he does not believe in any system of morality. His predicament is spelt in clear terms in his dialogue with Mr. Khemka: "You had a clear-cut system of morality, a caste system that laid down all you had to do. You had a God; you had roots in the soil you lived upon. Look at me. I have no roots. I have no system of morality. What does it mean to me if you call me an immoral man. I have no reason to be one thing rather than another." (136)

Consequently with this philosophy of detachment, of desirelessness, Sindi maintained that marriage is "one big illusion, that has been pounded into them by the society. For a while they go around bloated with their own pride imagining things which just are not there. And then gradually the whole thing crumbles and they begin to kill each other bit by bit." (106) Sindi's cynical indifference towards social institutions, his philosophy of detachment is not the result of any pragmatic approach towards life, but manifestation of the search of "wrong things in wrong places." (91)

In England he had a number of affairs but he remained "fancy free." He cherished the false notion that he could ever remain free and uninvolved. However his encounter with June gradually breaks down the barriers of detachment and non-involvement which he had built so painstakingly. "I stayed awake, counting the broken pieces of my detachment." (81) He wants to "inhale her fragrance" (27) but tries not to get attached to her for "one should be able to love without wanting to possess . . . and should be able to detach oneself from the object of one's love." (66) Sindi is forced to analyze this strange sensation and this analytic self has emerged out of a deep anguish and agony, asserting itself as an indication of his dormant philosophic potential: "one becomes what his memories made of him and at any one point in time the future is as inevitable for him as night follows day." (134) Again, he tries to compare himself with what he had been before he met June and finds that he has become "possessive, selfish and greedy." He also observes that he had permitted himself "to become a battlefield where the child and the adult warred unceasingly." (137)

This continuous analysis of the self does not permit him any occasion to evade the questions. The agony of living with unanswered questions, and unattained ambitions, is almost unbearable, as he says: "I wanted the courage to live without desire and attachment. I wanted peace and perhaps a capacity to love. . . . Above all, I wanted to conquer pain. What I could have done . . . if the ball of pain still hung around my neck like a dead albatross?" (146) This analytical approach is the cornerstone of the philosophy of the *Gita*. Sindi also wants to "know the meaning of life." (175) His questions pose the eternal dilemma of the nature of being." (79) He craves for a transcendental vision to create something permanent amidst the haze of quixotic experiences of contemporary culture.

While trying to analyse his experiences of initial trauma, Sindi realizes that the root of all evils, "his foreignness" lay within him only (65). He realizes his mistakes in his dealings with June and Babu, he holds himself responsible for Babu's death. June's accusation, "Look, what your detachment has done," (84) and finally her death crumbles his veneer of self-proclaimed detachment. His realization that sometimes "detachment lies in actually getting involved" (239) becomes the first decisive step in the direction of seeking harmony with the cosmic rhythm. He wants to redeem his past." (234) His sympathy with Muthu, other lowly paid workers and consequent actions represent a positive selfless association with them, which may eventually be the harbinger of a universal brotherhood: "Only the theatre has changed, the show continues." But gradually Sindi Oberoi's understanding deepens as he roots himself into the world of the miserable who live in rags. Human suffering purges him, awakens him, to the real meaning of detachment."[7] Muthu replies to Sindi's apprehension of getting involved: "But it is not involvement, Sir. Sometimes detachment lies in actually getting involved" (225)

Now Sindi, like Arjuna, surrenders to the right kind of involvement and the right kind of action with which his selfish desires have nothing to do. Realising the true nature of his situation, he gives a twist to his name 'Surinder' and calls himself 'Surrender'.[8] Now Sindi understands that detachment does not mean escape or alienation; it means involvement, devotion, sacrifice. Man's authentic existence manifests itself not in escapist philosophy of passive detachment but in active involvement and not with the self, but with the world. Through Sindi, Arun Joshi illustrates what the *Gita* said: "One has to understand what action is, and likewise one has to understand what is wrong action and one has to understand about inaction. And to understand is the way of the work." (IV, 17)[9]

Thus, Joshi seems to reject the deterministic position with its attitude of "wait and wait and let the past determine the future." The *Gita* has a pragmatic approach which inspires to 'act,' to make decisions and take chances in life, if they can lead to a better world. One cannot, therefore, afford to continue with an irresponsible existence but has to commit oneself. Arun Joshi rejects Sindi's excessive rationalism as a way of life. The myopic approach of Sindi distorts his attitude towards life and makes him sceptic about every human involvement.

Arun Joshi inspires to act, to make decisions. Life is not static. The world is dynamic, budding. Every moment springs new surprises and is pregnant with new possibilities, which, if exploited creatively, may lead to a better world order. And it is sheer folly to confront this budding world with a rigid set of preconceived notions and prejudices. These don't consist of the whole truth, the essence of life. Arun Joshi observes that "life's meaning lies not in the glossy surfaces of our pretensions, but in those dark mossy labyrinth of soul, that languish for ever."[10] In fact Joshi's subject is the dark night of the soul and his creations are hopelessly lost, lonely questers after the absurd in the benighted underworld of the inner, dark recesses of existence. Joshi is a connoisseur of souls divided against themselves. Sindi's cynical indifference towards social institutions and his philosophy of detachment are not the result of any pragmatic approach towards life, but manifestation of the search of wrong things in wrong places: "He did not have any morality. He did not believe in the institution of marriage nor did he think much of love, friendship or loyalty in the international context."[11] Although he loves June intensely and experiences a lot with her but in a bid to remain uninvolved Sindi refrains from responding to June's insistent pleas to marry her because he does not believe in marriage. But the reality of the situation is somewhat different:

> My love for June was streaked with hatred and anger. And every passing day my love fed upon my anger and both grew stronger. It was as if two high voltage electrodes had taken roots in my head and each of them kept spitting venom in my brain. The strain grew so great that I almost lost all ability to think logically for any length of time. Often I supposed I was going mad. . . . I had become possessive, selfish and greedy—all that I had struggled against for years. But the realization was that I had almost lost my will power. I had permitted myself to become a battlefield where the child and the adult warred increasingly. The child usually came on the top. (127-28)

Sindi's detachment does not seem to be wise, because it betrays his excessive obsession with himself, without taking into cognizance the larger social reality of life. This obsession becomes obvious from June's remarks. While explaining the reluctant transfer of her love to Babu, June tells Sindi: "You are so tied up with your own detachment, it makes little difference whether you love or you don't." (159) She further protests: "I had wanted to belong to you, but you did not want it. You are so self-sufficient, there is hardly any place for me in your life except perhaps as a mistress." (31)

Sindi's philosophy of detachment is not pragmatic because it overlooks the fact that one cannot live for oneself alone, because no human act is performed in isolation and without consequences. The conflict between the 'Saint' and 'lusty beast' in him leaves him divided against himself. Unable to identity himself with moral, ethical and religious values, he makes an effort to evolve his 'essence', his own system of values through his own life experience. Here begins the crisis in the lives of Joshi's protagonists. If they hear the call of the inner self which gives them subjective satisfaction, and act accordingly they are dubbed as strangers by the world. But if they are unable to act according to their true selves, they are not only alienated from their self but also rendered morally culpable. This predicament not only kills Babu and June, but also alienates Sindi from himself.

In spite of all his frustration and despair, Sindi still continues to search for a meaningful stance in life. His urge for knowing the meaning of existence still persists: "One thing was certain; my search had to continue. I had solved some of the questions my existence had posed for me; but many more remained to be solved." (175)

But ultimately Sindi learns that it is involvement and not detachment that can and does redeem a man. Realizing his past mistakes, he says: "We could have acted more responsibly, with greater detachment. And if I had been more irresponsible than any of them, that too was a result of randomness. Circumstances and events had led to my detachment from all of them. But as Shiela had pointed out, I could not be detached from the world and remain attached to myself. The long dark journey of the past had been an attempted escape from the world and remaining attached to myself. The dark journey of the past had been an attempted escape from the world's entanglements only to allow my passions a freer rein." (221) Though Sindi is still sceptical, yet he is hopeful about the future: "And the future? In an ultimate sense, I knew, it would be meaningless as the past. But, in narrower sense, there would perhaps be useful tasks to be done; perhaps, if I were lucky, even a chance to redeem the past." (221)

Sindi's dilemma lay in his indecisiveness and incapacity to take action. But if Sindi is a drifter, Babu is too much anchored to his parents, dispossessing him of free will, hampering his capacity to make resolutions and take actions in tune with growth. He is not different from Sindi. While Sindi does not make resolutions "because the pain of breaking them was too much" (78), Babu due to his conservative control is incapable of making them. Torn between the moral "chasm of this living" he becomes its victim: "Both Babu and Sindi are two aspects of the same psychology—one foolish and the other unwise. One could not take decisions, the other would not for fear of involvement. One was over-controlled, the other was under-controlled. Both were basically cowards, either haunted by the spectre of the presence of the parents or by the depressive memories of their absence."[12]

To quote Ralph Harper, "A natural orphan is not the most solitary of human beings; the metaphysically homeless is more desolate."[13] An individual may be alone in the physical sense for many years and yet, may be related to ideas, values, or at least social patterns that give him a feeling of communism. In fact, physical isolation becomes unbearable if it also implies spiritual alienation. Erich Fromm says, "Religion and nationalism as well as any custom and any beliefs however absurd and degrading, if it only connects the individual with others, are refuges from what man most dreads isolation."[14]

Arun Joshi reconciles both the oriental view of detached action which *The Gita* advocates, that of occidental view of action taken on pragmatic encounter with life. In fact, the wretchedness in which Sindi wallows is due to his rational view that his involvement would perhaps be of no avail. He allows the June-Babu affair to take its expected turn but himself remains an unattached spectator. He knows it fully well, more acquainted with the life of both the East and West, while June believes in pluralism. Babu cannot overstep the bounds of one-to-one relationship. Thus in the end the existential hero, who blundered into pride, greed, selfishness, withdrawal and cowardice under the mask of detachment, comes to learn its real connotation.

Thus from Boston to Delhi has been a journey from alienation to arrival, from selfishness to sacrifice, from anomic responsibility to himself to a member of mankind, from detachment to commitment.

NOTES

1. Shyam M. Asnani, "A Study of Arun Joshi's Fiction," *The Literary Half-Yearly*, 19.2 (July 1978), p. 112.
2. J.P. Sartre, "Existentialism is a Humanism," *Existentialism from Dostoevsky to Sartre*, Walter Kaufmann, ed. (New York: New American Library, 1975), p. 347. Qtd. Anup Singh Beniwal, "Existential Problems in Arun Joshi's *The Foreigner*, *The Strange Case of Billy Biswas* and *The Last Labyrinth*," M.Phil Dissertation (Kurukshetra: Kurukshetra University, 1988), p. 16.
3. Qtd. R.S. Pathak, "Human Predicament and Meaninglessness in Arun Joshi's Novels," *The Fictional World of Arun Joshi*, ed. R.K. Dhawan (New Delhi: Classical, 1986), p. 107.
4. Thakur Guruprasad, "The Lost Lonely Questers in Arun Joshi's Fiction," R.K. Dhawan, ed., p. 157.
5. Arun Joshi, *The Foreigner* (Bombay: Asia, 1968), p. 195.
6. R.S. Singh, "Facets of Consciousness in Recent Indo-English Novel," *Indo-English Literature: A Collection of Critical Essays*, ed. K.K. Sharma (Ghaziabad: Vimal, 1977), p. 233.
7. Hari Mohan Prasad, *Arun Joshi* (New Delhi: Arnold Heinemann, 1985), p. 42.
8. O.P. Mathur, "Arun Joshi and *The Gita*" in R.S. Pathak, ed., *Indian Fiction in English: Problems and Promises* (New Delhi: Northern Book Centre, 1990), p. 136.
9. *Ibid.*, p. 221.
10. Qtd. A.K. Mishra, Loneliness in *Modern American Fiction* (Delhi: Authors' Guild Publication, 1984), p. l6.
11. Erich Fromm, *Escape from Freedom* (New York: Avon Books, 1967), pp. 34-35. Qtd. A.K. Mishra, p. 17.
12. Qtd. Thakur Guruprasad, p. 156.
13. R.S. Singh, p. 233.
14. O.P. Bhatnagar, p. 32.

Feminism in Nayantara Sahgal's *Rich like Us*

SUBHASH CHANDER

Feminism is a concept whose focus is woman and the future of woman in society, which is at the heart of a radical movement striving to create a brave new world for woman. A feministically read text can lead to a better understanding of the woman's condition, thereby subverting the male strategies of oppression. Thus, the very basis of feminism is reformist. As the historian Linda Gordon says, feminism is "an analysis of women's subordination for the purpose of figuring out how to change it."[1] At the same time, while dealing with feminism as an ideology and also as a critical tool, it is essential to take note of the fact that it assumes different configuration in accordance with racial, class and cultural variations. As a literary discourse, it is part of the modernist search for new modes of conceptuality to change the existing pattern of gender relationships. Feminism, thus, offers a fresh perspective for critical analysis linking the study of literature with real life contexts.

Nayantara Sahgal's progress as a novelist, however, bears testimony to the fact that she has been moving towards a definite feminist position, so that the women's experience do not merely provide data but are actually organized in such a way that they become an exercise in raising consciousness and a critique of society with its unequal gender roles and the power distribution involved in them. Sahgal presents in her novel *Rich like Us* the problems that the contemporary women face in society and in their struggle towards self-realization. She not only deals with the questions of marriage, sexuality and woman's equality with man but also raises the question of love, hatred, jealousy and certain other human emotions and values. Moreover, she also presents an antithesis between idealism and pragmatism, illusion and reality. Sahgal has a humanitarian approach and is extremely sensitive to Indian womanhood as being wronged. In this novel, she reflects the tension between the predicament of the contemporary Indian woman and the traditional Hindu culture. She studies the social forces working on the psychology of the Indian woman.

In India, a woman must necessarily be virtuous, chaste, submissive, homely and devoted to her family as she is considered an embodiment of sacrifice, silent suffering, faith and knowledge. Women are expected to seek pleasure in these domains of life. A woman's status is based primarily on the simple fact that she is the bearer of children and their concern is her primary responsibility; thus her sphere is restricted to her familial roles.

Sahgal concentrates primarily on single and married women. She examines with keen sensitivity and perception the sufferings and problems of women in marriage who feel completely entrapped, depressed, oppressed, suppressed and doomed to the care of husband and home. Mona in *Rich like Us* is one such woman who submits herself to Ram. She is the example of a typical Hindu woman who dares not raise a voice against any action of her husband. When Ram brings home his second wife, Rose, she does not utter a single word against his action but weeps in silence. In spite of raising her voice, she keeps a fast and holds prayers to thank God for his safe return:

> The first one Rose remembered was the elaborate prayer chanted in thanksgiving by Mona's priest for Ram's safe return. And then Mona's voice instructing servants hurrying between kitchen and backyard, directing the feeding of beggars once a week, the voice of the mistress of the house, whoever else might be in it. The week had another day when the mistress fasted for her husband's long life and prosperity. And apart from Mona's fasts and prayers, there were Mona's loud insistent tears. (45)

Rose, the second wife of Ram, is so deeply in love with him that she leaves her home and country despite knowing the fact that he had a wife and an infant child. She had gone far ahead in love until Ram revealed the truth to her and it was not possible for her to look back.

Ram in *Rich like Us* seems to be very indifferent to the sentiments of a woman and inflicts great emotional violence on both the women he marries. He does not care about the feelings of his first wife Mona, and brings an English wife Rose after Mona has given birth to his son. Besides, he reveals the truth to Rose about his marriage with Mona and his infant child as though there was nothing serious about it, being very indifferent about her reaction to it. "And one afternoon he told her, in a natural everyday voice, that he has a wife and an infant child." (41) When Rose raises the question "How can we get married when you're married?" he has the audacity to answer: "My religion lets a man have more than one wife" (42)

Ironically, wronged by Ram, both Mona and Rose develop a hatred for each another. Mona tries to project herself as the mistress of the house and Rose desires in her heart to see Mona dead so that she may become the mistress of the entire house. One of Rose's more foolish fancies had been that everything would work out all right if Mona were dead: "If only she'd be dead, dead, dead, she had hammered out the thought night after night. It is wicked to think such thoughts. Rose, she has done you no harm, it isn't her fault. Mona was only two years older than herself, she wouldn't die for years. The three of them would live and die together, an impossible situation that entered the realm of possibility every morning when she went down the stairs into the household and tried to discover ways to make it work." (107)

The agony and pain of Rose is also not understood by Ram who talks to her in a jestful manner. Rose tells Ram:

> "I don't think I can make much more of this Ram" "Of what?" he had the temerity to ask: "You living with two wives." He was stretched out on his bed too good-humoured and too lazy to quarrel: "Lord Krishna had three hundred." (63)

The husband in the Indian set-up has the social sanction to do whatever he can to satisfy himself but he cannot tolerate his wife if she indulges in anything which he feels is not proper. In *Rich like Us*, Ram Swaroop already has two wives at home, Mona and Rose, but he continues to develop ardent love affairs. He has the audacity to disclose to Rose about his affair with Marcella; he does not even care to hide it from Rose to save her from being hurt. Rather he comes home with "his footfall open and normal on the stair at three a.m." (115)

Rose suffered for months after this incident and she could get no comfort from anyone. Men seem to take pride in the fact that they are encircled by many women and they usually deprive women of togetherness and warmth. Love is nothing but fun for Ram Swaroop who is engaged in affairs with many women at the same time. The question of bigamy, which entails suffering and sacrifices for the co-wives Mona and Rose, is dealt with in this novel. In spite of getting all the love and care from his two wives, Ram gets infatuated with Marcella, a young British lady, and falls deeply in love with her. Zafar, a friend of Ram, remarks: "You have the path to heaven all paved for you . . . with a cocktail party upstairs and prayer meeting downstairs." (77)

Rose takes care of his sensual needs and Mona provides security to Ram's household but he wrecks their life by inflicting mental torture on both of them. Both women, being dependent on him, are exploited by him and he continues doing whatever he likes. Marriage for woman means a life of total dedication to one person whereas for man it means getting comfort at every level.

A single woman has no importance in our society and the practice of 'Sati' is a glaring example of a woman's plight. It is difficult for a single woman to survive in this society. *Rich like Us* presents ghastly accounts of the way in which widows were made to perform 'Sati' forcibly. Sonali, on reading her grandfather's manuscripts written in 1915, finds how widows were literally thrown into the funeral pyre of their husbands. In case they resisted, they were beaten with logs of wood and were forcibly thrown into the funeral pyre to die with their husband. In the manuscript, Sonali reads the incident of an unfortunate Brahminee who of her own accord has ascended the funeral pile of her husband's bones (for he had died at a distance). On finding the torture unbearable, she threw herself from the flames by a violent struggle and fell down. Some gentlemen who were present there immediately plunged her into the river, which was close by and thereby saved her from being burnt. On recovering her senses, she complained of the badness of the pile and expressed her willingness to try again if they could improve it. They did not do so and the poor creature shrank with dread from the flames which were now burning more intensely, and refused to go on. When the inhuman relatives saw this, they lifted her and threw her into the fire, and held her there till they were driven away by the heat. They also struck her with large blocks of wood in order to deprive her of her senses. She again made her escape and jumped into the river. The relatives tried to drown her by pressing her under water but she was saved by a gentleman present there. She was then sent to the hospital but, after lingering in most excruciating pain for twenty hours, she died.

Sonali's grandfather raised his voice against this evil practice and was very happy when in 1929 its practice was abolished but ironically his wife too was cruelly burnt alive by his relatives when he died.

A woman had no choice in the matter of marriage and had to remain devoted to her husband even if he was the crudest person on earth. The man, on the other hand, could leave his wife any time he wished and remarry any other woman of his choice. The lines in the manuscript are worth-mentioning: "Yet the question remains: What kind of society is it that demands human sacrifice to appease the blood thirst of what kind of gods?"

The feeling of sisterhood where women develop solidarity and a deep social relationship amongst themselves is more pronounced in *Rich like Us.* In this novel, Sonali, a spinster and an I.A.S. officer, extends all her help and support to Ram's second wife Rose. Rose's stepson Dev intends to usurp her wealth and assets. Sonali not only arranges for a lawyer but also entertains Rose in the best possible manner in order to relieve her of her loneliness and misery. Though Sonali was younger to Rose, their relations were very intimate. After the death of Rose, Sonali seems to be the only person who laments her death. After her death, she spent a day in Rose's room and found it completely deserted. She began lifting her dresses off the hangers, taking clothes from drawers and laying them on her bed. She felt that with the end of her life, the use of these garments had also ended. She says: "In Kumar's haggard presence I sat on her bed on top of her dresses and cried as I had cried my heart out to Rose years ago in the hotel room in London." (286)

The relation of Rose and Mona is also another example of sisterhood. Although initially Rose and Mona could not accept each other and Rose in her heart of hearts wished Mona dead, later we find that they accept each other as sisters and Rose saved her life when she tried to commit suicide:

> Mona sat cross-legged, her eyes closed, a band of flame advancing up her cotton sari, consuming it soundlessly while she submitted to the inevitable like a woman in disciplined child birth, her short agonized gasps barely audible. Rose dragged the cover off her bed with Kumar's help, wrapped it round Mona's struggling bod·' and got her out of the room.

After this incident Rose does not hate Mona, rather she sits "in front of her long delayed breakfast telling herself she was carrying fancy too far, only there was no denying that houses breathe in and out, sighs sink into walls and walls exhale them." The incident also changes Mona's attitude towards Rose. She starts appreciating her and welcomes her with her heart saying: "We are sisters." (175) They become good friends and mutually run the house and are living examples of two women being agonized by one man. Rose considers Dev, Mona's son, as her own and Dev too calls Mona Mama and Rose Mummy.

Everyone supports Rose after the death of her parents. Mona ordered the household to revolve around Rose and perform a religious ceremony for peace of her mind. She takes the loss of her parents as her own personal loss.

> But said Rose feebly, "if the ceremony is for me, why should you be the one to spend the day fasting?" Mona, categorical as ever, replied if we're a family, then we're a family. She starved herself all day with the energy of one for whom a fast is a positive act, breaking it at sundown with a horrible concoction consisting of smoking hot milk and soggy jalebies. (178)

Through the characters of Mona and Rose, Nayantara Sahgal depicts the concept of sisterhood which means that women must develop friendship and assert their identification with each other.

In *Rich like Us*, Rose's musings on her childhood present a very poignant picture of women suffering because of pregnancies when abortion was not legally allowed. "Loving each other had fallen in to disuse" (66) between her parents as for her mother it was tired sex always accompanied with the fear of more mouths to feed. At a time when abortions were not legalized, "Miscarriages were better than nothing, but in the end you were back to full-term deliveries, your burnished and battered body returned, a loose empty sack to fIll up again." (66)

Rose herself longs for a child when she first sees Dev, Ram's son from his first wife Mona. She wants to produce a son so that she may also be termed as the mistress of Ram's household but her dream remains unfulfilled. Ironically she is murdered years later at her stepson Dev's behest whose care Mona had made Rose's duty at the time of her own death. Sonali in *Rich like Us* is a positive achievement of Nayantara Sahgal. She is born of intercaste marriage, her mother being a Kashmiri and her father a Maharashtrian I.C.S. officer. She escapes the net of marriage spread out by her parents by asserting her individuality. She tells her father: "I am going abroad after my B.A. I don't care if you didn't send Kiran, I'm not Kiran." She goes to Lucknow, works hard at her studies, sits for the I.A.S. exam and tops the list of successful candidates. On this occasion, she remembers her father's words: "Sonali, people like you, especially women like you, are going to Indianize India." (22)

Life for her is not easy in this male-dominated world, even though she is Joint Secretary in the Ministry of Industry. She refuses to make any compromises and finally is demoted and sent back to her home state and finally resigns her job. She says: "I hadn't merely been transferred without warning, I had been demoted, punished, and humiliated, and I had no inkling why." (27) She wrote about herself: "And then I had become the kind of woman, who highly concentrated on the subject in hand, is supposed to have 'a man's mind' and who disappoints the flirtatious and flippant." She has a strong individuality, is brave and opposes dictatorship, "not even of the proletariat, not even as a passing phase because who knows the phase might get struck and never pass."

Sonali is a soft and kind-hearted girl. After the death of Rose she brings artificial hands for a beggar who lived near Rose's house. Rose sympathizes with him and often warns him not to go near the well for it could be very treacherous for a person without arms. Ironically Rose herself is thrown into the same well by her stepson Dev. Sonali tells the beggar that she had arranged the artificial hands for him and that it would take him a day or two to get them fitted. After he had learned to use them, he would be taught a trade. She says: "He had been waiting for the news, and now that I had come, he said, his voice teary and rasping, he couldn't stay here any more, not after what he had seen, a youth camp tough suffocating her with a sack descending over her head, another pinioning her arms, both of them carrying her out, where else but to the well where her body was found?" (290)

Sonali, in spite of being unsuccessful in her personal and professional life, is not at all pessimistic. The remarks, with which the novel closes, reveal the mettle of which she is made: "I went to work immersed in the past; I was preparing all the while for the future beyond Brian's country and his exhibition. Marcella has reminded me of it, made a gift of it to me. Though it was really Rose's legacy again, the paths that had crossed hers now crossing mine, reminding me I was young and alive, with my own country stretched out before me, waiting to be lived." (301)

In *Rich like Us*, Sahgal also depicts the miseries and sufferings of the low class women and the treatment given out to them by the policemen. Their sufferings are beyond imagination and they are bound to live a wretched life. A servant tells Nishi, the daughter-in-law of Rose, about an incident when his wife had disappeared. He thought the police had grabbed her. The landowner who owned the cultivable land in the village and whom they worked for had sent for the police at the harvest time to make sure they didn't get off work, their full share of the crop, and didn't try any land-grabbing tricks as were going on in the area and could be catching. But the policemen, being jittered by feet marching in unison with scythes on shoulders and song being sung in the fields, had plundered the stored grain, smashed cooking vessels and set huts on fire if there was any resistance. They had made free and easy with the women, so lots of them had run away. His neighbour informed him that he had seen five women fleeing together towards Bakhadda. They were with eight policemen. Two of them lay on their sides chewing blades of grass. The rest were in a circle with one woman in the centre. He also saw through the shrubbery the top of a lathi raising the woman's sari above her waist, poke and prod and turn her round and round like marionette. Another lathi joined the first. The other lay like overlapping corpses on the ground. He had vomitted into the bushes but stayed crouched until he heard the clank of chains and the women being led away naked. After the crops have been harvested he heard his wife had been taken along with few others to one of the brick-kiln-pig hole places along the Ganges. Nishi tells rose: "Do't now Mummy me. If you and I get raped the militia is out looking for the rascal. But their kind nobody bothers about." (277) After hearing the account of the poor miserable women, Rose says: "I can't see any of it 'appening to you and me, can you?" (278)

In *Rich Like Us*, Nayantara Sahgal renders a living picture of the oppressed, depressed and suppressed life of women in India. She basically deals with two kinds of women: the first group of women is of those who are confined to a life of Hindu orthodoxy and the other of those who have a strong sense of individuality and an analytical mind but are shuffling between the traditional and modern values. There is also a juxtaposition of two worlds, the personal world of man-woman relationship and the impersonal world of politics. A point worth noting and mentioning at this stage is that Sahgal's aim is never to set one sex against the other. She, being aware of the feminist movement in the West, contributes to feminism in India in her own way. Her women characters try to become themselves by staying within the limits of the best Indian traditions and values.

A Saga of Women's Problems: A Sociological Study of Kamala Markandaya's *Nectar in a Sieve*

ASHA KHURANA

The early decades of the twentieth century witnessed the rise of many writers whose literary manifesto was to write for socio-political purpose. The purpose was not only to throw light upon the social evils and the malpractices prevailing in the society in those days but also to employ fiction to the cause of social amelioration. Mulk Raj Anand, Raja Rao, R.K. Narayan and Bhabani Bhattacharya, considered the four pillars of Indian fiction in English, have written with a social and ideological cause in mind. No less is the contribution of Manohar Malgonkar, Kamala Markandaya, Anita Desai, R.P. Jhabvala, Nayantara Sahgal and many others who have projected Indian society with all its dimensions be it religious, political or economic. The social evils and the societal problems interwoven in the web of their lives form major part of their thematic preoccupations. K.B. Vaid in his article "The Modern Indian Novel" opines that the Indian novelists are chiefly concerned with the "portrayal of poverty, hunger and disease, . . . widespread social evils and tensions . . . the innumerable dislocations and conflicts in a tradition ridden society under the impact of an incipient, half-hearted industrialization."[1]

Kamala Markandaya has given us an authentic depiction of the spectacle of peasant life in South Indian society facing the onslaught of modernization and industrialization in the post-Independence India. All her novels deal elaborately with the Indian economy and society of more than three decades. Kamala Markandaya has devoted a large space in each novel to the depiction and analysis of the women's problems.

Let us focus our study on her first novel *Nectar in a Sieve.*[2] We find that Rukmani, the narrator-heroine of the novel, becomes the mouthpiece of the writer not only to present an authentic picture of a village that is under the impact of severely inimical social and economic forces playing havoc with the lives of the folks, but also becomes an instrument to peep into the psyche of rural women folk with utmost honesty, sincerity and sympathy. She does justice in addressing not only the very personal and private feelings, emotions and reactions to various phenomena, social as well as psychological, but also in the universalized treatment of the some major problems of women in contemporary era. For instance, the problems of dowry, infertility, the necessity to have male-child, prostitution, the large unplanned families with meagre economic resources, the purdah system and women's safety, security and loss of privacy with the spread of industry.

In the very beginning of the novel, Rukmani compares her marriage with those of her three elder sisters who had been married long before her. At the time of their marriages, the headman, their father, had the power that money provides. Shanta, the first daughter, had a big wedding which lasted for many days, plenty of gifts and feasts, diamond earrings, a gold necklace, as befitted the daughter of a village headman. But the quantum of dowry went on shrinking with the decline in the economic status of Rukmani's father. Second daughter too, was married off well but the third one got only a diamond nose screw. Ultimately, the dwindling economic resources of the family compelled the village headman to marry off his fourth daughter to a poor tenant farmer. Her parents could choose no better than Nathan, for they could not offer any dowry. Even when Rukmani was moving towards Nathan's hut after her marriage, she felt it very low: "Such a disgrace for me. How shall I ever live it down." But her mother had commented: "What for you . . . my last born . . . four dowries is too much for a man to bear." If her father had money to give enough dowry, she could have been married in a prosperous family and could have lived happily. Learning a lesson from her own life, Rukmani prepares herself for the marriage of her daughter right from her birth. She never wanted to feel helpless like her mother. So, she saves right from Ira's birth despite her family's increasing demands for food and clothes. Thus, the dowry system in India having reduced marriage to the level of a business bargain is well depicted through this novel.

The issue of Ira's forced entry into prostitution and Murugan's wife following thereafter due to disintegration of self and pelf is also well highlighted in the novel. Ira, in fact, could not see her brother dying. Kuti, her youngest brother, had never had enough to eat. He could not stand starvation and fell ill. Rukmani was very much worried about her son but she was helpless. Ira could not stand it. She was left with only one alternative and that was to sell her body to save her brother's life. Nathan tried to stop her but she knew what she was doing—a sacrifice to save her brother's life. Rukmani however blames the tannery for Ira's fall and she says: "Ira had ruined herself at the hands of the throngs that the tannery attracted." (134)

How poverty drove a number of women into prostitution is substantiated to a great extent by Kamala Markandaya here. Kunthi also serves as a foil to Ira. Her reason for falling into prostitution is quite different. She is immoral and corrupt and does her very best to increase her sexual appeal. She walks the streets in search of customers with rose-petals in her hair and painted mouth and scented thighs. She is all for glamour and sophistication. It is the lure of money and sensuous gratification that degrade her and motivate her street walking. Thus Kamala Markandaya has shown the other side of the coin too, i.e., there may be other reasons besides poverty for women to take to prostitution.

The cruelty of family towards a woman not able to give birth to children is also highlighted in this novel. Ira does not get her share of happiness in married life on this count. Although she is beautiful and had her share of religion, music, noise and feasting at the time of her marriage but even this does not ensure happiness for Ira. She is rejected by her husband for being barren and is sent back to her parents. The husband quickly marries again.

while on the other hand, Ira's return to her father's house is a public humiliation for the family.

The social factors inducing a compelling desire for a male child show Rukmani the way to seek Dr. Kennington's help but at the same time it has been well highlighted that women did not have the courage to get even medical treatment openly but had to hide it not only from the society but also from their husbands for fear of opposition, especially when the doctor was a foreigner, a white man.

As time passes, Rukmani is caught into the dragnet of the birth of several children in quick succession accompanied by decline of fortune caused by hostile, natural, human and capitalistic forces. Unfortunately, the woman of her times which is true of crores of them today also might have had the slight courage to get herself treated for her barrenness but did not have the wisdom to seek ways to plan the family. A close study of the novel illustrates that in the beginning of the novel, although Nathan was not rich but having to support only Rukmani and Ira, they were happy and well-fed. But with six children to feed and every penny saved having been spent on Ira's marriage, the catastrophic monsoon forced them to starve till the next harvest.

The setting up of tannery in the village not only rudely ruffled the calm and peaceful social life of the village, it also effected a drastic change in the very mindset of the people of her village. "Now it is all noise and crowds everywhere and rude young hooligans idling in the street and dirty beggars and uncouth behaviour, and no man thinks of another but schemes for his money."

With such people around, Rukmani wanted to protect Ira, who was maturing fast. "I think the end of my daughter's carefree days began with the tannery." Not only Ira but the whole village community was adversely affected. The young girls, who otherwise moved freely and nobody looked at them with an evil eye, could not venture out confidently anymore. So, it has been pointed out that with the coming of industrialization, the social behaviour towards women changed.

Kamala Markandaya has also vindicated her feelings on 'burqua system' in this novel. With the setting up of the tannery, one could notice the arrival of the Muslims in the village and their burqua was something new to the village women. Rukmani feels curious about the women in veil who were "a queer lot and their way of life different from ours. What they did in their houses I do not know for they employed servants to do the work but they stayed mostly indoors or if they went out at all they went veiled in burquas. It was their religion I was told, they would not appear before any man but their husband."

Rukmani feels sorry for the burqua-covered Muslim women because they were deprived of cool breeze, warm sun and light. Although Kali feels that she could easily wear burqua if she was provided with a wealthy carefree life, Rukmani would not like to give up her freedom even for the comfort of money. Moreover, she was sceptic about the life behind those closed doors and shuttered windows. She never wanted to sacrifice the sight of open fields, the sky and the sun.

The writer has also portrayed the old Granny, a typical rural Indian woman, who ekes out a miserable existence sitting all day in the street, selling a few annas worth of nuts and vegetables. When Rukmani expresses her fear of such a life. Granny tells her: "It is not unbearable. One gets used to it."

Discussing her lot with the missionary, Kenny, Rukmani remarks: "Want is our companion from birth to death, familiar as the reasons or the earth, varying only in degree. What profit to bewail that which has always been and cannot change." Thus, the spirit of calm acceptance and fatalism is seen clearly in the psychology of the suffering, lonely women represented by old Granny in *Nectar in a Sieve*.

Rukmani, as Markandaya presents her, becomes an epitome of Indian womanhood, a typical daughter of the soil, deeply rooted in land. She suffers a lot because of land. She has to starve. Her sons die, her daughter is forced into prostitution and she loses her husband but Rukmani has faith in land intact "Still while there was land there was hope." Land was taken away but the hope was still there. If Rukmani, even after a series of sufferings, continues to have her mental equilibrium and sanity, it is because of her basic faith in God which sustains her in the hours of adversity. She, in fact, is the true replica of Indian woman of the folk with all her hopes and fears, doubts and beliefs, weaknesses and strengths that Kamala Markandaya has presented through *Nectar in a Sieve*

To conclude, Kamala Markandaya's treatment of Indian rural life is comprehensive and all-embracing. It is not idyllic, poetic or one-sided, but realistic and truthful. Through her novel, she has focused attention not only on the wretched plight of the poor and the destitute but has also dwelt considerably on some of the issues and problems related to women of her times and has shown their way of life, remarkable for its heroic endurance and innate goodness.

NOTES

1. *The Illustrated Weekly of India*, 26 May 1983. Qtd. C. Paul Verghese, *Problems of Indian Creative Writers in English* (Bombay: Somaiya, 1971), p. 113.
2. Kamala Markandaya, *Nectar in a Sieve* (Bombay: Jaico, 1950; 1982).

R.K. Narayan's *The Bachelor of Arts* and *A Tiger for Malgudi*: A Study of Social Reality

VINEETA

R.K. Narayan has written fourteen novels, set in the imaginary south Indian town he calls Malgudi. Malgudi, the locale of all the novels of Narayan, is a metaphor for India. In his creation of Malgudi, Narayan portrays a variety of south Indian characters who have in their blood and bones the community tradition they inherit and the ethos of the system in which they are born and brought up. The events narrated in his novels are like 'occurrences of the real life.' He catches the idiom, the tone and the rhythm of different categories of persons. The world he creates seems vivid, and the persons life-like and living. His novels describe numerous Indian myths, stories and legends. His vision is firmly rooted in the timeless values of life, as enshrined in the ancient Indian philosophy and religion, which attach great importance to self-discipline, non-violence, renunciation, reincarnation, and the law of Karma. In almost all his major novels these social values and the common features of the Indian philosophy such as the theories of Karma and rebirth, the doctrine of Mukti, the doctrine of soul, self-control, Maya, etc. find expression in one form or the other.

The Indian society is divided into several sets of life and it is guided by Vanashramdharma. In *Shrimad Bhagvad Gita*, there is also such classification of society:

> Chaturvarnyam maya srstam gunakarma vibhagash
> Tasya kartaram api mam viddhyakartaramavyayam.[1]
> (The four fold caste was created by Me by the different distribution of Guna and Karma though I be the author thereof, know Me to be the actionless and changeless.)

Ashrama, the ideal division of man's life, is studenthood, the status of a householder, and renunciation of the world. The place of householder is superior and youth is a training and preparation for it. Chandran in *The Bachelor of Arts* (1937) finishes his studies. He sees a girl named Malathi, sitting on the banks of Saryu river and instantly falls in love with her. The marriage negotiations fail as the horoscopes do not tally. Unable to find a job and the girl of his choice, he sets out for Malgudi and sees the magnificent Kapaleswar temple. The peace of the temple attracts him, and turns him into a Sanyasi. He then visits several south Indian villages and districts on foot, and lives on alms. He suddenly sees himself as he is a bogus Sanyasi. After eight months of these purposeless wanderings, he gets tired of his new role, and returns to his parents in Malgudi. He returns to the orthodox Indian ways even to the extent of allowing a marriage to be arranged for him to a girl named Sushila he has never met. The marriage negotiations with Malathi break on account of social bindings and customs. His mother believes in the sanctity of customs, the prescribed manners and order of the society: "She at any rate belonged to a generation which was no worse than the present one for all its observances and as long as she lived she would insist on respecting the old customs"[2] Chandran's mother cannot deviate even an inch from the social customs. She says, "If you want us to be there, everything must be done in proper manner." (91)

Chandran has to bear the social pressures, and he comes to terms with the situations of practical life. He never leaves the orbit of social norms. He does not become a true Sanyasi. In comparison to the life of a Sanyasi, he prefers other alternatives like suicide. He would have committed suicide but for its social stigma, perhaps he lacked the barest physical courage that was necessary for it. Starting as a Brahmachari, he skips the householder's stage for the Sanyasi's. Behind all this is hidden the idea of the utility of the Ashramas. Narayan here shows typical south Indian social customs. He portrays quite vividly the complex texture of the social and religious traditions governing a south Indian Hindu family. Rivers are considered sacred in India and a dip in the holy waters is supposed to purify the body and the soul. The river Sarayu and its banks serve the spiritual needs of the Malgudians. Chandran chooses the riverbank for his romantic experiences and later for shedding his youthful illusions and attainment of maturity.

According to the law of Karma, the entire universe is governed by an eternal moral order. This law stipulates that every action has its due consequences. A good action will lead to good consequences and a bad action will lead to bad consequences in this life or in the lives to come. All schools of Indian thought believe in transformation of the soul, and in the soul of every living being having a pre-existence and a post-existence and getting joys or sorrows, wealth or penury in accordance with the Karma of the being. This Karma theory is evident in the novel *A Tiger for Malgudi*. It deals with an aged tiger ruminating on its past. This is almost a spiritual odyssey of its life, beginning with its cubhood and wild days in the jungle and later life in humiliating captivity as a circus star. It attains freedom when it breaks loose from a film city camp and wanders into the town. Then a hermit saves it and adopts it as a companion. The novel takes us to the regions of metaphysical inquiry and search of the self. It is an autobiography of a tiger, Raja. Raja emerges as a champion as he tells his tale full of vicissitudes in a reminiscential mode. The magnificent tiger narrates his carefree king-like life in the forest; the way he was trapped to work in a circus; and finally how finding the human world too brutish and bewildering, he makes a dramatic bid for liberation, freedom and salvation. The most striking feature of the novel is that the tiger Raja is endowed with an intelligent, sensitive personality, spiritualized by the mysterious powers of his master, who is a Swami. About the Karma theory, Master tells Raja: "You probably in previous life enjoyed putting your fellow beings behind bars. One has to face the reaction of every act, if not in the same life, at least in another life or series of lives. There can be no escape from it."[3] (42) The tiger asks Master why he should have done that. The Master simply says, "I can't answer it; people only follow their inclinations, and sooner or later find their reward or retribution. That's law of life." (42-43)

Emphasis is also laid on yoga in *A Tiger for Malgudi*. The special interest of Narayan is in the practice of yoga as a means of the attainment of discriminative knowledge which is an essential condition for liberation. Yoga aims at cessation of all mental functions i.e. Chittavrittinirodha. It holds that God is the highest object for contemplation or concentration. Raja has not only undergone humanization, but also looks forward to his salvation. He understands Master's spiritual discourses on yoga. Narayan describes in the introduction to the novel certain yogic practices. He says: "Eight kinds of supernatural powers may be roused; one can become invisible, levitate, transmute metals, travel in space, control animals and men, live on air and so on and so forth" (9).

Time and again Master's spiritual powers are referred to. It is under the influence of Swami that the tiger has been spiritually transformed. Jayant K. Biswal observes: "The Indian psyche reared up in a tradition of the Vedanta and the Upanishads, the Panchtantra and the Jatakas finds it not at all difficult to accept the miracle of the spiritual transformation of a tiger."[4]

Narayan illustrates the spiritual thesis about the universality of soul and the oneness of the soul of all living beings—tiger and the man alike—its sublimation through gradual self-discipline and renunciation, and its final salvation from the bondage of Karma and the cycle of birth. By bondage it is commonly meant the process of birth and rebirth and the consequent misery to which an individual is subject. By liberation or Mukti or Moksha is meant the stoppage of this process. Swami realizes that the time for attaining Samadhi is near. He prepares himself for it by releasing himself from all bondage. As a first step, he releases Raja. The separation of Master and Raja has a close parallel with the mythical separation of Siddhartha from his family.

The myth of Buddha's enlightenment is used in the novel to indicate attainment of self-realization. There is a reference to Siddhartha, the founder of Buddhism. Master was once a man of the world like Siddhartha; one day he renounced the world because of an inner compulsion. He did so in order to merge his soul with the universal Soul, and attain the spiritual heights and the enlightenment of a real Sanyasi, a mystic. Narayan deals here with the theme of renunciation, and creates a real Sanyasi—instead of a fake Sadhu. Narayan differentiates between a real and a fake Sadhu in the introduction to the novel; "A Sañyasi is one who renounces everything and undergoes a complete change of personality . . . one obliterates one's past. . . . Apart from the genuine types, there are also fakes who adopt this life for its sheer vagrancy, or to exploit the public in the garb of holy man." (9)

Master is unquestionably a real Sanyasi who has attained spiritual heights. He never discloses his identity. He advises people not to probe too far into the origin of a river or a saint, for one will never reach the end.

In the novel, Narayan attempts a new dimension in the form of combining myth and fable. This form is deeply rooted in the cultural context of India. Narayan invokes the centuries-old religious and philosophical beliefs of his nation. In this connection, it is significant that the tiger escapes Captain, but submits to Master. The reason cited by Narayan is that the tiger and Master might have been brothers in their previous birth. The tiger is taught by Master to tread the righteous path. The basic form that the plot of the novel has is that of the long, strenuous odyssey of the tiger from callous arrogance and ferocity to tenderness and humility, from primitive ignorance and fury to the ultimate wisdom and tranquillity. Eventually, Raja abides by the Sattvic Gunas and is shown awaiting his final liberation.

The use of myth and legend in the novels of Narayan does not make them mere illustrations of abstract ideologies and beliefs. It rather provides the basis for a vision of the present-day reality, and enhances its appeal by linking the modern with the traditional. In this respect Narayan is in the line of old Indian saints and prophets who have interpreted the conditions of their time in the light of the ancient myths, legends and fables. In the words of William Walsh: "The religious sense of Indian myth is part of Narayan's grip of reality, of his particular view of human life and his individual way of placing and ordering human feeling and experience. What one can say about Narayan without qualification is that he embodies the pure spirit of Hinduism."[5]

A Tiger for Malgudi is undoubtedly a beautiful novel. Shyam Asnani views it as packed with "all the ingredients of a Narayan novel, such as delectable subtle humour, delicate irony, typical Indian social life as embodied in his imaginary town called Malgudi."[6]

Thus the novel deals with the Hindu philosophy particularly in respect of Karma, re-birth and transmigration of soul. Here, a tiger is shown behaving more humanly than even human beings. He undergoes humanization, and looks forward to his salvation. Master and the tiger return to the green foliage of Mempi Hills, far from the madding crowd, for peace of mind and sweet philosophical discourses on the teachings of the *Bhagvad Gita*. The tiger understands the spiritual discourses on Yoga and the *Bhagvad Gita*. In this way, *A Tiger for Malgudi* invokes centuries-old religious and philosophical Hindu beliefs.

NOTES

1. *Shrimad Bhagvad Gita* (Gorakhpur: Gita Press), Chapter 4, Shloka 13.
2. *The Bachelor of Arts* (London: Eyre and Spottiswoode, 1937), p. 75.
3. *A Tiger for Malgudi* (Harmondsworth, England: Penguin, 1984), p. 42.
4. Jayant K. Biswal, *A Critical Study of the Novels of R.K. Narayan* (New Delhi: Nirmal, 1987), p. 113.
5. In O.P. Saxena, *Glimpses of Indo-English Fiction*, Vol. 1 (New Delhi: Jainson, 1985), p. 139.
6. Shyam Asnani, *New Dimensions of Indian English Novel* (Delhi: Ajay Printers, 1987), p. 134.

Rohinton Mistry's *Such a Long Journey*: A Sociological Study

JAGDISH BATRA

The pioneers of the Indian novel written in English imbued their works with social realism. Stalwarts like Mulk Raj Anand, Raja Rao, R.K. Narayan and Bhabani Bhattacharya analyzed the social scenario and suggested remedies before the focus shifted to the individual psyche in due course of time. Anand, for one, used Auguste Comte's sociology, illustrating how such social phenomena as untouchability or poverty in *Untouchable* and *Coolie* could be read in terms of the three stages of development—theological, metaphysical and positivistic. These three stages can be traced in history but they also co-exist, as for example, on a single day in the life of Bakha. In the long journey of the Indian novel written in English, sociological reading of Indian milieu lost its hold, giving place to newer readings. However, the old emphasis on sociology has returned, as for example, in Rohinton Mistry's *Such a Long Journey* which presents sociological perception of human nature. Before we take up this novel in detail, it would be fruitful to ascertain how the sociologists themselves view life.

Sociologists like Max Weber claim: "modern industrial society is characterized by 'rationalization and intellectualisation.' The world is no longer charged with mystery and magic; the supernatural has been banished from society."[1] On the other hand, we have scholars like Vilfredo Pareto who have shown the weak foundations of a rationalistic approach to society. He believes that human actions, for the most part, are guided not by logic or reason but by sentiments. Pareto represents one of the most distinguished intellectual currents in the European tradition. "That broad school of thought includes such diverse figures as Burke,

Taine, Dostoevsky, Burckhardt, Nietzsche and Spengler and stands in opposition to rationalism, liberalism, egalitarianism, Marxism, and all of the other offspring of Enlightenment doctrinaires."[2] And it is this school of thought that seems to inspire Rohinton Mistry's work under study here.

In the first epigraph of the novel *Such a Long Journey*, quoted from Firdausi's *Shahnama*, Mistry has sought to underline the fact that the early rulers held populace subjugated precisely because the masses lived by beliefs, at times, transcending their minds such as the theory of the divine right of kings. That is why these early rulers exploited people's beliefs to the hilt, and as Firdausi learnt they left nothing worthwhile for the newer generations to fall upon.

As we open the reading of the novel, we find that it is not only the people in the past who have been gullibled at the hands of the Machiavellian rulers, our own lives are none too logically and scientifically lived. This novel is a story of a Parsee family. The head of the family Gustad, his wife Dilnavaz and their three children—Sohrab and Darius, both boys, and Roshan, a girl, live in Khodadad Building in Bombay. Their very ordinary middle class existence receives a jolt as they find themselves involved in a political scandal of international stature. This sensational event known as the Nagarwala scam is the one that rocked the Indira Gandhi government in the wake of the Bangladesh liberation struggle. The novel lays equal stress on the communal as well as the individual lives.

The novel has drawn heavily on that side of human life and activity which can be described as non-rational in the philosophical sense. Religious activity, for example, is one such facet which finds wide mention in the novel. The novel begins with the central character Gustad offering prayers to 'Ahura Mazda.' After finishing the prayer, as is the custom, Gustad cracks the *kusti* which action is symbolic of driving away the devil. But he does not resort to it merely as a religious gesture. In his mind are stored images of his childhood days when, with this action, he imagined driving away all sorts of ghosts and murderers. He continues to enjoy it with the same abandon even as a middle-age man.

The reader is now treated to the happy news of Gustad's eldest son Sohrab's admission to the I.I.T. That is a dream-come-true situation for any middle-class youngster and his proud parents. As such, Gustad plans to celebrate it on the ninth birthday of his daughter Roshan but surprisingly Sohrab is not amused. Things go haywire on the party day with an unbridgeable gulf developing between the father and the son. Sohrab would just not listen to the suggestion of entering the portals of the hallowed precincts of I.I.T. as he does not like the idea of getting separated from his friends, who ostensibly have taken up arts. All this appears so illogical and unreasonable to Gustad who blurts: "Throwing away his [Sohrab's] fortune without reason. What have I not done for him, tell me? I even threw myself in front of a car. Kicked him aside, saved his life, and got this to suffer all my life (slapping his hip). But that's what a father is for."[3]

His tiff with his son reminds us of the intransigence of his own father. 'One proud man's stubbornness' (101) is how Gustad referred to his father's soft corner for his dissolute uncle at the expense of Gustad's college fees. He never forgave his weak father for his 'effeminacy' and decided to grow strong as a rock. Now, that rock-like strength was being put to test by his own son who found him stubborn in wishing him to join I.I.T. Anyone would dub Sohrab's action as non-rational because it means honouring his emotional links with his buddies but Gustad also cannot be called a rationalist because it is his son who has to study and ultimately shape his life according to his own interests. The point Mistry makes is that our wishes, propped by beliefs and sentiments, are not necessarily realized because there is no logical connection between what we wish and what happens.

Mistry, through this fiasco of the central wish, underlines his views about human nature which for all its evolution is still steeped in non-logical ways of thinking and acting. Mistry was not the first to present this sociological perception of human nature. I.A. Richards, in his essay 'Pseudo-statements' said that most of our attitudes are determined by emotive responses rather than by scientific views. Poets are known for making pseudo statements such as the existence of God, of immortality, of freedom but such beliefs do serve some social purpose, when it comes to organizing society around rituals and ceremonies, around common beliefs and shared sentiments. Still, on the whole, these non-logical actions have also been exploited by those who are able to free themselves from these sentiments.

In the midst of the father-son standoff, it is Dilnavaz, Sohrab's mother, who suffers. The special chicken dish is hardly partaken of, its six out of nine pieces remaining in the pot. Sohrab's uttering a volley of audacious words right in the face of his father appears like so much blasphemy to his mother. This gulf, most unfortunately, goes on widening and at one point of time, Sohrab walks out on his father and his family. This is indeed shocking. As a mother, Dilnavaz's utmost concern is to see her son reconciled to his father and the family re-united. She cannot think of any reasoned solution to this malady and falls for the utterly irrational and superstitious counsel of her neighbour Miss Kutpitia (which in Gujarati means 'the quarrelsome one'), an elderly and freakish spinster who acts as the community advisor of queer medicines prescribing lemons and chillies to win over the estranged son of Dilnavaz, subjo leaves for Cavasji's hypertension and nails and lizard for Roshan's illness. Dilnavaz is also in the reflex habit of saying 'touchwood' and touching anything nearby—a table or a chair—whenever she hears about some accident or to avoid anything untoward happening to her family.

In his first book, *The Treatise on General Sociology*, Vilfredo Pareto has raised the issue in much the same vein as Mistry that actions resting on exact knowledge—purely logical or means-ends estimations and judgements—are very rare in human affairs. Only a very limited section of actions in society approximates to logic. The rest is relegated to specific kinds of human propensities, instincts and interests through which mankind seeks material gratification. They are the actions, as for example, the first action of Gustad, praying, is attached to sentiments or subjective desire, often without a definite orientation to ends, which are, in any case, vague, diffused and unattainable. In short, we aspire for such things which have no logic of causality. All this does some good at least psychologically; they have their utility but not their truth. Pareto calls these actions emanating as they do from primordial human nature residues.

Pareto examines multitudes of human actions that constitute the outward expressions of sentiments and classifies these residues into six major classes. Class I is the manifestation of sentiments in individuals and in society that tend toward inventiveness, and the desire for adventure. Class II residues encompass the more conservative side of human nature, including loyalty to society's enduring institutions such as family, church, community, and nation. In a society, both have their respective roles and functions and complement each other but what concerns us here is the fact that both these concepts are built around sentiments and not reason.

Another Italian thinker Machiavelli divided humans into two classes, foxes and lions. The qualities he ascribes to these two classes of men resemble quite closely Pareto's Class I and Class II residue types. Men with strong Class I residues are the "foxes," tending to be manipulative, innovative, calculating, and imaginative. Class II men are "lions" who place much more value on traits such as good character and devotion to duty than on sheer wits. They are the defenders of tradition, the guardians of religious dogma, and the protectors of national honour. Indeed, Major Bilimoria, who symbolizes 'Nagarwala' of the historical political scandal, appears to be a fox to start with but Gustad remains a lion throughout. Both are sentimental fools however. After the former withdraws himself from Khodadad Building surreptitiously, Gustad learns a bitter lesson—never to trust friends. And yet Gustad is noble enough to prove himself a true friend not only to Bilimoria and Dinshawji but also to half-wit Tehmul.

At times, Gustad resembles Roderigo of Shakespeare's *Othello,* who was advised to "put money enough in your purse" by Iago. This is the same line that occurs repeatedly towards the end of Act I and Gustad is asked by Bilimoria to mark it so that the former may be marked by his man, Gulam Mohammad. Roderigo is a poor gentleman—for he is a gentleman, though a "gulled gentleman—he has a sad life in the play, bled white by Iago, disappointed of his hopes . . . a pathetic figure . . . trying to swim in a sea much too rough for him."[4] Doesn't Bilimoria make Gustad a Roderigo? Tested on the touchstone of rationalism, Gustad's agreeing to see a languishing Bilimoria in Delhi does not appear any whit logical. However, as things unfold themselves later, Bilimoria himself is taken in by bigger foxes.

The Parsee community has been in India for quite a few centuries now and still their total population stands at a few thousands only. Seen from this angle, they can be categorized as an ethnic minority, but the sense of their great heritage, their rich contribution to the country of their adoption, i.e., India, their forward-looking attitude—all these have denied to them a minority syndrome that is normally characterized by low achievements, high crime rate and worry about amalgamation through inter-race marriages etc.[5] Parsees are also alleged to have gained a lot through collusion with the Britishers before independence in India. This is not to discount the valuable contribution made to the independence struggle by stalwarts like Dadabhai Naoroji and Sir Pherozeshah Mehta. Yet it is a fact that the bulk of the Parsees kept aloof from common Indians on account of their better economic and educational status. In the post-Independence India, their somewhat westernized life-style has ensured the continuation of the wedge between the two communities. Allowance must be made here for the very ordinary, economically speaking, Parsee characters portrayed by Mistry in the present novel. They retain residues of ordinary prejudices of their group. Durkheim believed that "the fundamental categories of thought have a social origin, and that they owe their necessity and their *a priori* character to the fact that they are the basis of all intercourse between individuals."[6] The members of the Parsee community have their thoughts fashioned by inadequate knowledge of the majority community. Dilnavaz is enchanted by the milkman's *choti* but does not know its name. She has a faint idea that some caste sports it. Born of this ignorance is the suspicion of the slum-dwellers whose eyes seem to be threatening to throw the Parsees out.

Sociologists are of the view that "every in-group constructs out-group stereotypes."[7] Therefore, all Maharashtrians could be lumped together as 'Maratha buggers' (330). Prejudices take the form of derogatory references like "The Maratha brigade ran like cockroaches" (40). The numerous jokes regarding various communities (70-71), though in good faith, do point to underestimating the value of the out-groups. Beef is humorously considered healthier "because it is holier." (23) The Parsees themselves are at the receiving end when they are referred to as 'crow eaters.' (39)

A common subject of societal conversation in India is politics. Now, the popular understanding of politics is simplistic rather than rationalistic. A fine specimen of this, couched in figurative language is provided by Gustad-Dinshawji tête-à-tête: "Where is *madar chod* America now? Not saying one word. Otherwise, if Russia even belches, America protests at the UN. Let Kosygin fart, and America moves a motion in the Security Council." (76) It is not that persons like Gustad are not aware of what goes under the title 'news.' Cautioning his son, he waxes, "Whatever you read in the paper, first divide by two—for the salt and pepper. From what's left, take off ten percent. Ginger and garlic. And sometimes, depending on the journalist, another five percent for chilli powder. Then, and only then, will you get to the truth free of *masala* and propaganda." (68) But when the son grows wiser about the activities of RAW, the self-same Gustad has a different approach, "I read the papers and I know what goes on. Rumours and allegations all the time, and no proof!" (93) Later, Gustad himself is at the receiving end of the RAW personnel's macabre modus operandi. It is Ghulam Mohammad's turn to remind Gustad of the doubtful nature of news, "You know everything that appears in newspapers is not the truth." (202) In the kind of society to which Gustad belongs, Peerbhoy Paanwala analyses news in his inimitable style for the benefit of his customer-audience.

In such a society, myths are born easily. Thus, Medhiwala Bonesetter, the one who set right Gustad's aching hip, is famed to have 'piercing eyes' because of which the X-ray laboratories suffer in getting business (130). Peerbhoy Paanwala makes umpteen varieties of the betel leaf to cure all sorts of ailments and weaknesses. The enthusiasm for deification is quite common. Mr. Rabadi, the 'dogwala idiot,' would like Dustoorji Bania's picture drawn on the municipal wall for he can prescribe remedies for all the ills of life related to health, job, business, social status and even pet animals (288). It is a world in which "roadside latrines become temples and shrines, and temples and shrines become dust and ruin." (338) In this world, where Tatas and Birlas are favoured as against the poor people (127), Cavasji finds God highly irrational.

However, when a catastrophe like the Chinese aggression of India takes place, a rare emotional camaraderie is seen. The aggressor is transmuted to the category of a bugbear. "The wicked Chino will carry you off if you don't finish your food," Dilnavaz would tell her son Darius (9). Even a much lesser problem like the demolition of the boundary wall of Khodadad Building brings about a feeling of camaraderie among people living within and without, regardless of their religious or regional affiliation. All this is achieved on impulsive rather than any rational consideration. One is reminded of the famous simile of freezing porcupines given by Schopenhauer, which "crowd together to save themselves from being frozen to death, but separate again as soon as they feel one another's quills until at length they discover a mean distance at which they can tolerably exist."[8]

Even though scientists and philosophers have failed to find final answers to the myriad questions of philosophy, a kind of obsession with rationalism, that El Dorado of epistemology has marked the thinking of man much against human experience in certain weak moments as is provided by the following peep into the life of the great apostle of rationalism. Descartes took it upon himself to find a body of self-evident truths which could appeal to common sense and the faculty of reasoning. He desired to see the kind of accuracy in philosophy as characterized Mathematics, "prayed for divine illumination, vowing a pilgrimage to the shrine of Loretto in case his prayer should be answered."[9]

There are perhaps limits to practical transformation of all human ideas. G.B. Shaw's "The Revolutionary's Handbook" in his magnum opus *Man and Superman* begins with the promise to unravel the 'golden rule' but deconstructs stating simply, "The golden rule is that there is no golden rule."[10] Major Bilimoria has learnt while working in RAW that one must not trust anyone howsoever near and dear. Unfortunately, if the worldly-wise Major had stuck to this golden principle, it would have been a rational approach and he would have saved his skin, but acting on impulse and taken in by the majestic charm of the Prime Minister, he signs his confession. (277) While the Major meets his doom at the end of the novel, Sohrab's estrangement and Roshan's illness also end. However, this latter happy development coincides with the last magic rites conducted by Miss Kutpitia before the laboratory of magic goes up in flames. The writer seems to be trying to achieve some kind of suspension of disbelief with regard to the miraculous impact of the magic.

Why does man leave the straight path of reason and get fascinated by the labyrinthine maze of sentimentality instead? The answer, if it can be called an answer, is provided by the footpath artist, "You see, I don't like to weaken anyone's faith. Miracle, magic, mechanical trick, coincidence—does it matter what it is, as long as it helps? Why analyze the strength of the imagination, the power of suggestion, the power of auto-suggestion, the potency of psychological pressures?" (289)

NOTES

1. Michael Haralambos, *Sociology: Themes and Perspectives* (Delhi: Oxford University Press, 1980), p. 484.
2. Fr. James Thornton, *Vilfredo Pareto: A Concise Overview of His Life, Works, and Philosophy* <http://www.google.com>
3. Rohinton Mistry, *Such a Long Journey* (London: Faber and Faber, 1991), p. 52.

4. M.R. Ridley, *Othello.* (London: Methuen, 1969), p. lxvi.
5. David C. King and Marvin R. Koller, *Foundations of Sociology* (San Francisco: Rinehart Press, 1957).
6. Morris Ginsberg, *Sociology (*Delhi: Surjeet, 1979).
7. Robert Bierstedt, *The Social Order* (New Delhi: Tata McGraw Hill, 1970).
8. Ginsberg, p. 103.
9. Frank Thilly, *A History of Philosophy* (New Delhi: SBW, 2005).
10. George Bernard Shaw, *Man and Superman* (Middlesex: Penguin, 1977), p. 251.

Raising Issues Related to Caste Defined Samskaras: A Study of U.R. Anantha Murthy's *Samskara*

TEJINDER KAUR

In this paper, I have chosen the novel *Samskar*a for discussion, originally published in Kannada in 1965 by a prominent Kannada novelist, short story writer, poet and essayist U.R. Anantha Murthy, a recipient of Jnanpeeth Award in 1995, Padma Bhushna in 1998, Ganakrishti award for literary distinction, Kolkata for the year 2002 along with a number of awards both from the Government and academies for his invaluable contributions in many fields. Since its publication, this controversial novel has received wide acclaim in the literary circles and from the readers and has been translated into many languages in India and abroad. It was filmed by Girish Karnad in 1970 and was translated into English by A.K. Ramanujan in 1976 and was published by Oxford University Press in 1978. In this novel subtitled "A Rite for a Dead Man" Anantha Murthy has portrayed a decaying South Indian Brahmin colony in a village in Karnataka and has dealt with very serious issues related to orthodox Madhva Brahmin caste order, its following the age-old traditions of the rigid caste-defined value system, its inherent contradictions and deviations due to human weaknesses, challenge to the oppressive rigidity of the system by new ideas and hypocrisy of high caste brahmins, slow shift in the ethics, exploitation of the low caste women and harlots, the value judgements on a person as per the caste in place of one's humane intentions and actions. While handling these issues in the narrative along with many other issues, the basic questions raised in the novel are (i) what is actual *samskara*? (This Sanskrit word is very important in this novel and has multiple layers of meanings). (ii) Is it achieved by blindly following rules and traditions or it gets lost when they are not kept? (iii) Are the good and bad caste defined? Such caste and religion based themes and issues in almost every cultural community have been interrogated, challenged and pondered over in literature all over the world and in many Indian literary texts written in regional languages and English also with a plea to transform the social orders to make them humane but the way Anantha Murthy has grappled with these issues (in an ironical and humorous way) which are being debated even now as ever, in this complex, thought provoking open discourse make it a unique narrative in many ways.

When the novel was published in 1965, it was criticized for assailing the traditions but Anantha Murthy as "a critical insider" boldly portrayed the realities of his own oppressive Madhva Brahmin past in a remote Karnataka village "when its orthodoxies were being questioned in the reformist climate of the 1930s and 40s," and also the slow shift in the ethics taking place and the agrahara system disintegrating. The novelist here has captured the spirit of the times by raising live questions giving no conclusive answers. There is a continuous deferment of the questions and their suggestive answers, producing new meanings during and after every reading which make this text a "writerly" one in Roland Barthes's term. The title and the sub-title of the text give us the impression of its being a narrative pertaining to the samskara, the last rite of a dead man. The central focus of the narrative is the dead body of a heretic, Naranappa—belonging to Madhva brahmin caste—lying waiting in the agrahara—a brahmin colony—of a Karnataka village named Durvasapuram to be cremated, since he was an orphan and also had no children to perform his last rites putting the brahmins into religious controversy as to who should do this task without risking his brahminhood and should his samskara be performed as per the prescribed norms for his high caste in the holy texts as he had been following the anti-brahmanic ways. The plot of the narrative is woven around this problematic to dwell and debate on so many issues in multiple voices which keep on mounting and conflicting as the action moves and even after the narrative ends but does not conclude in the text. In this polyphonic novel, to borrow Bakhtin's words, "everything is still in the future and will always be in the future."[1]

Another problematic of this text is the multiple meanings of the Sanskrit word 'samskara' "which refers to the concept central to Hinduism" e.g. forming well, making perfect, refining, refinement, making sacred, conception in the mind, preparation and making ready, realizing of past perceptions, making pure, purification, purity, a sanctifying or purificatory rite or essential ceremony (enjoined on all the first three classes or castes), any rite or ceremony, funeral obsequies"[2] which invite us to explicate the text and analyse the intentions and conduct of its characters from various angles. "Though the word 'samskara' does not occur obtrusively or too frequently in the narrative, its meanings implicitly inform the action. . . . The action depends on the several meanings being at loggerheads with each other," comments A.K. Ramanujan.[3] In Derrida's words, we can say, "The absence of the transcendental signified extends the domain and the play of signification infinitely."[4]

There are two male protagonists in the novel, both belonging to the upper Madhva brahmin caste—Naranappa, who has recently died of plague when the novel opens and the other is Praneshacharaya, the guru of this agrahara. Both these characters represent two different ideologies, which clash with each other. Naranappa, a product of the changing times, embodied the revolutionary spirit under the impact of western culture and new emerging ideas to abolish many social evils like untouchability and rigid caste barriers, and to spread education, develop one's personality and live a life of pleasure and fulfillment. In his lifetime he had openly flouted, mocked at and questioned the prescribed ideology and code of conduct for his caste, and exposed the hypocritical and sinful living of the narrow-minded, selfish, greedy, jealous fellow Brahmins whose brahminhood consists only of following age-old rules and rituals without caring to understand them and living in the fear that disasters would fall them if these rules and rituals were not observed. For their living they depended only on the alms, charity, donations and meals on various occasions and anniversaries where they performed various rites and rituals, samskaras. Instead of having holy thoughts, spiritual experiences and doing virtuous deeds as laid down, they disliked one another and made nasty comments and their wives mainly indulged in idle gossip.

Defying all the caste defined samskaras on finding them meaningless, repressive and non-progressive, Naranappa had been living a life of his own desire without bothering about the good or bad opinions of his fellow agraharians, by deserting his non-pleasure giving wife, living happily for the last ten years with a beautiful concubine Chandri, considered to be low caste, brought from Kundapura, eating food cooked by her, eating meat and catching fish from the temple pond with his Muslims friends, making friends with the low caste brahmins of other agraharas also, helping people in need, having cut his tuft growing the crop of hair in the western style, forming drama and dance troupes and goading the brahmin youth of his own and nearby agraharas to give up the orthodox and redundant thinking and way of life and join different professions, which agitated his fellow brahmins who blamed him for misleading and corrupting their children. He had openly challenged the virtues and idealism of the most virtuous brahmin of that agrahara Praneshacharaya who had earned the title "the Crest jewel of Vedic learning" because of his learning, scholarship and ability to argue in religious matters. The people of this and nearby agraharas respected him for his knowledge of the religious texts and ritualistic samskaras for every occasion for his moral and austere living and compassionate attitude towards all irrespective of their caste, his devoted and ungrudging service of his ailing and invalid wife. Above all, he believed "in typical brahminhood which he imbibed through great learning,"[5] and tried to maintain its observance in this agrahara. Even when Naranappa mocked at his perpetuating the rotten samskaras among these sinful brahmins and held himself responsible for their decadence and their corruption since he provided the protective umbrella of the ancient books over their sins, insulted him many a time by offering him liquor, argued with him asserting his anti-brahminic viewpoints and threatening him to roll up his "brahmin respectability" and throw it all ways for a little bit of "pleasure with one female," Praneshacharaya never shouted back. Rather out of compassion to reform him, he observed fast for two days a week to bring the lamb going astray back to the fold of the unprotesting ritualistic brahminic order which alone could redeem him.

Praneshacharaya's commitment to conform to the old order which alone was held right and pure and Naranappa's challenging it demanding a change in it as per the changing times and on humanitarian grounds, rising above the caste-defined values of samskaras has been the focus of Naranappa's arguments which Praneshacharaya used to listen patiently rather pitying the offender. Naranappa was condemned during his life time for his unsamskari views and ways, died unredeemed in spite of Praneshacharaya's efforts and now even his dead body has created a problem for the samskari brahmins leaving them hungry and angry because they can't eat and perform the daily rituals till a brahmin's corpse is cremated.

Though Naranappa had given up brahminhood yet the brahminhood had not left him. With his death, the agrahara is not only passing through a situation of Dharam Sankat as to who should perform the samskara of a fellow brahmin who had not been excommunicated, it also brings many situations which reveal the degraded inner selves and the unsamskari samskaras and actions of the upper caste samskari Brahmins and also lay bare the politics of religion. By presenting the humane attitude, good intentions, and acts of compassion of Naranappa's concubine Chandri in various situations who is considered to be unsamskari, impure, unrefined, uncultured because of her birth from a prostitute's womb vis-à-vis those of the higher caste brahmin men and women (supposed to be samskari—pure, refined, cultured since born in brahmin families), the writer shows the fall in their character and their foolish adherence to caste-prescribed rituals.

Profession-wise, Chandri is a whore, an outcaste and is dubbed by brahmins and their wives as "Mari," the dark goddess of death, plague, "a seducing witch" whose face should be branded since she had ruined Naranappa's married life and was mainly interested in his property and gold, whose corpse was lying "around like this without even the benefit of a rite" only because of her having distracted him from the path of righteousness. The gold she has been wearing around her neck and wrists should have adorned Narayana's lawful wife—now dead. These comments of the samskari men and women place Chandri in her defined caste and social order because of which she has to bear their wrath but if we analyze her role, conduct, intentions, attitudes, actions and impressions on a few characters in the novel step by step, these reveal her to be a grateful, kind, compassionate, humane, refined, cultured woman, in other words a samskari human being as compared to the male and female brahmin characters in the novel, who boast of their high birth and samskaras but actually are the committers of seven deadly sins.

Being a prostitute by class and caste, she is the 'other' among the community of upper caste Brahmins. Hence she holds a marginalized status but Narayana never ill-treated her. He rather defended his living with her and deserting his wife as who would live with a woman who can't give you pleasure. He declared his relations with her justified in the light of such relations of their sages mentioned in the Puranas and other holy texts from which Praneshacharaya himself illuminated and explicated the passages describing the beauty of the female body which had made many a sage like Parashara, Vishwamitra, Shankara have illicit sexual union in whom the fellow brahmins took much pride clamouring themselves to be their proud descendents. Durgabhatta, a brahmin from the smarta brahmin sect considered somewhat lower to Madhva brahmin caste, too approved of Narayana-Chandri relationship in the light of the conduct of their sages, not to favour Chandri but only to check and measure "the rival sect's orthodoxy with a questioning eye" whose many members visited the prostitutes quite often. Though the samskari brahmins loathed and denounced Narayana in public for his immoral living but many other middle-aged and young brahmins of this and other agraharas envied him for possessing such a beauty and secretly desired Chandri. Durgabhatta even ogled at her when after Narayana's death she was standing in a corner, aloof and isolated with her head covered and who seldom moved out of the house when Narayana was alive. Shripati, Lakshmana's son-in-law, whose wife Lilavati denied him physical pleasure as a punishment on her mother's advice, the formula applied on her husband also who secretly satisfied his lust with the low caste sweeper girl Belli off and on but he talks very high of Chandri's humane qualities and proves her more cultured and refined than the wives of brahmins in many respects.

Chandri used to dissuade Narayana from eating the food cooked by her, eating fish and meat as it was not allowed in his dharma but Narayana did not bother about these prohibitions; he called these "sheer pigheadedness" and shared his food and joy with her. She also used to advise Naranappa to be respectful towards the Acharya and behave properly with him. Thus though Chandri's relationship with Narayana was not socially approved yet both of them lived happily for ten years as if made for each other. She neither demanded anything from Naranappa nor did she meddle with his other affairs or tried to transgress her caste limits as she was aware of his and her own caste status. Though she behaved like a cultured woman but Narayana did not marry her and even visited other prostitutes.

Through Chandri's reveries and daydreaming we are also made aware of the fate and plight of the women of her class "ever auspicious, daily-wedded, the one without widowhood" who could not marry in the caste-defined set up and whose survival depended only on their remaining ever beautiful. She like every woman desires to be a mother. The only regret she had from this relationship was that in spite of her stay with Naranappa for ten long years "she still hadn't had a child." She regretted: "She had got everything, yet had nothing." (54) She used to think: "If she had borne a son, he could have become a great musician: if a daughter, she could have taught her to dance, classical style." (54) What is important here is that in spite of her having been born in a low caste family, she has progressive thinking of educating her children without any discrimination. Though not a legally wedded wife, she is not a money minting prostitute as declared by the brahmin women in the agrahara but a sincere human being who alone along with Praneshacharaya is grieved over the demise of Naranappa. Whereas other samskari brahmins are unwilling to perform Narayana's samskara because of many religious and property related reasons, it is only Chandri who is anxious and worried about the plague hit corpse of her paramour and wants it to be cremated as per the proper rites to help his salvation. No fellow brahmin is bothered about Naranappa. What they are worried about is the urgency of food, their loss of brahminhood and excommunication by their Guru if they performed the rites unless clarified by Praneshacharaya after consulting the Books. There is no consideration of fellow and humane feeling among this samskari clan.

Even when the question of meeting the expenses of the funeral obsequies of Naranappa is raised, it is Chandri who comes forward, removes all her gold and offers it to Praneshacharaya to meet the expenses for the proper rites of the man who had given her all the comforts and joys. The hypocrisy, greed, hatred, selfishness and jealousies of these samskari brahmins who are expected to be above these base feelings are exposed when instead of appreciating her act of offering her gold, Durgabhatta and Lakshmana and their wives, Sitadevi and Anasuya respectively (mythical names ironically used) stare at the heap of gold worth two thousand rupees and quarrel over the possession of this gold. These two brahmin wives had earlier warned their husbands, whispering into their ears not to agree in a hurry to perform the rites as the Guru will excommunicate them and now they persuade their husbands individually to claim before Praneshacharaya their rights as kins to cremate the dead body of Naranappa so that Chandri's gold could come to them. It is also interesting to observe that now instead of blaming Chandri for Naranappa's pollution, they start accusing each other for their nefarious practices and intentions with regard to Narayana to claim his property.

Praneshacharaya grows anxious: "Why did Chandri spoil everything with her good intentions?" (10) and he also starts realizing the sins of his fellow Brahmins. We see that this first act of Chandri of "compassion" which is called "human gold," "exposed the vacuity of the order."[6] Praneshacharaya is moved by this act of hers, appreciates it before his invalid wife, Bhagirathi: "how pure Chandri's heart was, how she laid down all her gold and what new complications arose from that generous act" (20) and he also becomes aware of the greed of the fellow brahmins. This lust for money becomes apparent in the guru of Madhvas also whom the brahmins ultimately visit to settle the issue of Naranappa's cremation and who wants the entire property of Naranappa to be attached to the monastery and threatens the brahmins of their excommunication if the money was donated somewhere else. After Naranappa's death and the new problem generated due to the greed of the brahmins, it is only Praneshacharaya who is compassionate towards Chandri in her distress and also returns her gold saying, "Naranappa is dead. But you've your life to live." (49)

In this scenario no brahmin is bothered about Naranappa's corpse or his entry to heaven or the dilemma of Praneshacharaya struggling to find the right answer from the Books of Law. Their concern is only food and to get rid of the body at the earliest. Here too Chandri is shown full of pity and compassion for the man who had been suffering for others. When he had gone to the Maruti temple to seek the answer for this dilemma so that the brahmins could cremate the dead body and take food, she carries plantains in the corner of her sari, waits for him under a tree. She remembers the words of her mother who used to say "prostitutes should get pregnant by such holy men" and she realizes: "Such a man was Acharya, he had such virtues; he glowed. But one had to be lucky to be blessed by such people," (46) though she has no intention of entrapping him. On Acharya's coming back from the temple without finding any answer, she follows him in the darkness, falls at his feet for seeking his blessings, and while lifting her up, he feels the warmth of her body and full breasts. Chandri holds him down, gives him the plantains to eat and caresses him. This tender love leads to sexual union. On waking up, he feels himself fallen but does not "scold" or "despise" Chandri for this. Rather he tells her that now he had lost the authority to decide for the agrahara. He asks her that this act must be confessed before the agrahara gathering and they must tell "this happened": "If I don't have the courage to speak, tomorrow you must speak out. I'm ready to do the funeral rites myself."

She lets him go ahead and reaching the agrahara goes to the room where Naranappa's rotting, stinking body is lying and considers it her duty to cremate it. It is here through Chandri's reflections that Anantha Murthy makes a dig at the frivolity of the rigid religion and caste-based structures built and fussed about when on seeing Naranappa's decaying corpse, she ruminates: "That's not her lover Naranappa. It's neither brahmin nor shudra. A carcass. A stinking rotting carcass" (70) over which so much furore was being created. Gathering courage, she goes alone in the night to the cartman Sheshappa's house and on his refusal to meddle with "a brahmin corpse," she seeks the help of a Muslim fish merchant Ahmad Bari (an outcaste for brahmins), a friend of Naranappa whom he had helped with a small loan to buy oxen when he was bankrupt, to cremate the dead body in the dark of night with the firewood lying in her house. No brahmin knows about this fact and the samskari brahmins including Praneshacharaya keep on wriggling over the ritual sanctities—samskaras—foolishly. Through this another humane act, Chandri breaks the tradition and caste barriers like Naranappa and even "gets the better of Praneshacharaya" and "exposes the inhumanity of orthodox Brahmanism that permitted itself to be trapped in ritual hairsplitting when faced with life-and-death issues."[7]

After cremation, she weeps to her heart's desire for Narayana, collects her clothes, money and gold and leaves in the dark to travel by road to catch a bus in the morning for Kundapura without even informing Praneshacharaya about the cremation and her intention to depart. Instead of taking advantage of the situation to blackmail Praneshacharaya and see Praneshacharaya's humiliation in front of others if he spoke about the last night's act, her decision to leave the place quietly speaks of her good samskaras as compared to those of Praneshacharaya's samskari fellow brahmins who would have left no stone unturned to downgrade him on knowing his inadvertent act.

Her decision of even not meeting him before her leaving, as it would make such a noble man feel small before her, too is an indicator of her greatness as a human being and regard for the genuine goodness of the Acharya and his kindness towards her throughout. Thus we see that Chandri's and Ahmad Bari's belonging to a lower caste in no way makes them base and lower human beings which they are in the eyes of the high caste brahmins. Rather they possess the basic human quality of "compassion, the right way of dharma," (48) which the other samskari brahmins except Praneshacharaya lack in this text.

Though Chandri leaves the stage at this point, right in the middle of the text and we are not told of her whereabouts afterwards, she leaves a great impact on the mind of Praneshacharaya, after exposing him to the world of flesh. His encounter with Chandri proves a turning point in his life. After cremating his wife who had died of plague, he leaves the agrahara, as he can't face people who had revered him as the most virtuous person. But though he flees from the surroundings, he cannot flee from himself. Through a peep into his mind, we are shown the fraud of asceticism practised by him. By his choice marriage with an invalid woman which would keep him away from the lust and his asceticism and service of her will surely guarantee him a passport to heaven and a seat there. Now his irresistible desire for touching Chandri's full breasts or even of the low-caste Belli and other young women and his fear of being discovered for his sexual act with Chandri and roaming around aimlessly bring a moral crisis for him, putting him in further dilemmas, conflicts and turmoil which have been shown through a series of interior monologues and self-introspections of the Acharya in the second half of the novel. He starts realizing the duplicity in his life, his winding between "asceticism and eroticism," "dharma and kama" and he feels himself "hung—suspended under two truths like 'Trishanku.'" (92) His contact with Chandri now makes him aware of the difference between the world of beauty which he now starts admiring and desiring and ugliness which he despises now. He starts understanding the willing submission of the ancient sages of the Hindu mythology and that of his studious ashram friend Mahabala and of Naranappa to the female beauty. He also finds Naranappa having victory over him who had earlier challenged him and wanted Praneshacharaya to listen to others' experiences and viewpoints also. His strenuous struggle with himself while passing through the world of real life's ordinary experiences in the company of Putta in their beauty, ugliness and ruthlessness, which he did not desire or experience earlier living in his samskara embowered ivory tower and now resolving to own the responsibility of his action boldly and his reaching the decision of living with Chandri openly like Naranappa as this way he will "remake" himself as a human being, shows him now a reborn person "a *trija, thrice born*." This transformation (samskara) of Praneshacharaya as a human being is a positive step towards correcting the falling human standards in that agrahara. He gets disillusioned "regarding the ethics he had strongly favoured and preached till then. The shift of ethics from the socialistic and religious to existentialism is quite prominent from this stage."[8] Now he starts thinking in terms of the existence of the individual as a free and responsible person.

Thus we see that through the good-intentioned humane acts of the subaltern Chandri which cross the boundary of caste-laid norms, Anantha Murthy as a critical insider not only lays bare the hypocrisy and shams of the decadent brahminic order but also shows the transformation of Praneshacharaya who ultimately decides to confess his act fearlessly before the brahmins cremate the dead body of Naranappa himself, go to Kundapura, start living with Chandri openly. He also floats his reformative vision of rising above the caste barriers, developing a humane approach and also the rehabilitation of the prostitutes like Chandri who are the product and victims of the patriarchal and rigid caste system. If the learned and virtuous religious men take lead in this connection, the victimization of the women of this class will surely end and social and religious systems can be overhauled. But whether Praneshacharaya will have the courage to go to Kundapura by breaking the tight shackles of the samskaras of his caste, own Chandri and her child socially and legally or will he just keep her as a keep like Naranappa or Mahabala is a question mark because at the end of the narrative, he is shown still grappling with himself: "How can I face all those brahmins alone?" (137) The "anxious, expectant" Praneshacharaya sits in the lorry going to Durvasapuram and the narrative itself ends with a question mark: "He will travel, for another four or five hours. Then, after that, what?" In fact, this is the dilemma of everyman of Praneshacharaya's mental make-up and social status in the given socio-cultural milieu. The text leaves us with two other questions: (i) what will be the fate of Praneshacharaya if he confesses his act and announces his decision? and (ii) what should brahmins do when confronted with the confession of Praneshacharaya?

Thus we find that "while narrating this tale, the author raises several questions and highlights various conflicts and contrasts in society, but it ends without offering any specific solution. Indeed, it confirms that there is no specific solution,"[9] because it was very difficult to break the established caste and social orders and live in total defiance in the times when the novel was written. Still we can say that though Anantha Murthy has not given any overt solutions to the questions raised in the text or a set of alternative order but by showing the sowing of seeds of transformation in the religious leader of a caste order preparing him for bringing a change in the sick social system, the writer has conveyed his message. Moreover, even if he has succeeded in raising questions in the readers' minds regarding the caste based rotting orders which need to make collective introspections, re-examine and re-define their caste ordained value system, the task of the literary text as means of social change gets well performed. Though the text does not lay down the defined answers about samskaras but to the two questions (i) who is a true samskari? and (ii) does your birth or caste determine your samskaras or your humane attitudes and actions? there can be no two answers. The latter question implies the most probable answer to the problematic of samskara dealt with in this text.

NOTES

1. Mikhail Bakhtin, *Problems of Dostoevsky's Poetics*, trans. and ed. Caryl Emerson (Manchester: Manchester University Press, 1984), p. 166.
2. U.R. Anantha Murthy, "Epigraph," *Samskara* (Oxford University Press, 1978).
3. "Afterword," *ibid.*
4. Jacques Derrida, "Structure, sign and play in the discourse of human sciences," *Modern Criticism and Theory: A Reader*, ed. David Lodge (Longman: London and New York, 1988), pp. 108-23.
5. Shard V. Bhat, "Shift in Ethics in U.R. Anantha Murthy's *Samskara*," *Indian Journal of Contemporary English Criticism*, ed. Mandal B. Beg, Vol. 1, No. 1, Jan.-June 2002, pp. 5-9.
6. P. Usha Sundari, "Ritual to Paranoia: A Study of Anantha Murthy's *Samskara*," *Ibid.*, pp. 64-74.
7. Rajagopal Parthasarthy, "*Samskara*: The Passing of the Brahman Tradition," *Masterpieces of Asian Literature in Comparative Perspective*, ed. Barbara Stoler Miller (New York: M.E. Sharpe), pp. 189-200.
8. Bhat, p. 7.
9. *Samskara*, a Book Review, Meghdutam com.

Gender and Caste Issues in Arundhati Roy's *The God of Small Things*

SEEMA JAIN

To begin with an age-old, oft-repeated cliché, it can be reiterated that literature holds the mirror to life and society and in turn, exercises an influence upon society—shaping, reshaping and transforming many of its conventions, taboos, values and beliefs. It has been rightly observed, "Literature is not only the effect of social causes; it is also the cause of social effects."[1] In spite of the formalist and structuralist critics' emphasis on the beauties of form and structure, on the literary and stylistic devices employed, the socio-cultural significance of a literary work still remains indisputable. In the words of the celebrated French critic Hippolyte Adolph Taine, "a literary work is not a mere individual play of imagination, the isolated caprice of an excited brain, but a transcript of contemporary manners."[2] The moment and the milieu do contribute considerably to the creation of pioneering literary works.

Coming to the Indian context, fiction has been an ever-growing, rapidly evolving genre, portraying the typically Indian sensibility placed in the Indian ethos. Apart from the celebrated writers like R.K. Narayan, Raja Rao, Mulk Raj Anand, Kamala Das and Khushwant Singh, the fiction of Salman Rushdie, Anita Desai, Arundhati Roy, Jhumpa Lahiri, Shashi Deshpande, Manju Kapur and Rupa Bajwa has lent a uniquely rich vibrancy to the Indian fiction. These writers, whether in India or abroad, display experiences and sensibility which are distinctly Indian.

Sometimes, the delineation of the Indian scene in these writers takes the form of a critique, an overt or covert indictment of some of the ancient Indian beliefs and value systems which still have very strong roots in the fabric of the modern Indian society. The present paper aims at analysing the limiting, restraining and constrictive influence of some aspects of our system and their tragic consequences on the lives of individual human beings, as depicted in Arundhati Roy's celebrated novel *The God of Small Things*. Arundhati Roy catapulted to fame with her maiden work of fiction winning the prestigious Booker Award in 1997. Her book has won accolades from critics for her narrative style and innovative use of language. But equally gripping and powerful is the way the novel depicts and rationalizes the socio-cultural realities of the Indian system. The present paper proposes to discuss Arundhati Roy's novel in the light of two social issues—gender and caste inequalities—which have existed in our society for centuries. The novel shows how the macrocosmic social reality, The God of Big Things as it is called, has the potential to annihilate the individuals' dreams of a meaningful existence—individuals who cling to small things. As Silva Peter says: "The small things are the trivial diversions the characters focus upon in order to avoid confronting the pain of big things."[3]

Arundhati Roy, in her novel, portrays the society of Ayemenem, a place in Kerala, which is deeply rooted in the patriarchal value system, and epitomizes all places where patriarchal structures reign supreme. Being a female author, Roy focuses upon some of the key gender issues like marginalization and oppression of women having no *locus standi*, lack of legal and inheritance rights for women and women being subjected to violence in marriage. These issues emerge through the portrayal of female characters like Mammachi, Ammu, Rahel and wives of Kathakali men. The novel also represents, through Baby Kochamma and Mammachi, the negative side of femininity where these women, having unconsciously and unquestioningly imbibed/ internalized the values of patriarchy, tend to derogate the members of their sex and collude in their subordination.

The prime focus of interest in the novel is Velutha and Ammu, seen from Ammu's daughter Rahel's point of view. Though the canvas of the novel is very wide, covering the lives of a Syrian Christian family upto four generations, the novel is primarily about the fate and fortunes of these two characters, Ammu and Velutha and of their twin children, Estha and Rahel.

Ammu has had unpleasant childhood experiences and has bitter memories of her male chauvinistic father, Shri Benaan John Ipe or Pappachi, who had been Joint Director, Entomology, at Pusa Institute, Delhi, and was charming and sophisticated with visitors. He donated money to orphanages and leprosy clinics. He did everything to build up his public profile as a sophisticated, generous and moral man. But when he was at home with his wife and children, he would become a monstrous bully and beat them in the same inhuman and callous manner as the illiterate and unsophisticated Kathakali men beat their wives. Ammu, "as a child . . . had learnt very quickly to disregard the Father Bear Mother Bear stories she was given to read. In her version, Father Bear beat Mother Bear with brass vases. Mother Bear suffered those beatings with mute resignation."[4] Ammu would spend cold winter nights in the garden of her Delhi house because Pappachi would beat her and Mammachi (Soshamma) and turn them out of his house. The novel is replete with instances of violence, psychological or otherwise, against women. Pappachi has double standards towards the education of his son and daughter. After Ammu completes her education in school, Pappachi insists that "college education is an unnecessary expense for a girl," (38) whereas Chacko, her brother is sent to Oxford for his education. Pappachi is full of resentment and sullenness at his wife starting a pickle factory. The narrator observes: "In the evenings . . . he would sit on the verandah and sew buttons that weren't missing onto his shirts, to create the impression that Mammachi neglected him." (48) Ammu gets desperate to escape from "the clutches of her ill-tempered father and long-suffering mother." (39) She marries a Bengali man at the first opportunity, much against the wishes of her parents. But her husband, who is a full-blown alcoholic, often beats her. In her married life, there is a pattern of "drunken violence and post-drunken badgering." (42) When her husband is ready to prostitute her to his English Boss, Mr. Hollick, in order to save his job and when the bouts of violence begin to include her twin children, Ammu decides to leave him and returns, unwelcome, to Ayemenem, where her status is that of a dependent, "because Ammu as a daughter had no claim to the property." (57) Baby Kochamma, Ammu's aunt and a spinster, dislikes Ammu because she believes "a married woman had no position in her parents's home. As for a divorced daughter, she had no position anywhere at all." (45)

If Ammu and her mother represent constrictive effects of patriarchy on the lives of women, Baby Kochamma is an example of women co-operating in the perpetuation of orthodox patriarchal values, a fact often labelled as women being enemies of women. Such women can be seen too often in life around us.

Mammachi, Ammu's mother, is also rooted in this patriarchal, phallocentric ideology. On the one hand, she is a victim of her husband's male chauvinism, but ironically on the other hand, she becomes instrumental in inflicting suffering on her daughter Ammu. She has concessional standards for her son Chacko whose sexual adventures with female factory workers are dismissed as "man's needs." She has a separate door installed for him so that he can pursue his needs unhindered. But when it comes to her daughter's affair with Velutha, her fury is unmanageable; hell breaks loose because she thinks Ammu "had defiled generations of breeding." (258) Her double standards are in conformity with the system and hence she contributes her share in the perpetuation of a system of which she herself is a victim.

Heidi Hartmann and Christine Delphy, noted American Marxist feminists, argue: "patriarchy exists as a distinct system of inequality . . . and that patriarchy is founded upon male control of women's labour."[5] Thus, even when Ammu does as much work in the factory as Chacko, he refers to it as "my factory, my pineapples, my pickles" and tells Ammu, "What's yours is mine and what's mine is also mine." (57) She has no say in the decision-making affairs of the factory. Even Mammachi, who started the factory, takes a back seat once Chacko returns to Ayemenem. He gets the factory "registered as a partnership and informs Mammachi that she was the sleeping partner." (57)

After Sophie Mol's death and after Ammu's affair with the untouchable Veluthais discovered by Mammachi and Baby Kochamma, she is locked up in her room. The narrator remarks: "Ammu was incoherent with rage and disbelief at what was happening to her at being locked away like the family lunatic in a medieval household." (252) The motif of a raging lunatic locked up in a medieval household brings to mind *A Madwoman in the Attic* by Sandra Gilbert and Susan Gubar and symbolizes the piled up frustration, anger and agony of the women for centuries.

When Velutha dies in the police lock-up, Ammu, contrary to the calculations of Baby Kochamma, revolts with the "reckless rage of a suicide bomber," is scandalized, humiliated and alienated. Chacko shouts at her to get out of his house. She is forced to return Estha to his father. Rahel is sent to a boarding school in Delhi. Ammu has to pack her bags and leave. She drifts from place to place, from job to job, dreaming to be on her own one day, to be able to keep her children with her. But tragically, that is never to be. Suffering from acute asthma, solitary, desolate, broken, Ammu dies alone in a dingy room in a cheap lodge with nobody by her side. The sweeper finds her dead body in the morning, to which the narrator remarks: "A platoon of ants carried a dead cockroach sedately through the door, demonstrating what should be done to corpses." (162) The cockroach motif symbolically points out the insignificance of creatures like Ammu. In this situation, the following remark of Stevi Jackson and Jackie Jones appears very pertinent: "We continue to live in a world where large-scale inequalities still have a profound impact on women's lives and the ways in which social structures are both constraining and enabling cannot be ignored."[6]

Ammu's predicament leaves a trail of trauma and misery for her twin children who drift through life without any emotional moorings or support and finally drift into an incestuous relationship with each other. Ammu's violation of Love Laws, "The laws that lay down who should be loved, and how. And how much" (33) leads to the society punishing her and Velutha, which in turn leads Estha and Rahel to once again break love laws, about which the narrator remarks: "But what was there to say? . . . Only that they held each other close, long after it was over. Only that what they shared that night was not happiness but hideous grief." (328) This incestuous relationship, confounding as it is, is like a big question mark staring us in the face.

Closely linked to the gender issue in the novel is the caste issue. Though caste discrimination was outlawed in our country in 1950, it still is an enduring social issue, the prejudice against untouchables having strong roots in the collective unconscious of the touchables in the Indian society. The plight of untouchables and the caste distinctions in Indian society have been handled by a number of writers like Prem Chand, Mulk Raj Anand, Rohinton Mistry, just to name a few. Arundhati Roy portrays with great empathy and sensitivity this horrendous evil of our society in its inhuman, barbaric and monstrous dimension through the character of Velutha who is a parvan, an untouchable in the novel. Velutha, a talented young man, is in the words of Mammachi, 'a parvan with a future' and according to Chacko, 'is indispensable for Paradise Pickles and Preserves as he practically runs the factory.' A skilled and accomplished carpenter, Velutha is the God of small things and has uncanny skill with his hands. Velutha who falls for Ammu, a caste Christian, has to pay the price with his annihilation at the hands of the police in a chilling and blood-curdling manner.

In a society where the touchables would not allow untouchables inside their house, where they are not allowed to touch anything that touchables—caste Hindus or caste Christians—touched, where they have to crawl backwards and wipe away their footprints with a broom so that no touchable should defile himself by accidentally stepping into them, where even after converting to Christianity to escape the scourge of untouchability, untouchables are still segregated and made to have separate churches and bishops, where communist leader K.N.M. Pillai donning the mantle of a saviour for the downtrodden masses tells Chacko that his wife would not allow *parvans* inside her house, where touchable inspector Mathews perfectly understands Baby Kochamma's contrived allegations against Velutha because "He had a touchable wife, two touchable daughters, whole touchable generations waiting in their touchable wombs," (259) there can be no glimmer of hope for a man like Velutha. He is a victim of the inexorable social prejudices and all his skills and talent cannot absolve him of his untouchable status.

The identities and destinies of Ammu and Velutha are fused into one, not just because they are drawn towards each other, but because of their affinity in their marginalized social status. Thinking about Velutha, Ammu "hoped that under his careful cloak of cheerfulness, he housed an anger against the smug, ordered world that she so raged against." (176) The struggle of Ammu and Velutha, these two marginalized creatures of society, for happiness in a social system where gender and caste inequalities are widely prevalent, brings to mind the noted French feminist critic Julia Kristeva who views femininity not in terms of essences but in terms of positionality and defines femininity as 'that which is marginalized by the patriarchal symbolic order.' Kristeva further observes, "Insofar as women are defined as marginal by patriarchy, their struggle can be theorized in the same way as any other struggle against a centralized power structure."[7] Here, it can be observed that Velutha unlike all other male characters in the novel, who are male chauvinistic in their attitude, can be viewed as a feminine, socially castrated creature, due to his untouchable status in society, due to his marginalized identity on the basis of caste and economic class both. He is described as "The God of Loss. The God of Small Things." (330) In order to break the shackles that tie him down, he seeks refuge in Marxism and becomes a card-holding member of the Communist party. Here, it would not be out of place to observe that Marxists and Feminists both aim at cultural transformation and struggle to end oppression on the basis of gender or economic class. But Velutha is betrayed by the new God, Marx, whose high-priest K.N.M. Pillai, the local communist leader, has his own political axe to grind, because for him, Velutha's death is more profitable than his life.

The novel can be seen as a saga of revolt against tyrannical and outmoded social laws and taboos and the tragic suffering ensuing from it. Ammu and Velutha are 'history's offenders' and history squares its books and "collect(s) the dues from those who broke its laws." (308) It has its own ways of "inoculating a community against an outbreak." (309) Unfortunately, Rahel and Estha keep the receipt of the dues paid by Ammu and Velutha. The novel, thus, is a bitter critique of some aspects of our rigid and orthodox cultural values.

In an age which upholds the notions of women's equality and empowerment on one hand and abolition of caste considerations and evils like untouchability on the other, the tale of the disastrous ruin of a woman just because she has no *locus standi* and a man's ruthless annihilation just because he is an untouchable by caste raises many perturbing questions. The novel is extremely thought-provoking and contributes greatly to the slow but unmistakable process of cultural transformation by raising consciousness and sensitizing the masses towards these social issues. It makes a very cogent case for the abolition of evils like untouchability and strengthens the notion of women's self-reliance and empowerment, though the message is by indirection it does not detract from the artistic richness of the work in any way. And as is the hallmark of a great work of art, the novel raises many questions, issues and concerns.

NOTES

1. Harry Levin, "Literature as an Institution," *Accent* (Spring, 1946), qtd. "Introduction to Sociological Approach," *Five Approaches of Literary Criticism*, ed. Wilbur S. Scott (London: Collier Macmillan,1962) .
2. Hippolyte A. Taine, "Introduction to the History of English Literature," *Twentieth Century Criticism*, ed. William J. Handy and Max Westbrook (New Delhi: Life and Light Publishers, 1976), p. 309.
3. Peter Silva, Book Review of *The God of Small Things*, *Literature and Psychology*, Dec. 2000.
4. Arundhati Roy, *The God of Small Things* (New Delhi: IndiaInk, 1997), p. 33.
5. Stevi Jackson, "Feminist Social Theory," *Contemporary Feminist Theories*, ed. Stevi Jackson and Jackie Jones (New York: New York University Press, 1998), pp. 17-18.
6. "Introduction," *Ibid.*
7. Toril Moi, "Marginality and Subversion: Julia Kristeva," *Sexual/Textual Politics* (London and New York: Routledge, 2002), p.163.

Colonial Consciousness in Jhabvala's *Heat and Dust*

SANTOSH K. BHATIA

Many critics and scholars of Indo-English fiction feel reluctant to include Ruth Prawer Jhabvala among the creative Indo-English writers,[1] not only because she is a European by birth and upbringing[2] but also because her sensibility is alien and un-Indian. Verghese says, "Her citizenship is British; she sees no reason to change it."[3] Jhabvala herself admits: "When one writes about India as a European and as English (as I do), inevitably one writes not for Indian but Western readers."[4] The angle of her vision has certainly affected her craft of fiction so that her subject is not just India but, as she says, "myself in India."[5] That makes her position and point of view quite different from the rest of Indian English writers. She may have knowledge of Indian character, Indian family and Indian society but she lacks Indian sensibility. In this respect, her position, though parallel with that of Kamala Markandaya, is quite different because the latter, though she married an Englishman, is basically Indian in her sensibility. She is an insider living outside and yet writing about India as a historian of its culture, whereas Jhabvala brings a "foreigner's perspective" and her "voice has unmistakable foreign inflexions."[6] She writes about India as its critic and her European sensibility, basically colonial, presents numerous case-studies of European characters in the Indian context but her vision, says Shahane, is rather "one-sided, un-balanced and incomplete." (127) It is difficult to agree with R.S. Singh when he calls her "a true cosmopolitan" who "views the cultural clash of the East and the West with un-prejudiced eyes."[7] On the contrary, her novels reflect the consciousness of a Westerner in all its colonial manifestations. There is a strong undercurrent of irony and sarcasm in all that she writes about India. Even her apparent sympathy and concern for India reveal her condescending attitude which is quite self-obliging. It is intended to present herself and the westerners as noble missionaries who leave the comforts of their country and come to India—a country not only lacking in material comforts but also full of dreadful pollution—in order to display their humanistic concern. But it is like someone who can only sigh for, show lip-sympathy to, the wretched and yet shun them. She writes about India or Indians not because she has any humanistic motive similar to that of Mulk Raj Anand, but because it gets her recognition in the West. Her novels epitomize the art of presenting India through the eyes of a westerner and since she stems basically from a colonial culture her novels project the author's colonial consciousness.

Jhabvala's attitude is clearly different from that of Mulk Raj Anand and R.K. Narayan who are no less critical of Indian society and Indian character. It is also different from that of Kamala Markandaya and Bhabani Bhattacharya who like her depict poverty and hunger in India, who, too, may be indignant but never sneering, critical but never contemptuous, harsh yet always sympathetic. Narayan, even when exposing the fake and phoney character of Swami, makes Raju acquire that status which he was merely 'simulating; Markandaya enshrines the exemplary heroism of Rukmani in spite of all the dust and squalor, poverty and hunger of an Indian village that she depicts in *Nectar in a Sieve*. In other words, the attitude of the Indian writers in English is much more humane towards their native land and its people whereas Jhabvala's attitude lacks empathy, understanding and compassion. Her exaggerated courtesies only seem to conceal her contempt for India. It merely exposes her pretence of adopting the country of her in-laws without giving up her neo-colonial outlook. It is mostly the negative aspects of India that she highlights in her fiction. There is hardly anything Indian that is appreciated by her. She specialises in drawing a satirical portrait of India and her aim, says Verghese, seems to be "to ridicule the pseudo-idealism and pseudo-romanticism of Indians and westerners who are in love with India and come to India seeking spiritual solace." (34)

If it be true that an artist remains invisibly present in his work, then Ruth Prawer Jhabvala's unseen presence can always be felt in her fiction. Her novels reflect better their author's psyche and neo-colonial outlook rather than a complete and authentic picture of India. In fact, as Verghese says, "Jhabvala's understanding of India is not deep and she just skims over the surface of urban life in India." (33) What Dr. Hochstadt, a visiting Professor of Economics in Delhi, says about himself in *A Backward Place* is equally true of its author: "However much we may read and discuss and observe, we can never have that understanding of India in all her depths which comes to those who are in touch with the humbler people of this land."[8]

As a writer, Jhabvala paints only a facile picture but misses the spirit of India. She lacks an inward understanding of its culture and tradition, of its rich social heritage and ancient civilization. Verghese says that she seems to suffer from an inability "to get inside the skin of her Indian characters owing to the linguistic and cultural gap between them and her." (37)

Her story "The Aliens" epitomises the spirit that pervades her work. The interaction between the European and the Indian cultures which forms the major theme of her fiction proves invariably detrimental to the interests of Indians because the Europeans are mostly projected as seekers and sufferers. There are at least three visible dimensions of the East-West relationship in her novels—the social which also includes the familial, the cultural, and the spiritual. The relationships tumble and fail at all the three levels. It is invariably the westerners who are disillusioned with India and migrate. In the whole process, the weaknesses of India are brought out more sharply and critically compared with the limitations of the west. For instance, *A New Dominion* (1973) which Jhabvala herself considered her best novel, presents the Indians, says Shahane, as "invariably sensual, sex-hungry, hypocritical, pretentious, egotistic, self-willed." (118) She presents a highly sensual and distorted picture of the Indians which she repeats again in *Heat and Dust* (1975). Mrs. Saunders tells about a lady from Somerset whose "dhobi" felt excited "ironing her undies."[9] In the first place, Mrs. Jhabvala forgets that a "dhobi" in India is seldom given women's under-garments for washing or ironing; secondly, she conveniently ignores the prudery of women like Olivia and her remote grand-daughter who is the narrator of *Heat and Dust*. Both of them give themselves to Indian men, conceive, try abortions by native Indian methods, fail and then recede into the mountains for childbirth. The sting of her irony is directed solely against India and the Indians. The total effect is very disturbing because her viewpoint is rather biased and one-sided. Mrs. Saunders, in her loathing for the Indians, develops almost paranoiac tendencies and her abnormal fears of the Indians' sexuality need psychological probing which the novelist doesn't provide. Similarly, the westerner's spiritual quest in India gets warped with sexual desires. Lee and Margaret in *A New Dominion* and Chid in *Heat and Dust* are unable to resist sex. About Chid who is a westerner turned into an Indian ascetic, she herself writes: "He is always hungry, and not only for food. He also needs sex very badly and seems to take it for granted that I will give it to him the way I give him food." (65)

His "constant erections" remind her of "Lord Shiva whose huge member is worshipped by devout Hindu women" and it seems that "his sex is engendered by his spiritual practices, by all that chanting of mantras he does sitting beads in hand on the floor of my room." (65) What is noteworthy here is Jhabvala's attitude. Instead of exposing the hypocritical nature of Chid and the westerners who in the guise of spirituality try to fulfil their carnal desires, she puts the blame on Indian spirituality and its practice that, according to her, engender such sexual desires. Not only her treatment of sex is superficial, her whole understanding of Indian spirituality is lop-sided and shallow. Sexual appetite, from her point of view, is, says Shahane, "most intricately compounded with religion or spiritual pursuit in *Heat and Dust*." (127-28) He adds that the India of *Heat and Dust* that Jhabvala presents is an "odd combination of the sacred and the profane, the spiritual and the sexual, the ideal and the earthy." (128) And this does not go with the truth. The picture of India that emerges from her variegated descriptions is neither very pleasant nor very attractive. The pity is that it is neither wholly commendatory nor truthful. It is somewhat distorted and biased. Says Shahane: "She consciously as well as unconsciously brings to bear upon the Indian ethos the western scientific and rational attitude which inevitably become the criteria for judging Indians, their moral behaviour and their emotional or sensuous responses to environment." (26) As a European, she has the advantage that "she can afford to be critical and theatrical without offence. She can steer mercifully clear of political and religious controversy."[10]

India that she projects is "a backward place" full of nothing but "heat and dust." Such a biased and negative attitude to India can be seen in *Heat and Dust* in the sneering comments of the two English tourists—a young man and his girl. About Indians, the girl said: "they were all dirty and dishonest." (21) And when the narrator, who is only an alter-ego of the author, asked her, "Why did you come?" "To find peace," she replied. "But all I found was dysentery," (21) she added. The authorial comments disguised under the narrator's voice are equally noteworthy and add insult to injury: "She had a very pretty, open, English face but when she said that it became mean and clenched, and I realized that the longer she stayed in India the more her face would become like that." (22) It is only her alien sensibility which is reflected through such remarks. Further, the three characteristic smells—that of "spices," "urine" and betel"—associated with India in Chid's letters reveal her bias. The smell of the soil is only a prerogative of the native and cannot be enjoyed by an outsider. Nor can it ever be enjoyed by a native like Karim, the Nawab's nephew, who distances himself and settles in London and keeps only a business interest in the country of his birth.

India may have enough to invite criticism and even contempt but it is not without objects to appreciate and praise. For example, there is the warm hospitality of its people towards their guests which is amply displayed by Inder Lal in *Heat and Dust* but which remains unacknowledged by its foreign recipient. The unmatched capacity of the Indian women to suffer and endure is revealed in the characters of Ritu, Inder Lal's wife, and

Leelavati, the beggar woman. But Jhabvala sees only what she can through her coloured glasses and everything looks to her murky and dirty. Her blinkered perspective does not allow her to see beyond a certain patch of dust. For that reason alone the India of 1970s reflected through the narrator's journal is only an extension of the picture of India of 1920 presented through Olivia's diary; it is rather a shade worse. In other words, the author fails to see the tremendous progress and modernisation of India that had taken place in those 50 years especially after Independence. Her treatment of Indian poverty and misery from the beginning to the end seems highly exaggerated and unrealistic. Satipur, far from being an Indian township or village, seems to be an imaginary place having little connection with reality.

Even her seemingly objective narrative technique of reporting things, first through Olivia's entries in her diary and then through the narrator's journalistic entries, helps little to disguise the authorial voice. In fact, both these western women betray themselves as the thinly disguised alter ego of the author herself. There is almost little or no perceptible difference in their mode and manner of reporting, in their choice of language and vocabulary and, above all, in their attitude towards India. Even the experiences that they undergo, though fifty years apart, are almost identical as if the journalist-narrator were a reincarnation of dead Olivia.

Jhabvala's consciousness which is unmistakably that of a neo-colonist keeps filtering through her unsparing irony directed against India and all that India embodies. Her racial bias in favour of the Westerners is revealed through the narrator's comments on Olivia who "was by no means a snob, but she was aesthetic." (27) If we trust the tale and not the teller who, according to D.H. Lawrence, is a "dribbling liar," we find ample evidence of Olivia's snobbery the way she keeps "alone in her big house with all the doors and windows shut to keep out the heat and dust" (14), and the way she yields to the Nawab and the call of the flesh. She is attracted to the Nawab partly because her own husband, Douglas, has no time for her but even more because the Nawab embodies all those qualities of a colonist which she herself represents.[11] She does not want to go to Simla with Mrs. Crawford to escape the heat and dust of Satipur not because she loves Douglas (whom she eventually deserts) but because she enjoys the Nawab's parties. The result is that she bears the Nawab's child and ultimately elopes with him.

A theme that is frequently attributed to Jhabvala and that she constantly depicts in her novels, according to Meenakshi Mukherjee, is: "What India does to a foreigner?"[12] But she does not address herself to a corresponding theme, namely, what the foreigners do to India? They are never able to merge themselves completely with India. It is not just India which fails to absorb them but it is the foreigners themselves who fail to get absorbed because their contact with the country and its culture is superficial and their love for it somewhat romantic which soon withers away. They never become one with its soil. That is why an impasse develops in their relationship with India. Even though transplanted, like Jhabvala herself, they never feel deep-rooted in its cultural soil, fail to grow and ultimately migrate to the west.

Like her theme, Jhabvala's aim too is limited. It is, says Mukherjee, "to explain, within the limits of Western terms and concepts, what it is like to live in India?[13] More than anything else, it reveals the hidden recesses and contours of her own colonial psyche when she brings "an European sensibility to work upon material which is non-European."[14] Her novels go beyond political protest and racial anger but the Prospero-Caliban complex, according to Mukherjee, which "combines the racial issue of colour and the political issue of power under one psychological theory"[15] persists in them.

When *Heat and Dust* won her the Booker Prize for 1975, the feeling in India, as pointed out by Ramlal Agarwal, was: "Jhabvala was awarded the prize for her damning of India, the country in which she had lived for over a quarter of a century."[16] Nissim Ezekiel found it "viciously prejudiced in its vision of the Indian scene."[17] In the texture of the book she weaves in sharp juxtaposition scenes from pre-independence, colonial India (1923) and post-independence India, thereby revealing the psyche of the ruler vis-à-vis the ruled. Douglas, for example, "sitting at his desk rather stern and serious over his interminable files" (36) and the local rich men who come to pay their respects would "sit on the verandah with their offerings to the Sahib which were baskets of fruits and trays of sweetmeats and pistachio nuts." (37) Later, when Olivia asked him, "Why were they laughing? What did you say?" Douglas said: "I just told them in a round about way, that they were a pack of rogues." "And they like being told that?" "If you say that in Hindustani, yes." (38) So deeply entrenched in the native's psyche is the colonial experience that he not only swallows such insults but also shows a natural preference for what is western.

The post-Independence scene recorded side by side through the narrator's entries in the journal reveals that even after a gap of fifty years and the change in the political scenario, the psyche of the colonist and the colonised has not changed much. In Dr. Gopal's love for the English language, for example, the psyche of the colonized is well revealed. Mukherjee says that this is so because the "acceptance of the values and standards set up by the ruling cultures have in most cases become so absolute, that the recipient culture is sometimes even unaware of its hold."[18] Inder Lal, a petty office clerk, for example, has the same attitude towards the foreign narrator. He feels inferior to her in every way and says: "he is perfectly well aware that. by western standards, his house as well his food and his way of eating it would be considered primitive, inadequate—indeed, he himself would be considered so because of his unscientific mind and ignorance of the modern world." (95-96) Just as the colonizer once consciously wanted it to be, so the native now looks up to him and his superior culture as a model, feeling at the same time quite ashamed of his own backward and inferior culture. As Viney Kirpal says: "Clearly colonisation has meant not just geographic—political occupation or economic plunder of today's third world but also a spiritual and moral stunting of the native's character and confidence."[19] This fact is amply borne out in Inder Lal's character.

The subversive impact that colonization has had on the consciousness of native people is perpetuated in Jhabvala's novels, especially *Heat and Dust*, in as much as she tries to accentuate the cultural inferiority of India. The transformation of Chid, an English man, into an Indian ascetic with all his adoration for India in the beginning is matched with his re-transformation into a westerner with all his hatred for India. The contradiction in his character seems inexplicable because no psychological depth is provided by the author to his character in the novel to warrant his disillusionment with India. R.S. Singh says that it is perhaps "the inner tension of Ruth, the European, who chose to be Mrs. Jhabvala, but is unable to merge with India as long as she is alive" (163) which is transferred into Chid's characterisation. When asked about the change in her attitude to India and the unmistakable note of bitterness after her third novel, *Esmond in India*, Jhabvala said: "I loved everything during my first years here—I really loved it and was wildly excited about it and never wanted to go away from here. But later that changed. I saw a lot I didn't like. I'll go further: a lot that horrified me."[20]

After *Heat and Dust*, Jhabvala changed her residence from New Delhi to New York. And if proximity is said to breed contempt; one can only hope that the distance of thousands of miles will breed objectivity in her and that she will have more love and less hatred for India.

NOTES

1. Meenakshi Mukherjee, "Preamble," and "Notes," *Twice-Born Fiction* (New Delhi: Arnold-Heinemann, 1974), pp. 14-15, 16.
2. "Her Polish parentage, German upbringing, British schooling and finally, life in India after marriage and her living in New York only heighten the complexity of this problem," says Vasant A. Shahane. *Ruth Prawer Jhabvala* (New Delhi: Arnold Heinemann, 1976, rpt. 1983), p. 17.
3. C. Paul Verghese, "A Note on *Esmond in India*," *The Journal of Indian Writing in English*, Vol. 4, No. 2 (July 1976), p. 33.
4. Ruth Prawer Jhabvala, "Moonlight, Jasmine and Rickets," *The New York Times* (April 22, 1975), p. 35.
5. Ruth Prawer Jbabvala, "Living in India," *London Magazine* (Sept. 1970), qtd. Shahane, p. 21.
6. Raji Narsimhan, *Sensibility under Stress: Aspects of Indo-English*

Fiction (New Delhi: Ashajanak, 1976), p. 138.

7. R.S. Singh, *Indian Novel in English* (New Delhi: Arnold-Heinemann, 1977), p. 149.
8. Ruth Prawer Jhabvala, *A Backward Place* (London: John Murray, 1965), p. 34.
9. Ruth Prawer Jhabvala, *Heat and Dust* (London: John Murray, 1975), p. 119.
10. H.M. Williams, *The Fiction of Ruth Prawer Jhabvala* (Calcutta: Writers Workshop. 1973), p. 10.
11. I do not agree with Ramlal Agarwal who says, "Her sympathy for the Nawab is part of her attitude to the Natives which is radically different from that of the others in her community." Ramlal Agarwal, "A Critical Study of *Heat and Dust*," *Studies in Indian Fiction in English*, ed. G.S. Balarama Gupta (Gulbarga: J.I.W.E. Publications, 1987), p. 55.
12. Meenakshi Mukherjee, "Journey's End for Jhabvala,'' *Explorations in Modern Indo-English Fiction*, ed. R.K. Dhawan (New Delhi: Bahri, 1982), p. 211.
13. *Ibid.*, p. 212.
14. Meenakshi Mukherjee, "Inside the Outsider," *Awakened Conscience: Studies in Commonwealth Literature*, ed. C.D. Narasimhaiah (New Delhi: Sterling, 1978), p. 90.
15. Meenakshi Mukherjee, "Caliban's Growth: Impact of Colonialism on Commonwealth Fiction," *Colonial Consciousness in Commonwealth Literature*, ed. G.S. Amur and S.K. Desai (Bombay: Somaiya, 1984), p. 218.
16. Ramlal Agarwal, "A Critical Study of *Heat and Dust*," p. 53.
17. Nissim Ezekiel, "Cross Cultural Encounter in Literature,'' *The Indian P.E-N.* (Nov.-Dec. 1977), p. 5.
18. Meenakshi Mukherjee, "Caliban's Growth," p. 220.
19. Vinay Kirpal, "The Third World Fiction," *Recent Commonwealth Literature*, ed. R.K. Dhawan P.V. Dhamija, A.K. Shrivastava (New Delhi: Prestige, 1989), p. 12.
20. Ramlal Agarwal, "An Interview with Ruth Prawer Jhabvala," *Quest* (Sept.-Oct., 1974), p. 34.

Salman Rushdie's *Midnight's Children*: Major Themes and Issues

P.K. DEY

"To understand just one life, you have to swallow the world," (109) so observes the narrator Saleem in Salman Rushdie's epic novel *Midnight's Children* (1981). In this text, the narrator hero is philosophically obsessed with a desire, rather Indian desire, for the whole, he attempts to swallow all of India. This desire for the whole, the multitude, may be understood as a veritable Indian disease. Noted critic Srivastava sees this desire 'as a specifically Indian urge to encapsulate the whole of reality.'[1] Therein lies Saleem's ambition and downfall.

Salman Rushdie's *Midnight's Children* was "hailed as a "postcolonial meta-fiction, a novel about third world novels."[2] Since the 1980s, a wave of novels by Indian English writers appeared that were clearly influenced by this seminal Rushdie text and its conception of national literature. Rushdie's examination of the relationship between the self and the nation, and his advocacy of the concept that there are as many equally valid versions of the truth as there are Indians, proved liberating for the Indian English writers. *Midnight's Children* has been the major postcolonial novel in English which fictionalises the events of Indian history from the moment of the birth of nation state in 1947 till the declaration of the emergency by the Congress Prime Minister Indira Gandhi in 1976 which did a death knell to the monolithic dream of a secular-democratic nation-state perhaps insufficiently imagined and expressed in the midnight speech by the first Prime Minister. Dreams of the founding fathers since the 1960s turned into a veritable myth, and writers expressed disillusionment with the corruption and failure of the nation-state. In opposition to the monolithic concept of the nation, of the history, *Midnight's Children* advocates plurality of our mongrel selves. The narrative is determined from the outside, by a pretext of the epical myths, orality and religion.

Role of Ancient Myths, Fantasy and Orality in Explaining Contemporary History

Notwithstanding their absolute involvement in history, their individuality, the narrators in a Rushdie text are, more often than not, fantastic and yet are real. Rushdie returned to India in the late 1970s as a young man of thirty in the aftermath of the Emergency when many Indians expressed outrage at the Congress party's betrayal of the secular-democratic ideals on which the early post-Independence generation had been raised. In *Midnight's Children*, Rushdie re-affirms and seeks to re-create, in a postmodernist way, the lost nationalistic democratic ideals for the underdog and the underprivileged. Postcolonial history thus reproduced is fictionalized and mythicised.

Saleem, the principal narrator, the most gifted of 1001 midnight's children, has been endowed with a magical power and a vision. His physical impotence and deformed shape may be read as a caricature of the political map of India. All the midnight's children are born with special power with hundred and thousand possibilities but all these possibilities are simply wasted. Saleem and Shiva are born with contrasting qualities. They are the leaders of the group but they have their double, one in reality and another in the realms of myth. Saleem stands for the whole, abundance. He contains within him the mythical creator Brahma. Shiva is the god of destruction and hence is a rival to Saleem. The novel remains an allegory of Indian history and may be read as a literature of subversion of every form of convention and authority. The narrator patterns his own story telling on oral narration and deploys fantasy in order to be faithful to the reality of India, a country and a nation where millions believe in the world of spirits. In *Midnight's Children*, Rushdie presents an ideological post-colonial critique of the linear, imperialist discourse of meta-history which represses, rather distorts, Indian's own account of history.

India is a vast and ancient land teeming with millions of people of different races and colour. Ancient epics, myths and oral tradition inform the lives of the people even today. The elephant-headed Ganesh is the great storyteller in the ancient epic, the *Mahabharata*. He is the patron-deity of arts and literature. In *Midnight's Children*, Saleem the powerful narrator is portrayed as a storyteller of Ganesh-like-skill. He is born with elephantine nose while his alter ego Shiva is all knees. Saleem is a reporter of the events of history; he creates alternate history by creating things out of memory and imagines truth as opposed to the truth of history; he preserves his materials in the chutney of fantasy and myth (pickling process). At daytime he works in the chutney factory and during night he writes his stories for the imagined listener Padma (Lotus). Lotus has an association with mud. Padma likes listening to stories of sensation and thrill. She has no power of intellection and thought. She believes in stories and more stories. Indian subaltern multitudes are gullible and are swayed by the rhetoric of the politicians and vote catchers easily. Saleem has the potential of an omniscient and omnipotent narrator, creator as well as preserver. He is a modern Vishnu. Empowering himself in mythology, the all-knowing narrator chutnifies his own version of history and truth. It is "memory's truth, because memory has its own special kind. It selects, eliminates, alters, exaggerates, minimizes, glorifies and vilifies also: but in the end, it creates its own reality."[3]

The entire narrative is clothed in fantasy. Myth and reality overlap boundaries. Fantasy may be seen as seriously narrating political reality when the readers and the author share certain views. In this novel, numerical exactitude is a feature which relates fact to fantasy. In his 1983 interview, Rushdie states his fascination for figures when he says: "It seemed to me that the period between 1947 and 1977 the period from Independence to emergency had a kind of shape to it. It represented a sort of close period in the history of the country. That shape became part of the architecture of the work."[4]

Saleem's narrative is valuable precisely because it is self-conscious and invites judgment and criticism. He claims omnipotence and omniscience as a narrator, but more often than not, he laments his inability and his impotence. There is a kind of postmodern playfulness and trivialization which inform Saleem's narrative and which instills in the mind either faith, doubt or questioning. Why and how should the alternative to Saleem be Shiva, a figure of violence? What is the lesson of Emergency? If the idea of a secular nation-state and history be rejected, would the rule of anarchy and lawlessness descend on the life of the nation? Shiva represents the dispossessed without a stake in the dream of the nation and constitutes a political threat to Saleem's plural India. Shiva, very like his mythical origin, is made to signify chaos and unmeaning. He, in the text becomes Indira Gandhi's henchman during the Emergency when the sterilization of *Midnight's Children* metaphorically nullifies the hope and possibilities with which they were born. Only he, Shiva, escapes the bulldozer and thus fathers the next generation. There is a glimmer of hope in the end that Saleem can claim one of Shiva's off-springs as his own son. He thus becomes able to write his autobiography for his son, the elephant-eared son born of Shiva and Parvati, Saleem's wife. Thus Saleem is not the biological father of his own son, just as he himself is not the biological son of Amina Sinai and Ahmed Sinai, his foster parents. But then the theme of illegitimate birth can be traced back to the grand epic *Mahabharata*. Is it not the fact that the mythical gods of Ganesh, the god of fortune, Kama and many other mythical figures are bastards? In *Midnight's Children,* the theme of illegitimacy perhaps constitutes a critique of the concept of the purity of race, class and nation and may be seen as an item of criticism of the concept of Hindutwa vis-à-vis the concept of multiculturalism which may adequately explain Indian nationalism. Narrator Saleem is born of Vanita, a Hindu wife of a magician singer, by an Englishman, Methwold, and nourished by Muslim parents, that too, because of a magical act of the exchange of children at birth in the hospital. Thus he is allowed to be bathed in the confluence of world religions: Hinduism, Islam and Christianity.

Metaphorically the narrator is endowed with plural identities and stands for postcolonial India.

In his personal heritage, the identity of the country emerges His birth coincides with the birth of a modern nation, nay two nations and subsequently three (Bangladesh). Birth of the narrator and the birth of the nation take place precisely at the same hour, thus at birth, Saleem is 'handcuffed to History.' He is the child of history as other midnight's children are. He grows, develops and finally goes into cracks and fragments in the same way as the nation grows and develops and experiences fissures in the body politic. This interplay of the personal and national histories gives the narrator shape and a sense of unity to the novel. This metaphoric consciousness of history, awareness of oneself as a blend of past and present, makes the narrator Saleem realise that history operates on a grander scale than any individual:

> Who, what am I? My answer: I am the sum total of everything that went before me, of all I have seen been done, of everything done to me. I am everyone everything whose being-in-the-world affected was affected by mine. I am anything that happens after I've gone which would not have happened if I had not come. (457)

Critique of the Concept of Postcolonial Nationalism vis-à-vis Indian Writing in English

Rushdie once referred to Indian English writing as 'Empire's bastard child' (Rushdie talk 4/4/97). Is not Saleem, the principal narrator of the same status? In *Midnight's Children*, the chief protagonist Saleem can be seen as Indian writing in English claiming centrality of position. But by now, English language has achieved centrality by virtue of the fact that among other things Rushdie, as a technician, has made it the fit medium for conveying indigenous consciousness. Rushdie's position as a man and as a writer needs to be understood in this context. He lays claim to India, a kind of centrality and also a sense of engagement with the history of the sub-continent. He, like his hero Saleem Sinai, has been 'handcuffed to history' in a special sense. He was born in June 1947 and two months after, the British left India.

Midnight's Children portrays the delirious joy of the people which accompanies the formal dissolution of the Empire and birth of Indian nation state at the precise hour of the midnight in 1947 when Mountbatten hands over power to Nehru, the first Prime Minister. Nehru's famous, midnight speech coined in the finest English language sounds metaphoric and ironic: "years ago we made a tryst with destiny. . . . A moment comes, which comes but rarely when the soul of a nation long suppressed finds utterance"; the sub-text of this metaphoric speech turns out to be a text of collaboration with the English educated nationalist elite. The leaders of the new state will, no doubt, reproduce the colonial method of control and exploitation. It becomes the story of a new nation, 'insufficiently imagined.' Chances of forging a new nationalist discourse are simply lost sight of, as the subsequent happenings will prove. The Raj leaves behind hollow men like Ahmed Sinai. Methwold's transfer of property to indigenous elite like Ahmed Sinai, who ape an Oxford drawl and who are secretly pleased when they lose pigmentation due to skin-disease, because it makes them resemble the Europeans, is an eloquent testimony to the nature of independence. This tendency still persists with our academics and professionals. Colonial institutions still have a surprising spell over our mind. It is resolved that Methwold estate is to be preserved and retained. Saleem describes the estate thus: "Methwold's Estate: four identical houses built in a style befitting their original residents—large durable mansions with red gabled roofs and turret towers in each corner, ivory-white corner towers wearing pointy red-tiled hats . . . houses which their owner, William Methwold had named majestically after the palaces of Europe." (94)

This allegorical statement by the narrator suggests the passing on of the colonial mantle to the Indian nationalist elite which not only inherited power from the colonial masters but also love for the exotic as opposed to the indigenous. In the new dispensation, progress means back-pedalling, rise of fanaticism and the cracking up of Indian independence. "India had been divided anew. But the boundaries of these states were not formed by rivers or mountains or any natural features of the terrain: they were instead walls of words. Language divided us." (189) In the same process, the sub-continent was divided. The departing imperialist did a parting kick by dividing the sub-continent on religious lines and installing a class of people who would carry Macaulay's legacy—brown in skin and English in character. Eloquent Nehru and Ahmed Sinai belong to this class. *Midnight's Children* thus constitutes a critique of nationalist rhetoric which makes a linear downward journey from 1947 to 1977—the year of the declaration of national Emergency which means the curtailment of democratic rights of the people. The episode of the Emergency and Mrs. Gandhi is described as an allegory which is an indictment of the state-controlled media. The media projects the dictator as god and Mrs. Gandhi as devi, the mother Goddess in her terrible aspect with a centre-parting hair. The fascist slogan "Indira is India" (427) is relayed over the media. The Nehruvian dream of secular democratic nation comes a full circle and post-Emergency period sees the dethronement of the fascist god, end of one party rule and installation of a Janata Coalition govt. which, henceforth, becomes the shape of Indian politics. Democracy demands a plural society as opposed to unitary one.

However despite the sense of despair, the journey from wholeness to fragments, the novel ends on a note of hope, rather political one; that is the intensification of the struggle of polarised political forces in opposition to Congress model of nationalism. As the narrative progresses, the disintegration becomes quicker. Saleem mentions the cracks in his body: "My poor body, singular, unlovely, buffeted by too much history, has started coming apart at the seams. In short, I am literally disintegrating slowly for the moment. . . . I shall eventually crumble into six hundred and thirty million particles of anonymous and oblivious dust." (37) With his final words, the disintegrating Saleem prophesies his fate and articulates the post-colonial condition of the generation of midnight's children. "Yes, they will trample me underfoot. . . . Reducing me to specks of voiceless dust . . . because it is the privilege and curse of the midnight's children to be both masters and victims of their times." (63) At the end, Saleem's body cracks into as many parts as there are Indians and there are as many stories to tell. Saleem has told his story, maybe imperfect and unreliable but nevertheless his own, "Stubbornly and against all odds, victim transforms himself into protagonist, simply through the telling of his own story."[5]

The crisis of the unitary nation state opens up space for thousands contending claims and it seems that the "crisis of the once dominant nationalism opened up space and for new discursive models."[6] Thus there is a tension between the narrator and the narrative. Saleem, the narrator, may sound pessimistic but the feeling of the book remains affirmative in its abundance, multiplicity and urbanism. At the impressionable age, Rushdie feels deep attachment for the urban city of his birth, the metropolitan city of Bombay for its spirit of abundance, secularism, cosmopolitanism and urban culture.

Midnight's Children as a City Novel

This epic novel was conceived in a dream about the large Indian city of Bombay, an industrial city, a city of film, and also of a young man's dream. For a long time, the author had cherished a desire of writing a big and voluminous book about Bombay where he was born in June 1947. The city was in his dream because of its uniqueness, its films, cosmopolitanism and urbanity. He left Bombay in his teens for England for higher education as James Joyce left Dublin for Paris, Bombay was to Rushdie as Dublin was to Joyce. In both cases, the relationship of the artist with the city of his birth remains problematised. For a migrant writer, the concepts like home and nation are imaginary constructs. The city as a metaphor defines the authorial self and in a way informs the novel. In his collection of essays *Imaginary Homelands*, Rushdie observes "to be a Bombayite and afterwards a Londoner was also to fall in love with the metropolis." (404) The metropolis embodies hybridity, impurity, intermingling . . . culture, ideas, politics, movies, songs." (394) Post-colonial subject can find no better paradigm than the city to define his self. In the colonial times, the culture of the city was considered alien and non-pure. In the novels of Raja Rao, R.K. Narayan and others, an ideal village was considered a true signifier of Indianness and Indian values. In Raja Rao's *The Serpent and the Rope*, the hero rejects the metropolitan India as un-Indian.

Bombay being an industrial city had no meaning for a Brahmin like Raja Rao. Indian fiction has travelled a long way from the 1960s, and in Rushdie's 1980s novel, the metropolitan and industrial city of Bombay appears to be a true signifier of Indianness. Politically, Indian nation state prefers the Nehruvian dream of secular and democratic modern industrial India to "the rural handicraft-loving sometime medieval figure of Gandhi" (*Attenborough's Gandhi*, 104). If the villages are considered to be the site for Indian values and if true Indianness is supposed to be constituted by Brahminical hierarchy and the purity of race and caste, modern fiction has no future. Modern city is the site for plurality, multiplicity and hence, the modern Indian villages must go the city way in respect of culture which is not unitary but plural. In its cosmopolitan nature, the city of Bombay represents an India which through the ages, has been the confluence of many nations and races, East and West.

In the postcolonial situation, the terms like 'pure country' and 'complicity' do not exist. Postcoloniality and hybridity go together. The reading of *Midnight's Children*, a postcolonial text in the context of other cultural productions may be meaningful. We know Rushdie's focus is not the realistic portrayal of the events of postcolonial history but rather a third world consciousness of history, truth and nation shaped through myth, fantasy, dream and orality, the tools that constitute an umbrella term magic realism.' Bombay cinema has all along remained a site for fantasy, hallucination, dreamland wish-fulfillment for the Indians irrespective of class affiliations.

The narrative of *Midnight's Children* parodies Bombay cinema's fantasy operations. Stock narrative situations like mistaken exchange at birth and stock cinema figures like good "ayah" Mary Pereira recall Bombay films. The most frequently discussed cinematic element of *Midnight's Children* is the exchange of the infants Shiva and Saleem at birth. Rushdie himself in his essay "*Midnight's Children* and *Shame*" makes a significant comment on this particular cinematic convention:

> This melodramatic device . . . was a genuine kind of Bombay Talkie, B-movie notion and I thought that a book which grew out of the movie city ought to contain such notions. These are children not so much of their parents but children of time, children of history.[7]

Other cinematic operations are that of natural mothers who are perfect and stepmothers who are evil. Virtuous male protagonists are contrasted with evil counterparts and so on. Shiva, Saleem's alter ego, combines the role of rebel-hero with the villain of Bombay film. In the 1970s and 1980s, the reach of Bombay cinema and its influence on Indian mind can easily be imagined. By sheer volume of production and star-charisma, Bombay film dominates the dream of the millions even in the anti-Hindi Southern states. Thus Bombay film industry becomes "an important agency for Hindi-speaking cultural hegemony in post-Independence India."[8] Benedict Anderson's thesis about the fictional component of nation, the role of print in helping people imagine themselves as nationals along with others they have not seen, is powerfully pertinent to a consideration of cinema (Imagined communities). Thus the Bombay film, with its apparatus of myth and fantasy, provides a site for mythic unity in the face of the body politic of the contemporary India.

On the realistic level, such conventions suggest the plurality of postcolonial identities. Saleem represents, the multiple and complex identities of the postcolonial Indian because he is born of British father and Hindu mother, exchanged at birth by Christian nurse and brought up by Muslim businessman as his son. This comic epic novel is a blend of literary genres and is coined in a mood of irony, satire and fantasy but the author has serious purpose in mind. The narrative is devised in a mood of playfulness, non-seriousness, trivialization as postmodern fictions mostly are. Rushdie's act of juxtaposing myth and contemporary postcolonial Indian history serves a model of intertextuality which informs among other texts, Shashi Tharoor's work *The Great Indian Novel*. But in the case of Rushdie, the classic myth only explains the contemporary situation. Tharoor trivializes the epical heroes in a mood of hilarity. Juxtaposition of trivial and serious, elitism and mass culture of Bombay film, centrality and marginality of positions and vice versa, purity and hybridity of racial and national identities and postcoloniality of history are the major themes and issues which the epic novel *Midnight's Children* successfully addresses.

NOTES

1. Aruna Srivastava, "'The Empire Writes Back,' Language and History *in Shame* and *Midnight's Children,*" *ARIEL*, 20.4.
2. Timothy Brennan, *Salman Rushdie and the Third World: Myths of the Nation* (Basingstoke and London: Macmillan, 1989), p. 25.
3. Salman Rushdie, *Midnight's Children* (1981; London: Picador, 1982).
4. C. Pattanayak, "Interview with Salman Rushdie," *The Literary Criterion*, XVIII, 1983.
5. Josna E. Rege, "Victim into Protagonist? *Midnight's Children* and the Post-Rushdie National Narratives of the Eighties," *Rushdie's "Midnight's Children": A Book of Readings*, ed. Meeenakshi Mukherjee, p. 200.
6. *Imaginary Homelands: Essays and Criticism 1981-1991* (London: Granta, 1991).
7. *Ibid.*, p. 4.
8. Nalini Natarajan, p. 167.

David Davidar's *The House of Blue Mangoes*: The Petit Grand Saga

JASPREET MANDER

The word trend is given in the thrust of the present book does appear to be a problematic entity. It conjures up images of something decidedly short-lived, practised, followed or even aped rather unthinkingly, inherently shallow as also tawdry. Even if tried to be understood, trends remain rather vague and amorphous. Everyone just flows with them because that's just the way trends are, meant to be taken on, stretched over and then worn off and out.

To my mind, the word trend which breathes in the given thrust area is not so much as a fashion, fad, style or a mere sartorial design but it is more as an authentic orientation, tendency or a direction adopted by Indian English literature, particularly fiction in the post-1970s. This direction marks a decisive shift in the understanding of what India is in the eyes of the novelists of last quarter of the twentieth century. This direction points out candidly, sometimes almost brutally, what it means to be an Indian given what the vast multitudes of India have gone through, experienced, resisted and given way to. This direction unseen, experienced, resisted and given way to. This direction unravels how extraordinarily the so-called ordinary Indians have wrestled with seemingly larger than life but equally stifling realities of caste and its endless manifestations.

This tendency is neither new nor entirely divergent, so to say. To a certain extent, no fiction during any historical epoch or period has ever remained or can remain untouched by the various striations of this tendency. Literary activity has always been furrowed by these strands. But the biggest motivational shock that occurred for the followers of this movement was and, to a certain extent, still is Salman Rushdie's *Midnight's Children.* The personal and the political lie interwoven here like never before. Saleem Sinai gets born with the birth of modern India, ages literally with the unfortunate aging of India and finally gets dismembered with the imminent dismantling of the country. Apart from a host of other things, questions such as what is India and what does it mean to be an Indian or to put it slightly differently, what does it mean to have and carry an identity as that of an Indian's, are paramount for an understanding of Rushdie's novel.

Running the risks involved in over-simplification and over-generalizations, I would venture to say that Rushdie's *Midnight's Children* gave an immense impetus to the personal-political sagas. It broke fresh ground and became the hotbed of fictional muse, imparting not only inspiration but also giving rise to intrepid investigations undertaken to explore the personal and the political sagas. These investigations particularly focussed on the various points of conjunctions and, equally importantly, of disjunctions marking stages whereby one affected the other, resisted the other, gave way to the other in their mutual contestations and capitulations. In this sense, *Midnight's Children* can easily be regarded as initialling a second renaissance in Indian English fiction. It virtually broke the flood-gates open. From this point onwards, for the personal-political sagas, there has been no looking back.

Amitav Ghosh and Arundhati Roy are fiction writers who can easily be studied from this vantage-point. Ghosh's *The Glass Palace* can also be read as the saga of at least two generations of Indo-Burmese tangled and webbed in the socio-political upheavals of Rangoon, Ratnagiri and Calcutta. Amazingly well-researched, *The Glass Palace* undulates through the unnerving ululations of British India transforming and transfiguring the lives of Rajkumar, Dolly and their children Neel and Dinu, among others. To a certain extent, Arundhati Roy's novel *The God of Small Things* also portrays, among other things, how Ammu, Velutha, the twins and the village Ayemenem lie enmeshed in the larger constructs such as caste, socialism and the almost ineradicable caste-discriminations and prejudices. The microcosm and the macrocosm have the strongest bearing on each other, stretching, testing, modifying and finally rupturing each other. The small village Ayemenem, in Roy's fiction, becomes the focal point for the interplay of the individual, the familial and the socio-political. The points of contact as well as the blind spots in the interactions of this triumvirate are essential to comprehend the text and its varied convolutions. Once again, the family saga and the anguishing individual tales are entrenched in the over-arching power-constructs of the state and of the socio-cultural set-up.

David Davidar's *The House of Blue Mangoes* is a continuation, delightful and sad, in the same vein. Davidar recreates history, from 1899 to 1947, fleshed, boned, emotioned and lived through the three generations of the Dorai clan living and struggling in their ancestral village of Chevathar located on the southern extremity of the country. In a sense, history happens to them and in turn becomes real, concrete and personalized through their lives. From a lifeless amorphous mass of facts and figures, it becomes a formed entity, graspable for readers and protagonists alike. On the other hand, the members of the Dorai clan, especially Solomon, Daniel, Charity and Kannan plunge at the pliant-and-not-so-pliant clay of the history and politics of the village Chevathar as well as of the British India. The larger socio-political realities and the individual realities of the members of the Dorai family are linked inseparably, kneaded together and textured into new and sometimes not-so-new patterns in each of the three generations portrayed in the novel. In this sense, the relationship of the petit and the grand is a relationship of contestation, capitulation, resistance, absorption, rejection and of acceptance too. Besides, it is an ongoing relationship with no final answers, solutions and trouble-proof, perennial remedies.

In this regard, a few instances and observations in connection with some of the protagonists, come handy for the explication of this two-way process between the personal and the larger politico-historical. Solomon Dorai—the patriarch and the able headman of the village—in spite of his sensitiveness and realisation about the potentially catastrophic nature of a casteist clash and his sincere intentions of thwarting any such mishap in his beloved Chevathar, falls victim to a bloodied caste battle fought between Andavars and Vedhars on the village beach. Indeed, Solomon jumps into it of his own volition, all exit-routes, in his view, having closed off. The man who is the keenest to save his village from the scourge of casteist violence, lays down his life and of others too for the sake of his caste—the Andavars. Daniel, the elder son of Solomon, having suffered exceedingly at the hands of dirty caste-politics along with the other surviving members of his family, chooses to found Doraipuram—an extended family commune—at the very place where the family had lost their seemingly unassailable position, prestige, pelf and power. In Doraipuram, Daniel shuns and prohibits any and every kind of political activity and yet the internal squabbling and pulls and pressures of the commune bring about Daniel's demise. Kannan, Daniel's only male heir, gives up the seeming imponderables and inflexibilities of Doraipuram to seek individual accomplishments and freedom in the British-monopolized tea-plantations at Pulimed only to get sucked up in a different kind of white-brown politicking and politics. The more he tries to rise in the entrenched tea-echelons, the more mired and disenchanted he grows. Finally, enervated and defeated, he comes back to his native Doraipuram to be a part of it and its running. In a nutshell, the personal and political are so closely knitted together in the lives of these protagonists that the skeins can neither be separated nor analyzed separately. Each explicates the other and becomes the refracting medium for the other. In a way, the family saga is played out in the very convergences and divergences occurring on the personal-political axis.

An important aspect of this individual-societal, micro-macro or the big-small dialectics is the inner-outer tension that is played out in *The House of Blue Mangoes*. Time and again, the chief protagonists venture out to realise their potentialities and also to respond and relate to the world outside and the outsiders. Solomon resents the building of the road in Chevathar precisely because it is an unwanted channel with the world outside and also because it begets trouble and troublemakers from outside into the village. Left to Solomon, he would seal it off permanently. And yet, one of the most trusted confidantes and friends of Solomon happens to be a complete outsider—Father Ashworth—who ultimately lays down his life in trying to stop the Andavars and Vedhars from spilling more blood in the name of safeguarding caste-affiliations and caste-segregations.

Similarly, Daniel is helped to the maximum with regard to his revolutionary younger brother Aaron, by none other than the wonderfully kind and helpful ICS officer Chris Cooke. If Aaron is mutilated and wrecked most inhumanly by the Briton—Superintendent Rolfe—he is also sought to be saved by not only his brother Daniel but Chris Cooke as well. On the other hand, if Kannan and Helen face the freezing and fossilized racism of Mrs. Stevenson at Pulimed, they also encounter the friendship of the Frasers. Kannan, in particular, is the recipient of the main concern and companionship of Freddie Hamilton as also the final rescue at the hands of the nativised Harrison. All this is surely not meant to exonerate the third-grade subjugative, dehumanizing, imperialistic designs of the British, their racism, cruelties, conmanship manipulations and drying up of the native resources so as to bring prosperity and well-being to the mother country back home. The idea here is to bring about a fresh thought to the question of outsiders and insiders, colonizers and colonized and the subjugators and subjugated. Such divisions and categories are more often than not misconstructions and misleading too.

Obviously, what often goes unnoticed are the divisive, fissiparous, seemingly centrifugal and many times the destructive forces and elements working and living right amidst all families, communities, communes and other forms of collectivities. One of these forces is the overarching reality of caste and the huge chasms and ravines that exist among people of India in every sphere, stratum and segment. Even Christianity could not lessen these cast(e)-iron divisions and affiliations. In fact, these divisions and sub-divisions thrive, flourish and perpetuate themselves despite everything. Very significantly, right in the beginning of *The House of Blue Mangoes*, the young Andavar girl Valli has been raped by none other than the ruffians and rapists hired by Vakeel Perumal. A little later in the text, the caste-conflagration is gained and brought to the boil by none other than the chief of the Vedhars, Muthu Vedhar. Even the group of revolutionaries, joined by Aaron and others give out entirely skewed definitions and rationalizations for carrying out killings necessary for bringing about revolution and independence. The senseless killing of the head constable, by Aaron and his comrades, has neither any justification nor meaning.

Finally, the decline and disintegration of Doraipuram is brought about by none other than the residents of the commune. Undoubtedly, the youngsters have to move out in search of better opportunities and prospects but many of those who choose to stay behind are neither committed to the common cause nor do they value the Herculean efforts put in by Daniel, Ramdoss and others in putting together and raising of the tremendous family settlement, Doraipuram. This shows that there are enough chinks in the collective Indian armour, enough fault-lines in the seeming terra firma of the Indian reality. This surely is not to decry the rich diversity and multiplicity of Indian social fabric; it is meant to show the sheer inability of a people to come together on anything whatsoever; it is meant to show the incapacity of a people to rise above the individual even for worthy causes; it is also meant to show that collective experiments have a limited life-span and they need to be revisited and revised if they are to remain viable.

Another significant facet of this inner-outer dialectic operating in the novel is the all-important question of belonging, boundedness. In other words, what are the limits of one's self—one's self-space and consequently of one's living space? One can possibly exist or better still live reasonably ethically and justifiably without defining, re-defining and living out these limits of boundedness and ways of going beyond them. *The House of Blue Mangoes*, on various occasions and stages of the story, attempts to grapple with some of these above-mentioned issues. Solomon unhesitantingly extends the purview of the individual or the self. Both as a thalaivar and as the head of an ancient family of Chevathar, Solomon not only believes in but also lives out the enlarged zones of self and responsibility concomitant with these zones. His boundedness takes in not just zones. His boundedness takes in not just the caste of Andavars but also the entire village of Chevathar. He remains a traditionalist since the outside world represents a threat for him and his village but at the same time his self-zone is uninhibitedly large. His life and actions are much closer to the contours and rhythms of the ancient land whose proud custodian he is. Successful or unsuccessful, Solomon tries to find answers to the nearly intractable problems of his village, as is also suggested by his favourite cousin, Joshua. Daniel, guided by his teacher and mentor, Dr. Pillai, learns to temper his knowledge of Siddha medicine with certain useful concepts and techniques of the Western medicine. In other words, appreciating, understanding and absorbing significant aspects of medicinal science as it developed in the West allows a Siddha physician much better comprehension, appreciation and accurate evaluation of the uniqueness and intricacies of his own stream of medicine. Thus, tradition that is unmixed, unalloyed and hence unrevised and unchanged is a lot of deadwood. In this context, it is relevant to point out the dismal failure that Helen, Kannan's wife, comes out to be. Apart from other things, her concept of her self, her identity is a hopeless prisoner of her Anglo-Indian tradition. She is just not ready to re-consider the notions of her selfhood. She bangs her head, blindly and fruitlessly, against the nauseating and noxious walls of Mrs. Stevenson's White tea-community. She gets defeated and runs to the old, weary grooves of the received notions of the collective Anglo-Indian identity which anyway happens to be mistakenly more Anglo than Indian.

Traditional understanding thus remains viable only till it is open to the influences of the outer, the other and those which are beyond the bounded. In this way, the text oscillates between the bounded and the beyond. Any search of the self or of identity, for that matter, proceeds from the zone of the bounded and leaps into the areas of the beyond. It has to partake of the roots and the routes thereof. In other words, it has to, in order to be worthwhile and not self-defeating, participate in the traditions and a studied, conscious irreverence towards the traditional. Looked at in this vein, *The House of Blue Mangoes* becomes a remarkable exploration of the roots of the family as well as the directions chosen away from these roots. In this light, Daniel's life can be seen as a painful move away from the Chevathar of magical blue mangoes. He makes the most of this move and gets very hefty returns on his Moonwhite Thylam by cashing in upon the prevailing trends and tendencies. After this, the native Chevathar beckons him and he can no longer ignore its call. He goes back to savour the traditional cup as also to redeem the family name. His son Kannan's life traverses a pattern which is the exact opposite of this. The beyond beckons him in the form of his love Helen, freedom and the headiness of self-determination. Like any third-generation member, he heeds this call of the beyond and readies Pulimed and indeed does make a substantial success of himself. He goes on aspiring, trying and endeavouring to the best of his capacity to reach the pinnacle of success at Pulimed. He tries especially hard to wear the British mask and be as near perfection as he supposes the British to be. In a sense, his efforts become as painful as those of Helen. In the end, it takes the efforts of the trio comprising his old friend Murthy, Freddie and the much-reluctant Harrison to waken him to the awful reality that he has tried so very hard to wear a mask on a face whose existence and basis he has no conception of. Consequently, he comes back to the Doraipuram of his childhood and early youth. Strangely enough, the wheel of bounded and beyond and the issue of identity that lies wedged somewhere between them, comes full circle for Kannan as well.

This brings this brief exploration to the last related issue of Indianness in the text. Is there something called the characteristic, unique or the essential (to use a forbidden word) Indianness? Or to put this question slightly differently, is there any essential way of being a Chevatharian or a Dorai? Another related question, in this context, could be and rather should be: Is there any essential India that exists at the moment or has existed at some time in the past which is recoverable from a study of this past? To my mind, this set of questions can be understood by briefly looking at the trope of mangoes, in general, and the blue mangoes, in particular. A tour across the vast stretches of India to taste and assess the various well-known and even the relatively lesser-known varieties of mangoes assures Daniel that the blue mangoes grown in Chevathar and later in Doraipuram are indeed the best, the most delicious, the sweetest and also the most fragrant. With blue mangoes adjudged the best, the essential Indianness too is found and approved. So far, so good till the text takes the readers along towards the end of the second section of the novel entitled Doraipuram to a point where Daniel acknowledges to Ramdoss that the blue mangoes may look and taste the best but the fact of the matter is that, every season, the blue mango houses plenty of mindless and headless maggots that twirl and curl in their dark tunnels made in the fleshly mounds of mango-mountains. This statement is once again repeated at the end of the next section entitled Pulimed when Ramdoss reads out Daniel's will to the residents of Doraipuram. This clearly shows that the idea of any essential or essentialising Indianness is a mere hoax. There is nothing quite like that. Every family, every community, every settlement and every nation has its own set of maggots that exist at the very heart of the life-centre. They can neither be blown away nor wished away. Perhaps, the only chance of saving the crop of blue mangoes is to make the good, edible mango-flesh healthier and stronger.

So says the petit—the small—to the grand—the big: 'This world-house is indeed a pretty maggoty, mangy place but it also does have quite a few succulent, supple blue mangoes which make living and struggling worth one's while alright.' There are sagas and sagas of this kind in this multitudinous land waiting to be discovered along with their set of blue mangoes.

Raja Rao's Portrayal of the Ganga in *On the Ganga Ghat*

ROSHAN LAL SHARMA

The present paper aims at analysing Raja Rao's use of the Ganga as a leitmotif in the latest collection of his short stories entitled *On the Ganga Ghat* published in 1989. After briefly discussing Raja Rao as a short story writer, a mythological overview of the archetype of Mother Ganga will be given, followed by an assessment of his use of the same as a fictional tool in this work.

Essentially known for his novels, Raja Rao has also contributed considerably in the field of short story. Among his contemporaries (such as R.K. Narayan, Mulk Raj Anand, Bhabani Bhattacharya, Manohar Malgonkar, Khushwant Singh), Raja Rao holds a markedly distinct place on account of his use of myth, choice of themes, and his peculiar Vedantin stance. Due to his Vedantic vision, distinction between the creator and the creation does not exist for Raja Rao. As such, he moves with fluency from the mundane to the metaphysical. Moreover, writing for Raja Rao is an exercise in Truth, or a kind of *Sauhana* as he explained to Shiv Niranjan in an interview. "It is an attempt to come in contact with the ultimate reality."

Another point of divergence in Raja Rao's style, as compared to the major contemporary exponents of this genre, is his peculiar Indian stance as he is soaked in Indian culture, thought and mythology. The point of Rao being a writer with a difference is suggested by A.N. Dwivedi thus: "Raja Rao is definitely of a different make up both. . . . He is soberer and more serious in evoking a proper atmosphere in the flowering of Indian thought and tradition. He writes mostly on . . . social scenes around him with a natural ease and philosophical resignation."

Indeed, Rao is an innovator who uses myths, legends and folk-tales in his stories to achieve Puranic effects. He has infused the genre by creating his own 'monomyths.' M.K. Naik rightly observes, "Raja Rao seems soon to have realized that to resurrect an old art form only to make it do the old things in the traditional manner is a far less significant endeavour than to adapt it to the needs of the living present, thus tapping the innate vitality that is always latent in such forms." Raja Rao's profound mythic imagination and his knack for "mythologizing contemporary reality" make him distinctly unique thereby distinguishing him from other short story writers.

Raja Rao began his literary career by writing short stories. His first collection *The Cow of the Barricades and Other Stories* (1947) included most of the stories that had been published prior to *Kanthapura* (1938). *The Policeman and the Rose* (1978) included several stories from the earlier collection with the exception of the three (the title story, "India—A Fable," and "Nimka"). A novelist of world repute, Raja Rao has undoubtedly enlarged the scope of the short story both with respect to content and form. The variety of themes and the "levels of consciousness" that Rao has explored in his short stories are exceptional and justify Rao's evaluation by critics as an "innovator" in Indian English shorter fiction. The publication of *On the Ganga Ghat* has demonstrated with finality that the short story, far from being a stage in the process of Raja Rao's evolution as a novelist, is a unique, independent entity in the existing body of Indian English literature. In the epigraph to *On the Ganga Ghat,* Rao quotes a maxim of his Guru—"Water does not flow"—which is highly symbolic. The secret of unflowing water is disclosed by Rao in the concluding part of the book where water connotes *jnana ganga* or the stream of inner knowledge which Rao perceives as unflowing. Hence his final request to the unflowing "water". i.e. *jnana ganga* is to "flow." (127)

There is no denying the fact that these stories did provide inspiration for the novels such as *Kanthapura.* But it is worth mentioning that for Raja Rao, short story is a complete genre. As such, to place, or to analyse his stories in a linear developmental mode as be the wont with critics is to limit their scope and to undermine his achievements as a unique short story writer. Rao's accomplishments as a short story writer have to be evaluated independently, without confusing them with Rao the novelist though one can always establish linkages of these stories with his later novels. In fact, Rao's stories present a complete and conspicuous world of their own which is semantic. Thus the contention of the critics such as Narasimhaiah, Naik and others that Rao's stories are merely a preparation for his novels, in no way seems to be tenable. As Shyamala A. Narayan affirms: "The range of Raja Rao's short stories is amazing. Every facet of India is present in them. . . . Even if he had not written any novels, his stories by themselves would have assured him a permanent place in Indo-English fiction."

II

Mother Ganga is a perennial and timeless archetype in Indian mythology signifying purity and sanctity. Ganga is the most sacred river in India "whose waters are said to have the power of cleansing from all past, present, and future sins [and] is believed to be divine." In Hindu mythology, Ganga is the eldest daughter of Himalaya (Lord of Mountains), her younger sister being Uma (Parvati), Lord Shiva's spouse.

The Ganga is celestial, of divine origin. The great sage, Bhagiratha, provided a spiritual instrument for mortals to taste divinity by bringing about the descent of Ganga from heaven to earth. Once this was accomplished, the ashes of his dead kinsmen in particular, and humanity in general could experience and enjoy eternal heavenly bliss through the purification of the cremated ashes in holy Ganga waters. This feat, however, was almost impossible, as Ganga became wrathful due to her reluctance to descend to earth, the world of mortals. Bhagiratha invoked Lord Shiva to stem the mighty torrential wrath of Ganga who, unappeased, attempted to sweep away even Shiva, 'the Great God down to the nether regions.' The tide was stemmed by Shiva and released from the tangled coils of his hair to form the seven sacred streams. Thus, Bhagiratha's ancestors, including sixty thousand sons of the mythic king Sagar, were purified. Wilkins quotes from Griffiths' *Ramayana:*

> Soon as the flood their dust bedewed,
> Their spirits gained beatitude,
> And all in heavenly bodies dressed
> Rose to the skies' eternal rest.

Ganga is the symbol of ultimate purity as far as freedom from the continual cycle of birth, death and rebirth is concerned. The great sage Shankara elucidated the origin, evolution and culmination of Ganga and all its aspects referring to her as the Lovely Goddess.

> Descending from the king of Mounts (Himalaya]
> Saving one and all that dip in her waters
> Sporting in (the company of) the Sea
> Removing the fear of rebirth once for all,
> Imitating (in her course) the curved shape of the
> Serpent Adisesha.
> Assuming the form of the fresh creeper
> Sporting in the region of the Kasi
> Excels Ganga: the Lovely Goddess.

Thus, we can see that Ganga is a purifier, protector and liberator. The myth of the descent of Ganga from the heavens is somewhat parallel to the dispersion of fire to mankind by Prometheus. Nevertheless, the Ganga myth embraces more cosmic proportions as it embodies purification of karma, which is ever present, and of a regenerative and liberating nature in a larger sense. This is evident in *On the Ganga Ghat* as "traditionally a celestial river comes down to earth in compassion for human suffering. . . . A bath in her is supposed not only to wash away our karma--the accretions of all our past lives--but also free us from rebirth for ever."

III

Esha Dey rightly opines that Raja Rao's *On the Ganga Ghat* "marks a brilliant achievement as a classic of tabulation." (248) This collection as suggested by Rao "is meant to be read as a novel." (5) This draws attention to the fact that all the stories have the same background. The stories seem to have a 'unity' derived from their background. The stories are not titled; nor do they follow traditional formal mode. They 'flow' like the Ganga, which along with Benares, serves as a setting. The stories or "vignettes" are episodic and Puranic in tone, method, and narration. Viewed as a whole, the world of Rao's latest collection of short stories is complete, as it presents a holistic view of life in the sense of the *Viraat* in the infinitesimal, and not in the traditional Indian epical sense of the *Ramayana* or the *Mahabharata.*

Critics have pointed out various elements such as the dense texture, whimsical manner, and the light-hearted narratorial tone in Rao's stories in *On the Ganga Ghat.* For instance, Vijay Shankar observes, "All through the book, there is a virtual cavalcade of well-focused characters whom you almost touch as you walk by the lanes, the funeral ghats and the temples of Benares." K.S. Duggal, on the other hand, views *On the Ganga Ghat* as "a sheaf of perceptive sketches of the social scene and the spiritual milieu in the city of Varanasi, done with consummate skill by a master artist." However, the Ganga serves as the epicentre of the stories in *On the Ganga Ghat* as it binds as well as arches over everything, be that worldly or spiritual, sacred or profane.

River Ganga is a powerful archetypal leitmotif in Raja Rao's fictional world. In *On the Ganga Ghat* in particular, Rao has woven a beautiful pattern around the Ganga, which "flows fierce and fresh" purifying all (59). At yet another level, Ganga signifies progression; it flows perpetually, representing 'flow' or 'continual going.' Etymologically, the root word for Ganga in Sanskrit is 'gam' which means 'to go.' Generally, a river has always been a source of inspiration for poets and creative writers. As such, the Ganges (more aptly Mother Ganga as it is much more than a mere flow of water for Indians—a venerable and divine Mother, a giver of life, a protector, a symbol of purity and vitality) has inspired a large number of creative artists and writers in India. As a result, an enormous body of literature has grown around this archetype. The archetype of Mother Ganga forms an important part of the mythic imagination of Indians.

The Ganga myth has been considerably dealt with in the great Indian epics and other scriptures such as The *Ramayana,* the *Mahabharata* and the *Puranas.*

The archetype of Mother Ganga forms the warp and woof of the world of Rao's stories in *On the Ganga Ghat.* Interestingly enough, river Ganga with its different dimensions becomes the canvas on which life in its variegated form has been painted. In Rao's *The Serpent and the Rope* also, Mother Ganga flows vibrantly, perennially enrapturing the protagonist, Ramaswamy. It is like consciousness itself, a parallel of Ramaswamy's quest for truth. Ramaswamy is the microcosm. The Ganga is the macrocosm. For Rao, Ganga is Truth (the Absolute) and is ever 'pure.' Ganga liberates one from the endless karmic cycle. Ganga represents humanity, which nevertheless can aspire to Truth. Rao elaborates in *The Serpent and the Rope:*

> Truth is the Himalayas, the Ganges humanity. That is why we throw the ashes of the dead to her. She delivers them to the sea, and the sun heats the waters so that, becoming clouds, they return to the Himalayas. The cycle of death and birth goes on eternally like the snows and the rivers.

In essence, Rao views Mother Ganga as a metaphysical truth. The Ganga for Rao is not just a river on the physical plane; it rather has a profound spiritual implication, as its flow is perennial. It is like the flow of thought emanating from the mind but the state of the mundane is not denied or negated. At the mundane level, the water of Ganga is just water. It can be perceived, heard, touched, felt, tasted, seen and smelt. At the spiritual level, however, Ganga signifies eternal truth and pure consciousness.

The world of *On the Ganga Ghat* is peopled by a diverse variety of characters. Some of them are born and brought up in Benares only whereas others have come from various parts of India to seek salvation on the stone steps (*ghats*) of the Ganga, which is the river of redemption. Muthradas has come from Vrindavan with a hope to attain absolution from the cycle of birth-death-rebirth. Similarly, Rani Rasomani has come from Calcutta. She is serenely riveted on death in the sense of deliverance without any evil or love in her heart. Nanna, the fat Panjabi prostitute, is sincerely committed to her profession, which she takes for her *Dharma,* After a foul-tongued, short-tempered Sadhu gives her a "mantra," Nanna is shown to assume the proportions of "a great big rock" (111) who will, for sure, seek salvation. Ranchhoddoss Sunderdoss has come from Bombay to seek his daughter, Sudha, who, because of the Grace of her Guru, (121) has evolved considerably in terms of spirituality. They meet, and instead of bringing her home, Ranchhoddoss Sunderdoss himself seeks initiation from Sudha's Guru and decides to meditate on the Ganga ghats every morning until he attains *Moksha.*

Interestingly, most of the characters in *On the Ganga Ghat* have theistic bend of mind for they have faith in God, the *Vedas,* and the *Rebirth.* In other words, the psyche of Raja Rao's characters is steeped in Hindu thought and mythological lore. M. Hiriyanna has summed up two of the most significant aspects of Indian thought thus:

> These are two elements common to all Indian thought—the pursuit of *Moksha* as their final ideal and the ascetic spirit of discipline recommended for its attainment. They signify that philosophy as understood in India is neither mere intellectualism nor mere moralism, but includes and transcends them both. . . . They have been represented as the two wings that help the soul in its spiritual flight. The goal that is reached through their aid is characterized on the one hand by jnana or illumination which is intellectual conviction that has ripened into an immediate experience and, on the other, by vairagya or self-renunciation which is secured by reason of the discovery of the metaphysical ground for it.

Most of Raja Rao's characters have a religious disposition as exemplified in their repeated intoning of mantras, frequent prayers and recurring references to the holy scriptures like the *Vedas,* the *Puranas,* and the *Ramayana.* The quintessential aspects of Indian thought have contoured their consciousness. Most of the characters are in pursuit of *Moksha* and follow a tough code of moral discipline for its attainment.

In the story of Bhedia, Jhaveri Bai, a cow, takes the reader for a dip in the Ganga. Jhaveri Bai tests the temperature of the water and gradually eases in immersing herself up to her neck: "The Ganges flows fierce and fresh on Jhaveri Bai's back. Head inturned and her horns unshaking, Jhaveri Bai contemplates her own face in the moving waters. There's magic in this, picture that appears and disappears." (59) This act is symbolic of the cleansing of sins, or rather gradual spiritual evolution through immersion in the Ganga—the metaphor of consciousness. Unlike *On the Ganga Ghat,* in *The Serpent and the Rope* and *The Chessmaster and His Moves,* the evolution towards spirituality is more technical in nature. In these two novels, the connotations of Mother Ganga are more faithful to epic literature as the Ganga is primarily a symbol and cannot be experienced to the same extent by the senses as in *On the Ganga Ghat.* The Ganga in its perceived existence or as an entity evolves rapidly to different states. C.N. Srinath observes: "It is fascinating to see how the fact becomes image, the image symbol and the symbol, myth. The Ganga is all these, perhaps less of a fact. For, no river can be a fact and certainly not the Ganga." There are no such absolute compartmentalisations in *On the Ganga Ghat* as the mundane and the divine exist side by side.

Rao's Ganga serves all types of devotees whether their method is *Bhaktiyoga, Rajyoga* or *Jnanayoga.* The literal Hindu belief that a dip in the Ganga ensures *moksha* (liberation) is also in the foreground and the background. Rao remarks: "Ultimately, when the time [the moment of death] comes, you ask your son, uncle or grandfather for the Ganga-jal as you begin to have a heavy breath and you sputter yourself in, and now move into immortality." (125)

The purification power of Ganga is most strikingly present in the story of Bhim, the parrot-siddha, who in his previous incarnation as Rani Prabhavati, rejects palatial splendour and glory in favour of wilful death by drowning in the holy Ganga thinking that "a Ganges death were better than a palace rot." (21) Due to this act, the Rani is reborn as the enlightened Bhim. For the Hanuman bhakta, Madhobha who is an illiterate simpleton, the

Ganga is a 'real Mother.' Innocently, he apologizes to the Mother for not observing the ritual:

> 'Gangaji,' says Madhobha, 'do be kind to me. You know I never pray--I just forget to pray. You know I have no time to come and bathe in you often. I sit under a tap, by the shop, and have a quick shower. *But all water is Ganga water* [Italics mine]. Gangaji, you know my heart is all with you. I worship you, Mother, as a calf worships its cow.' (33)

The essential oneness of water, circular in being and origin, also finds place in *The Cat and Shakespeare:*

> 'Where does water come from?'
> 'From the tap?'
> 'And the water in the tap?'
> 'From the lake?'
> 'And the water in the lake?'
> 'From sky.'
> 'And the water in the sky?'
> 'From the ocean?'
> 'And the water in the ocean?'
> 'From the rivers.'
> 'And the river waters?'
> 'They make the lakes.'
> 'And the tap water?'
> 'Is river water.'
> 'And so?'
> 'Water comes from water'. . . .
> 'And the river flows.'
> 'And then?'
> 'The lakes give water to taps.'

The same thought is reflected in *On the Ganga Ghat:* "O, let water flow, Lord, that the earth turn not away from its fulcrum, whirl, earth, that the Ganga flow, round and around on herself, from earth to sky and from the heavens back to the Himalayas. The circle is the end of all beginnings as the Ganga is of water." (124)

In the story of Shankar, the Ganga is viewed as a "giver of gifts" by the protagonist. Shankar is of mathematical bent of mind and equates 'zero' (shunya) with the Ganga. He likens mathematics to the Himalayas as he believes an ascent is necessary to understand mathematics or reach the Himalayan peaks. It is a 'mantra' for him (73). This brings to mind the Buddhist concept of Shunyata. This is not a negative state but rather one of supreme bliss, the receptacle being the evolved soul. In the seventh story, the protagonist Bhola is lost in a perpetual trance on the banks of the Ganga. Bhola states: 'Man lives for happiness, as Vishwanathji [his guru] says. And if happiness is on the Ganga I say take it, eat it, be submerged in it, as you're with the Ganga. Sometimes when the red dawn breaks on the Ganga, I cannot bear the veiled white silence over the river—it brings tears to my eyes. I do not know why, but never for father or mother have I wept as I do for the Ganga—this Ganga is my father, this Ganga is my mother.' (83-84)

Thus, for Bhola, Mother Ganga represents the Absolute Truth, which can be realized after taking dips into the holy Ganges: "You plunge and plunge again into the Ganga. And you are suddenly aware of a fragrance of holiness and the touch of a deep white truth. And when you spit that water out, how your belly gurgles in happiness." (84)

In the last story, Rao depicts Ganga as the Mother of Compassion. The Ganga and its flow are likened to knowledge. "When knowledge, as Ganga, as Jnana Ganga, flows, death is dissolved into truth. She is as Sri Shankara said: "She is nija bodh rupa, she the form of consciousness pure" (127). Rao sees the Ganga as an outer symbol of consciousness representing wisdom. Benares is the hub of the Ganga and is indeed a living human organism (i.e. *Jivatma/Shariram).* It is the focal point of consciousness, the epicentre of connection with spirituality:

> My body, the holy site, in Benares,
> Spreading within me as knowledge, the Ganges,
> Mother of the three worlds.

In *On the Ganga Ghat,* the archetype of the Ganga takes on human qualities like compassion of a magnanimous nature and temperament. She gives the bounty of "song to the songstress, limbs to the brave, paddlepush to the boat, and child to the wife" (73). The progression of the Ganga culminates in "I" or "Jnana Ganga" in the last story. The perennial flow seems to have come to a standstill. The Ganga has become the 'self,' the inner being. But something is missing and that is flux through which one identifies and comprehends illusion and reality, truth and untruth. An invocation follows to reassert the dynamic as opposed to the static—Mother Ganga, "flow on." (127) This contention is echoed in Rao's Guru Atmananda's epigraph: "Water does not flow" quoted at the beginning of the book. This is a pointer for questers to tell the true nature of Maya (illusion) from Moha: "a bewilderment, and inability to understand the totality of a situation, of a thing." Finally, Raja Rao ends up entreating and imploring Mother Ganga who, in fact, signifies the inner "jnana Ganga," the "I" and also the "Self," to flow:

> One cannot go to the Ganges. One cannot go to the "I." For if you dare have a deep look on the Ganges evenings, and see the Ganga unflowing, then you know there is no Ganga. Water is just water. So, O Mother Ganga, please be gracious, and—flow. (127)

In this way, Rao goes beyond the mythological perspectives of the Ganga, which is the most completely personified of all the holy rivers in India. Besides using the archetype of the Ganga as a fictional device permeating through all the stories thereby linking them up, Rao enlarges its scope by portraying it as *Nija-bodha-Swaroopa/* the consciousness pure. She is all knowing—the "I"/ "Self having cosmic proportions. The perennial, ageless, timeless and eternal flow of the Ganga has answer for every conceivable query that man can raise. For instance, Rao makes the Ganga resolve the fundamental riddle of existence concerning the meaning of death:

> Man, you think you die. Burn yourself on my banks and know that what flows cannot but unflow. Death is a superstition, like the flies that sit on the baby's rags, and find nothing there. Is the donkey's bray a song? How can you, who have a name, die? If the Ganga cannot grow dry one will never know death. Hence is she, the Mother of Compassion. (127)

The Pragmatic World of Kamala Markandaya's English Characters: A Study of *Nectar in a Sieve* and *Possession*

KARAN SINGH YADAV

Notwithstanding the typical pangs of gestation, Indian English fiction has come of age. It has matured fast, expanding its sweep over the Western world, matching with the best of the writers writing anywhere in the world. This is to its credit that even from its inception, instead of presenting a narrow and exclusive solipsistic view of Indian cultural ethos and values, it has always revelled in an equally satisfying delineation of Western mind and attitudes. As a result, Indian English novel can be seen, in the words of Hari Mohan Prasad, as "an extended area of Indian literature, for in addition to embodying Indian ethos, it reflects an enhanced consciousness of Western life and culture."[1]

Among the galaxy of Indian writers writing in English, Kamala Markandaya has rightly been hailed by Stephen Hemenway as "one of the most productive, popular, and skilled Indo-Anglican novelists and a superb representative of the growing number of Indian women writing serious literature in English."[2] She has attained an important place in the Indian writers of fiction due to her imaginative fecundity and maturity in drawing English as well as native characters and their social milieu. Her sympathetic portrayal of landless farmers and poor people caught in the vortex of poverty and exploitation has brought wide acclaim to her. Her status as an expatriate writer, the fact that she started writing when Britishers had just left India and, of course, her own peculiar liking for English way of life have equally contributed in crowding her pages with European characters, mostly English. Her pages teem with English characters from various walks of European life. The prominent among them are—Dr. Kenny, Caroline Bell, Ellie, Annabel, Richard Marlowe, Clinton, Mr. Rawlings, Mackenderick, Helen, Millie, Sophie and Sir Arthur. It has been pointed outby Madhusudan Prasad, with some justification, that Kamala Markandaya "appears to be more at home with her English characters."[3] A.V. Krishna Rao says that she has been fittingly praised for "her artistic juxtaposition of the sustaining values of the Indian spiritual tradition and the soulless, prurient pursuits of a Western vittuoso."[4] The curious amalgam, in which she juxtaposes Indian sensibility with the Western one, brings to fore the need to explore the world of these English characters more fully than what attempts have been made so far in the form of well-known theme of East-West encounter in the novels of Kamala Markandaya. Since the English characters painted by her in her novels are admired, says Harish Raizada, as "not mere types but individuals infused with vitality of their own,"[5] it would be worthwhile to look at them closely with the kind of world they inhabit. These characters bring in their wake the rationality and pragmatism of European life. Working in a milieu characterized by peculiar Indian sensibility, these English men and women constitute a cerebral world of practical commonsense and astute rationality. Their universe is strongly marked by its matter-of-fact and commonsensical overtones. The materialistic world of West where they come from is undeniably unidealistic and rational. The irrationality and illogicality of East repels them and they are puzzled by the incoherence and chaos of the Oriental world. The pragmatism of their own worldview makes them reject the passivity and acquiescent nature of Indians.

Possession, described by Krishna Rao as "a probe into an alien onslaught on the auto- chthonic cultural matrix," (9) presents the story of an illiterate, simpleton goatherd boy Valmiki who possesses an unusual talent of painting. Living in abject poverty and apparently degrading environment of a remote South Indian village where he has no one else except a Swamy to fall back upon, he is spotted by Caroline Bell, a rich aristocratic English lady who takes him with her to London. There under the possessive zeal of Caroline, Valmiki learns the skills of the trade and achieves renown and fame as an upcoming painter. In the meantime, he falls in love with first Ellie, an orphan concentration camp victim, and later with Annabel, a young girl of eighteen. Both these love affairs come to naught mainly due to envious stratagems of Caroline. Ellie commits suicide with the unborn child of Valmiki, who now out of remorse leaves London with the help of Anusuya to join Swamy on the hills. Caroline's further attempts to secure Valmiki do not fructify mainly due to spiritual effects of Swamy and partly due to Valmiki's own newly attained wisdom.

Caroline, described by H.M. Williams as "one of Markandaya's most memorable and indeed terrible figures,"[6] is a shrewd, levelheaded woman who had a lot of devotees, both in India as well as abroad. Caroline is a confident woman who dazzles everybody around her with her self-composure and sedate behaviour. In the very beginning of the novel, she is spotted by Anusuya instantly after her entering the room where Caroline was stowing the fruit in her mouth a "daring behaviour which delighted the crowd by which . . . she was surrounded."[7] She makes Anusuya accompany her to the village despite her protests by virtue of her strong will-power and once in the village, it is she who controls the action and makes Anusuya act as her second fiddle. Caroline finds the cave where Valmiki worked and decides that Valmiki should follow her to London. Her conversation with Anusuya shows her marked straightforwardness and no-nonsense approach:

> "You forget," I said. "He may have a family. He may not want to leave them. They may not want him to leave."
>
> "We'll ask them," she said briskly. "Let's go. You can ask them for me."
>
> "You can ask them yourself," I said.
>
> "Do you mean do your own dirty work?"
>
> "I didn't say that."
>
> "I think it's what you meant." (10)

Caroline's attempt to westernize Valmiki is seen by Krishna Rao as "the commercial vulgarization of his art under the tutelage of this 'white narcissus'" (10) whose world is "a 'wasteland of spirit' that depersonalizes the individualistic Valmiki." (9) However, it is to the credit of Caroline that she is absolutely confident of her mission and once she makes up her mind she doesn't falter. Despite all the misgivings and apprehensions of Anusuya and the seemingly impossible nature of her task, she never wavers. This aspect of her character draws praise even from Anusuya, her otherwise recalcitrant critic: "She was supremely confident, born and brought up to be so, with as little thought of fallibility as a colonial in the first flush of empire, as a missionary in the full armour of his mission, dogged by none of the hesitancies that handicap lesser breeds." (15) Though Anusuya is seen as Caroline's opposite in her ethics, mores and sensibilities, she feels more than once praise for her more rational and materialistic companion. What hampers Anusuya is not just her high moral position, but her lack of confidence and initiative taking drive. It is what she admits before Caroline on her departure from India with Valmiki: "You're doing what I wouldn't do," I said, "but it's only because I know I wouldn't have the nerve or the strength to carry it through." (39) There is a tinge of truth in this admission as despite her protestations, Anusuya herself is a part of the same English culture by virtue of her choice and preference, which advocates action and rationality in place of philosophical subtleties and compliance. That is why she feels praise for Caroline who "had the courage and the imagination to secure for the boy a milieu in which he could breathe." (43) Once Caroline chooses a course of action, she follows it with all her resources. After taking Valmiki in the town, she, the rich aristocratic English lady, is ready to sleep even on the floor of Ashram for his sake.

Caroline's arguments regarding the vocation of Valmiki and his conditions are compelling and persuasive. The sheer rationality of arguments carries force and conviction which can be felt easily:

> But the conditions Val was working in were gross, disgusting. He couldn't have kept going for long—he'd have been washed up by twenty. That's why I took him away, and when I did I meant him

> never to have to grovel like that again. I wanted him to be free to work as he wanted, and never anything else. (47)

Caroline possesses strength of determination and resolution. Her decision to take Valmiki with her to London and her plans to launch him as an artist there involve a great risk. Nevertheless, she does it without flinching and with the precision of a shrewd planner. Even when Valmiki faces a bad patch, Caroline does not lose patience and never chides him even once. Although by nature a frank and forthright person, she shows "a forbearance so strongly against her nature that she must have torn her guts to achieve it, though the bleeding was kept internal." (76) Further, she very shrewdly guesses about the spiritual domination of Swamy on Valmiki and sends him forged letters thus precipitating in him artistic surge for creation.

When Valmiki falls in love with Ellie and makes her pregnant, Caroline does not discourage him in the beginning. She knows that Valmiki's urge for painting is stimulated by his contact with Ellie and thus encourages him to have his fling with her. But when she finds the intervention of Ellie in the life of Valmiki too much for her, she claims back her pride possession and very easily throws Ellie out of the life of Valmiki. Anusuya, the narrator, accurately guesses that Caroline had "never lost her balance. Ellie could have been dismissed out of hand at any time: but Valmiki would have followed. Caroline had elected to wait, and Ellie had been edged out, incredibly, fully acquiescent and consoling." (137) Similarly, Caroline strikes at the appropriate time when Valmiki falls in love with Annabel. Through her one masterful stroke, she reveals to unsuspecting Annabel the gory details of the affair between Valmiki and Ellie which leads to separation between Valmiki and Annabel and Valmiki's realization of his guilt. Caroline would have easily secured Valmiki for her, his resolution breaking at the death of Minou, but for the intervention of Anusuya. We see the same reflection of "iron and steel in Caroline" (230) till the end of the novel who, despite Valmiki's desertion, is resolute in her attempt to secure Valmiki and Swamy's troubled eyes at the end of the novel reflect his own doubts regarding Valmiki's capacity to resist her for long.

Annabel, another English character in the novel, is a rebel who leaves her family and enjoys a free life. Thus, in a way, she becomes symbolic of free and uninhibited English woman. She too, like Caroline, is rational and astute and possesses "something of Caroline's forthrightness in dealing with events, a belief in as well as an addiction to uncomplicated patterns of living." (197) Her decision to leave Valmiki is as much to do with Valmiki's failure to inform her about Ellie and his child as much as her own rationality triumphing over the muddle and lack of 'decency' in Valmiki. She may find herself temporarily bewitched by the exotic oriental charm of Valmiki but her accusations reflect more than what she outwardly raves.

The novel *Nectar in a Sieve* highlights contrast between the Oriental mystical acceptance of life and Western advocacy of unidealistic and pragmatic approach. Hence the reason that in her novel "people of East are passive and submissive whereas the people of the West are active and conscious of their rights."[8] Dr. Kenny, referred to by Rudra Prasad Mahto as "an ambassador of the ratiocinative West,"[9] is present in the novel mostly as a voice whose main purpose in the novel is to present an alternative worldview of rationality and pragmatism. He is an English missionary who loves Indian people but whose pragmatic outlook is pained to see their passive acceptance of suffering and exploitation. He seems upset to see their silent humility and lack of wisdom in finding the real cause of their degrading conditions. That is why he shouts before Rukmani: "I go when I am tired of your follies and stupidities, your external shameful poverty. I can take you people in small doses."[10] He chides Rukmani more than once for her passive acquiescence and acceptance and advocates a life of action:

> 'You must cry out if you want help. It is no use whatsoever to suffer in silence. Who will succour the drowning man if he does not clamour for his life? [. . .] Acquiescent imbeciles,' he said scornfully, 'do not think spiritual grace comes from being in want, or from suffering? What thoughts have you when your belly is empty

or your body is sick? Tell me they are noble once and I will call you a liar.' (113-14)

Dr. Kenny's analytical temper is once again revealed when he objects to the habit of the villagers to use dung as fuel which is an invaluable fertilizer for the land. Further, his outbursts over the meek surrender of the Indians without any protest in face of adverse conditions depict his own conclusions based on reason and a hatred for useless, mystical philosophies: "Times are better, times are better," he shouts. "Times will not be better for many months. Meanwhile you will suffer and die, you meek suffering fools. Why do you keep this ghastly silence? Why do you not demand—cry out for help—do something?" (44)

Kenny is an exponent of western concept of unbridled freedom, a much-touted western value. His advocacy of freedom in relationships has led to the branding of his contact with his wife and children as "usual encumbrances that men have—wife, children, home-that would have put chains about me." (71) He professes no commitments and works among rural people "when my spirit wills it." (71) The assertion of his free will led to his complete alienation from his wife and children. While his wife refused to come with him to India and his children forgot him.

The much-repeated rational remedies for the ills of Indian society, as prescribed by Dr. Kenny to Rukmani, present him, says Srivastava, as a "retarding force, injecting a sense of realism and sanity, attempting to make holes unsuccessfully in their excessive faith and hope and their blindness to reality."[11] The world of Indian mysticism, superstitions and irrational faiths with its own attractions is too much for him and beyond his comprehension. To his trained rational westernized mind, these matters present a constant puzzle over which he can frown but never comprehend fully. That is why he decides not to entangle himself in obscure philosophies of East and chooses to remain aloof without fully entering into them. Thus, in conclusion, it can be asserted that Dr. Kenny, an epitome of realistic "Western ideas like liberalism, progressivism and protest" (Mahto, 147) brings a whiff of rational and pragmatic world of Europe in a novel otherwise full of characters retaining their oriental values of fatalism and resignation while remaining mired in poverty and exploitation.

Thus, Kamala Markandaya's English characters dwell in a pragmatic world which is always in contrast with the numinous oriental world around them. The pragmatism of these "western rationalits"[12] makes them view the scenario around them with bewilderment and incomprehension. They preach from their own pulpit and thus despite their best efforts remain alien in a cultural context which they can neither understand nor appreciate.

NOTES

1. Hari Mohan Prasad, "The Quintessence of Kamala Markandaya's Art," *Response: Recent Revelations of Indian Fiction in English*. ed. Hari Mohan Prasad (Bareilly: Prakash, 1983), p. 165.
2. Stephen Ignatius Hemenway, *The Novel of India: Vol. 2 The Indo-Anglian Novel* (Calcutta: Writers Workshop, 1975), p. 52.
3. Madhusudan Prasad, "Introduction," *Perspectives on Kamala Markandaya* (Ghaziabad: Vimal, 1984), p. xxx.
4. A.V. Krishna Rao, "Continuity and Change in the Novels of Kamala Markandaya," *Perspectives on Kamala Markandaya*, p. 12.
5. Harish Raizada, "East-West Confrontation in the Novels of Kamala Markandaya," *Perspectives on Kamala Markandaya*, p. 38.
6. H.M. Williams, "Some Characters in Markandaya's Novels," *Galaxy of Indian Writings in English* (Delhi: Akshat, 1987), p. 113.
7. Kamala Markandaya, *Possession* (Delhi: Jaico, 1967), p. 1.
8. Jaydipsinh K. Dodiya, "Cultural Conflicts in Kamala Markandaya's Novels" *Indian Women Writers: Critical Perspectives*, ed. Jaydipsinh K. Dodiya and K.V. Surendran (New Delhi: Sarup, 1999), p. 3.
9. Rudra Prasad Mahto, "Angrez in the Novels of Kamala Markandaya" *Kamala Markandaya: A Critical Spectrum*, ed. M.K. Bhatnagar (New Delhi: Atlantic, 2002), p. 146.
10. Markandaya, *Nectar in a Sieve* (Mumbai: Jaico, 1956), p. 171.
11. Ramesh K. Srivastava, "Hope and Fear in *Nectar in a Sieve*," *Six Indian Novelists in English* (Amritsar: Guru Nanak Dev University Press, 1987), p. 128.
12. Pravati Misra, "Crisis of Transition," *Class-Consciousness in the Novels of Kamala Markandaya* (New Delhi: Atlantic, 2001), p. 79.

Preaching from the Pulpit: The Enigmatic Reality of Dr. Kennington in Kamala Markandaya's *Nectar in a Sieve*

SANJEEV KUMAR

In *Nectar in a Sieve,* Kamala Markandaya depicts realistically the feelings, culture, prejudices and deep-rooted psychology of rural Indians who become victims of natural calamities in the face of flood and drought. The novel is "mainly a depiction of rural life in which vagaries of nature and ill-planning of farmers make them feast or fast. [It is] a spicy work of art [that] makes the novel more palatable."[1] This significant novel "explores the themes of hunger, poverty and misery, the relentless logic of which compelled man to violate the established codes of morality, and the "disintegration of village life under the impact of industrial change."[2] There is also an emphasis on the subjugated conditions of the peasants and women whose obstructive ideas and beliefs, due to lack of education and learning, hinder their vision and knowledge.

Dr. Kennington, the "lord" and "benefactor" of Rukmani, plays a very significant role in Rukmani's life and also in the lives of other deprived people who had to suffer indignities due to their poverty and also because they were illiterate. Although an English, yet Dr. Kennington can speak local language, and he has a heart that beats for the needy and the poor Indians. He devotes himself whole-heartedly to the cause of the wretched and the exploited poor and has a sympathetic and serious consideration for them. Notwithstanding his virtues of head and heart, Dr. Kennington does not appear to be a psychologically convincing character. The present paper attempts to bring before the readers of the novel this particular weakness of Dr. Kennington's characterization by the novelist. An allied area of enquiry will be to highlight the pulpit preaching of Dr. Kennington to the native and poor rustics who do not really understand him and his western philosophy. An attempt will be made, thus, to enquire about his character which, however, remains enigmatic.

We first meet Dr. Kennington, an English missionary, in the paternal house of Rukmani—"a house of sorrow" where he is called in to treat her mother who was afflicted with consumption.[3] The English doctor, popularly known as Kenny, was "tall and gaunt, with a pale skin and sunken eyes the colour of a Kingfisher's wing, neither blue nor green." (19) Like an acute observer and expert psychologist, he asks Rukmani if she had any problem for he could not read her face. After a little hesitation, however, Rukmani reveals her innermost thought and the incessant desire to have a son. The doctor treats her and, as a result, she becomes a mother of not one but six sons. With the help of medical science, he succeeds where the heroine's prayers failed. He also helps her family in kind also. When, after many years, he finds that Rukmani is unable to feed her children properly, he starts visiting her and brings along "half a coconut or ladus made of nuts and rolled into balls with jaggery, which the children loved" or cow's milk for the suckling Selvam. (33)

There is, however, an aura of mystery that hovers around the English doctor. He disappears after helping Rukmani and her family at this juncture of their life. Nobody knows about his whereabouts. Rukmani says about his mysterious comings and goings: "Nobody knew where he came from or who paid him, but there he was, and people spoke well of him, though he was a foreigner." (18-19) She also says: "he came and went mysteriously . . . but when he left the village, for days or years at a time, nobody knew where he went or what he did." (34) A cautious reader, however, may find it deliberate, that is, the English doctor may have intentionally created a sense of mystery and suspense which could fill the rustic villagers with awe and wonder. This self-made suspense, by and large, helped Dr. Kennington win respect from his admirers and, at the same time, maintain a safe distance from them. The readers, after a close scrutiny, may find this rather crude and enigmatic for he becomes, in a way, a character who could hide his ways of life in his occasional appearances and thus, the reality is turned into an enigma, difficult to understand.

In our next meeting with Dr. Kennington after a fair interval of time, we find him serving the suffering humanity with "a long line of men waiting" for their turn with full devotion and dedication. (58) Rukmani meets him and talks about Ira and her barrenness with a request to cure her. The English doctor, after little annoyance agrees and treats her too. He recommends the name of Murugan, Rukmani's third son, for the job of a servant in the house of Dr. Birla who has been living in the city. When she meets Kenny to thank him for his timely help, he says: "It is nothing. You ask little." (70) Rukmani asks him, out of her whims, if he was alone. He, with little annoyance, replies: "I am never alone. Do you not see the crowds always at my door?" (70) With a shrivelled face, he says:

> I have the usual encumbrances that men have—wife, children, home—that would have put chains about me, but I resisted, and so I am alone. As for coming and going, I do as I please, for am I not my own master? I work among you when my spirit wills it. . . . I go when I am tired of your follies and stupidities, your eternal, shameless poverty. I can only take you people in small doses. (71)

Rukmani, however, fails to understand what Kenny has said. "A strange nature," she says, "only partly within my understanding. A man half in shadow, half in light, defying knowledge." (71) The English doctor reveals himself to be a peculiar Englishman fired with missionary zeal, who leaves his wife, children and home to serve strange people in an alien country. It is, indeed, ironic that he doesn't think of his own countrymen as those who were largely responsible for the "shameful poverty" of Indians. Why doesn't he realize that "follies and stupidities are the natural products of ignorance, illiteracy and poverty?"[4] The "strange" man, after this incident could not be found by Rukmani when she went twice to see him. As usual, he was away without the knowledge of anybody. His "own master," Kenny works and lives with poor farmers till his spirit "wills it" but when he leaves them after taking them in "small doses," where does he go? (71) The question remains unanswered, as nobody knows about it. The answers, however, may be many but their authenticity remains dubious. This is what remains under the carpet, thus turning the doctor into an enigma.

Notwithstanding his mysteriousness, he is liked by all and is a much sought after man. When, after a long time, he reappears, Rukmani immediately runs to meet him having "a garland of roses and jasmine to welcome him, and a lime for good luck." (106). Rukmani, however, soon realizes that she was not the first to come; others have already welcomed him. She was a bit anxious but Dr. Kennington starts laughing which made him look young and amiable and she felt better because the "strangeness vanished." (107) This incident highlights Kenny's humorous aspect which otherwise remains buried in his busy schedule and which he rarely allows to come out. It also helps relieve the tense Rukmani and create a healthy environment for interaction.

There is a tinge of sadness in his life which Kenny would not share with anybody but Rukmani. He tells her that his wife has deserted him and his "sons have been taught to forget" him. (108) Rukmani tries to comfort him by saying that he has "solicitude [for the poor peasants] and love for [their] children" despite the fact that it was not his country and not his people whom he serves. (109) He replies in a sad tone, "Sometimes I do not know which is my country. Until today I had thought perhaps it was this." (109) This incident throws a significant light on the pious and emotional relationship between the doctor and the heroine of the novel. They share their hidden and hitherto unexpressed feelings and the readers come to know more about their personality and the humanity that binds them with affection. Although the English doctor thinks "this" as his own country where he could serve humanity with heart and soul yet he can take the native villagers in "small doses" only. This is rather contradictory, for Kenny, no doubt kind and sympathetic toward the poor and suffering peasantry, fails to condition himself emotionally and physically with the people among whom he lives.

There is a significant contrast between Dr. Kennington and Lady Caroline Bell of *Possession,* another important novel by Kamala Markandaya. A "puppet master," Lady Caroline seriously involves herself to possess Valmiki not only physically but morally and spiritually also.[5] There is no doubt, however, that she recognizes the genius in the shepherd boy—a painter par excellence, and brings him to London to be widely acclaimed painter in the salons of London. But she is cold, selfish, mercenary and indifferent to human values, and manipulates every opportunity she gets to achieve her goals. Dr. Kennington, on the other hand, is warm-hearted, kind and sympathetic, helping and deeply attached with the Indian peasantry. He does not exploit Indians and their pathetic conditions to achieve his goal which is to serve humanity. Lady Caroline attempts to turn Valmiki into a passive character having no choice of his own. Dr. Kennington, by contrast, wishes the native villagers to be active and voice protest against all injustices inflicted upon them by the landlords and the rich.

Dr. Kennington is a sympathetic observer of the Indian way of life. He is pained to see the miseries of the underfed, exploited and downtrodden Indian peasants. He is very kind and sympathetic toward these rustics among whom he willingly lives. He builds a hospital there in order to treat the patients who would otherwise suffer for lack of money. He keeps Selvam, Rukmani's fifth son, as his assistant who had a knack for this profession. The study of the novel makes it evident that the English doctor had qualities of head and heart and won a special place in the heart of the people he lives with. Unlike Mrs. Pickering, an English character in Kamala Markandaya's *The Nowhere Man (*1972) who helps Srinivas at certain points of his life in London "out of pity first, and then through mutual friendship,"[6] Both Kenny helps the poor villagers on humanitarian grounds. Both these angel-like characters help other characters but whereas Mrs. Pickering, although a good-natured lady, gets success in acclimatizing Srinivas to British social culture and its manners and ways of thinking, Kenny feels helpless in altering the deep-rooted psyche of the poor Indians who rely on their destiny and bear injustice passively.

Kamala Markandaya has invested liberal humanistic outlook in the English doctor who fails to imbibe the reality and complexity of Indian peasantry because of his lack of conviction and clarity of perception. Although he is rational, having scientific temper, and a man of astute judgement, he occasionally fails to provide remedy to the common, day to day matters which he doesn't like. When he finds Rukmani using dung as fuel, he feels annoyed and chides her not to use it as manure for the land: "I thought you would know better, who live by the land yet think of taking from it without giving." (32) When, however, Rukmani demands an alternate, he becomes dumbstruck. His disapproval to the use of dung as fuel and providing no substitute for it exhibits that he is a man of queer nature who is moved with sympathy for the suffering humanity but cannot provide any solution to their sufferings. It also shows us that Dr. Kennington appears to be preaching the prejudiced Indians from the pulpit from where they hardly listen anything and, in turn, understand nothing. In this particular sense, his preaching seems to well out from his Western outlook which is beyond the reach of native Indians.

Nectar in a Sieve shows us that Dr. Kennington is dedicated wholeheartedly to improve the poor farmers' lot. He, however, departs from their philosophy of being fatalists all the time. He is against fatalism and injustice inflicted upon the wretched peasantry by the landlords. He finds it impossible to explain things to Rukmani because she, he opines, had "limited" view (108). He objects to the patient suffering of the peasants and asks them to protest against it: "you must cry out if you want help. It is no use whatsoever to suffer in silence. Who will succour the drowning man if he does not clamour for his life." (113) He further adds that there is "no grandeur in want—or in endurance." (113) He is irritated and angry over Rukmani's response to remain noble and spiritually high even when she faces harsh and unfavourable conditions. The following interaction at this point between Dr. Kennington and Rukmani is worth considering:

> "Acquiescent imbeciles," he would scornfully say, "do not think spiritual grace comes from being in want, or from suffering? What thoughts have you when your belly is empty or your body is sick? Tell me they are noble ones and I will call you a liar."
>
> "Yet our priests fast, and inflict on themselves severe punishments, and we are taught to bear our sorrows in silence, and all this is so that the soul may be cleansed."
>
> He struck his forehead. "My God!" he cried. "I do not understand you. I never will. Go, before I too am entangled in your philosophies." (114)

The interaction that took place between Rukmani and Kenny amply shows the stark difference between their ideology. "By projecting their respective viewpoints," Kamala Markandaya has put before the readers "a glimpse of those choices in life that are made both by man and his circumstances, as also of the havoc caused by an uncritical acceptance of the dominant ideology."[7]

Dr. Kennington appears to be entangled between two worlds—one is rational and the other is emotional, fatalist or irrational. He could not forget or discard the values of his western culture and the rationale that goes with it in a country where people are irrational either because of their superstitious nature or because they are illiterate. He, time and again, finds himself uncomfortable and sometimes irritated while living within a community of people that is mired in fatalism and passivity. He is pained to see the suffering humanity that is poor and unable to make two ends meet. He becomes angry with the poor peasants who, by and large, do not believe in labour or hard work and remain dependent solely on their destiny. He, for instance, does not like Rukmani's idea when she says that it was not in their hands to gain what they desire but on the Almighty that gives to one and all. Dr. Kennington, however, fails to understand what she means and why she, along with other native peasants, is so fatalist that it is quite difficult to accept. A focus on the study of the English doctor reveals that the readers of the novel remain confused about the reality of his personality that remains "half in shadow, half in light." In addition to this, his preachings which are aimed at correcting the prejudiced society prove futile because of their primordial heritage or because they do not wish to alter themselves or because they have no other choice. And hence it seems that Kenny is preaching from the pulpit to a public whose ears are either shut or unwilling to hear anything that is beyond their understanding.

NOTES

1. R.K. Dhawan, ed., *Explorations in Modern Indo-English Fiction* (New Delhi: Bahri, 1982), p. 179.
2. Bhagwat S. Goyal, *Culture and Commitment: Aspects of Indian Literature in English* (Meerut; Shalabh, 1984), pp. 45-46.
3. Kamala Markandaya, *Nectar in a Sieve* (Mumbai: Jaico, 2002).
4. Goyal, p. 109.
5. Shantha Krishanaswamy, *The Woman in Indian Fiction in English* (New Delhi: Ashish, 2001), p. 203.
6. Dhawan, p. 200.
7. Goyal, p. 108.

Dispossession and Displacement: A Quest for the Lost Home in Rushdie's *Midnight's Children* and *The Moor's Last Sigh*

PANKAJ SHARMA

Indian fiction in English is a tale of continual growth and evolution. It has evolved out from the imitative to the optative and then towards the innovative phase. The real evolution started with Bankimchandra Chatterjee (the Zeus of Indian fictional pantheon) and his *Rajmohan's Wife* becoming a foundation stone of Indian fiction.

There grew out a cluster of writers in India who started writing in English about and for India despite belonging to different regions, traditions and vernacular languages. They came as different generations. Most recent to be associated with this cluster are the writers of Indian Diaspora, of the expatriate sensibility, writers like Salman Rushdie, Amitav Ghosh, Vikram Seth and V.S. Naipaul (a writer born in foreign land writing about his ancestral land). The writers of this phase have new trends and innovative modes to present, stuffed with myriad of themes, motifs and meaning in the fiction. They are the children of the post-colonial era.

Salman Rushdie is a name with which almost the entire literary world is familiar. It won't be wrong to call him the bold voice of the contemporary Indian subcontinent with a host of other trendsetters after him like Chaman Nahal, Sasthi Brata, Shashi Deshpande, Arun Joshi, Shashi Tharoor, Arundhati Roy, Amit Chaudhuri, Rohinton Mistry and Jhumpa Lahiri.

Rushdie's *Midnight's Children* became a seminal book for most of the writing that has come from the third world. A generation of the authors was labelled as "Rushdie's children" viz.

Allan Sealy, Shashi Tharoor, Amitav Ghosh, Rukun Advani, Rajiva Wijesinha, Adam Zameenzad and Chitra Banerjee Divakaruni. He, hence, is followed as a novelist of conflicts. Rushdie became a "cardinal" writer for the progeny, who is anti-authoritarian. "Until the appearance of Rushdie, it is almost impossible to map a clear decent influence in Indo-Anglian writing."[1]

Salman Rushdie stands apart from all these writers with his ability to peel off the cicatrice of reality to show beneath it the raw flesh of deep feeling of dispossession and displacement. In his works, he has used the takes from various genres viz. Fantasy, mythology, religion and oral tradition. His narrative technique has connected his fiction to "Magic Realism."[2]

Rushdie has been associated variously by the critics to Milan Kundera, Gabriel Garcia Marquez, Gunter Grass, John Irving and V.S. Naipaul. He has been acclaimed as a fictional realist. *Grimus*, *Midnight's Children*, *Shame*, *The Satanic Verses*, *The Moor's Last Sigh*, *Haroun and the Sea of Stories*, *Ground beneath Her Feet* and recently in *Shalimar the Clown*, he recreates the real Indian subcontinent in a fictionalized manner. He acts as a minute observer, sitting out, with his antennas fixed over India and presents a similitudous reality. The things which are to be understood are a Pandora's box of dismantling and dispossession, which ultimately results in the "death of the Democracy," more particularly freedom which can be called the base of liberty, equality and justice. But, how the individual and the nation could come out of such crisis, if reality is not followed? And the reality has been that there remained a continuous dispossession and displacement, which Rushdie himself has felt:

> I cannot avoid the fact that my life has been constructed in a series of such displacements of which only the last, the decision to stay in England, was my own choice. . . . There are a lot of dislocations there! . . . I do feel that physical and geographical displacement makes you self-conscious about your position, obliges you to establish the ground you stand on.[3]

(Ahmad) Salman Rushdie was born in Bombay on June 19, 1947. Being a Muslim, Rushdie has brought out the fact in almost all the novels about the subcontinent. The fact of his being from a Muslim family in the newly partitioned subcontinent enters the fiction in diverse ways. According to Sameen, the eldest of Rushdie's three sisters: "There were questions about my family's loyalty to India: as Muslim who had not left." She notes that there were "court cases" and "the government took my father's properties"—the situation has been brought and reincorporated in *Midnight's Children*. Sameen also conveys that they were "conscious as a Muslim minority in India."[4] There comes a sense of alienation that has been featured by Rushdie in most of his fiction. Like his father and grandfather, Muslims were, according to Rushdie, part of a subcontinental Muslim tradition that was more lenient than it has become in recent years. That is why Rushdie has particularly waged a tirade against any kind of orthodoxy against which he has written boldly.

Rushdie's family has migrated from one country to the other. The fact that Rushdie and his family migrated first to Pakistan and then to England supports the argument that warring nations aggravated the sense of loss and dispossession in Rushdie, which he has brought in his novels too. Rushdie also feels that he belongs to both and neither of the countries. The feeling of homelessness has been expressed in an interview: "In Pakistan there is suspicion because I'm Indian and in India because I'm Pakistani. Both sides vie to claim me. Both sides find it hard that I don't reject the other side."

Rushdie has faced hard blows of direct check and censorship of his works, engaged in antagonism against orthodox Pakistani religion and culture in *Midnight's Children*, *Shame* and *The Satanic Verses*, creating a feeling of bitterness. He had to go into exile to settle in London and from there to U.S.A. It was after his settling in London that he started writing as a novelist in the days of "hand to mouth." In the fiction, there is representation of this loss through the plight of the protagonist.

Rushdie has become an icon of "postmodern metafiction."[4] Given his metafictional style, his sense of metamorphic self, and extensive use of metaphysical realism, we, the readers, might take him as a metacist which makes one understand the disjunction, dispossession and displacement as a postmodern reality, a tendency to have a look at reality from a distance which gives a room to doubt and faith, hope and despair. This gap makes one understand the complexity of the situation. Rushdie's mastery makes it easy for him to convey the meaning lying deep down.

The objective of this paper, however, is not to go into the details of the metafictive styles of Rushdie. His volatile mix of magic realism, history and metafiction, tradition and rebellion exists simultaneously in every novel, giving space to the novels rife of ambiguities and paradoxes.

In his novels, Rushdie constantly attacks the notion of beliefs related to cosmology, mythology and mysticism—the binary opposition of Heaven and Hell, gods and demons, vision and possession, angels and devil, to be taken as determinants for political and social upheavals. In his essay, "In God we trust," he argues that his secularism makes sense in terms of Indian history of the last half-century: "After the terrible communal\killings of the partition riots, it was plainer than ever that if Indians remaining Muslims, Sikhs, Buddhists, Jains, Christian, Jews, Harijans (untouchables), as well as the Hindu majority, were to be able to live altogether in peace, the idea of godless state must be elevated above all of the 330 million deities."[5]

Rushdie allows himself to explore myth, religion and metaphysics to a great extent. Being a sensitive writer, he cannot ignore to bring out realism in a tabulated garb. It remains based on the fact that no one has any authority over truth and reality. He has strived "to develop a form which does not prejudice whether your characters are right or wrong. . . . A form in which the idea of the miraculous can co-exist with observable, everyday reality." (*Ibid*., 377)

This includes the vast realm of the dilemma of dispossession and displacement resulting in an enigma, the havoc that has come with the credulous orthodoxy and religious fundamentalism. Religion is the base of his novels—to focus on the brutality, violence and suppression associated with it. It can really make the people like Ayatollah Khomeini to shudder and declare fatwa (death-sentence) against him.

All of this does not mean that Rushdie is against religion or religious values, or he cannot see any way to accommodate religious values under the rubric of a secular society. What he questions is the condition prevailing, the loss of the nation and the nationals at the hands of fanaticism, authoritarian sentimentalism and crooked crouched politicization of which he and his family became victims in search of a home. In the early novels, Rushdie has brought a symbolic and metonymic picture of rootless, fragmented and confused identity expressed through migration and alienation. He appeals for a sane, rational and humanist world order. The sense of migration becomes a recurrent theme in Rushdie's novels. The loss conveys the defeat of humanity and human spirit at the hands of perverted and crooked malignance, social, political and religious as well. Rushdie thus becomes a quester for the lost home. Jean-Pierre Durix says:

> Rushdie stresses the importance of what he calls the "Literature of migration" in the twentieth century. For him "a migrant suffers, traditionally, a triple disruption; he loses, his place, he enters into an alien language, and he finds himself surrounded by beings whose social behaviour and code is very unlike and sometimes even offensive to his own.[6]

It surely refers to the growth of cultural relativism when Rushdie or other similar expatriate or migrant writers play the game of cultural relativism, he juxtaposes fragments from different cultures, even when he knows that he may get violent reactions from people who feel in their most basic beliefs, but it's his urge to get settled and relate himself even when the reaction is both positive and negative. Rushdie has been successful to achieve this in his fiction.

Rushdie's characters have observed the several codes of cultural behaviour, basically those belonging to a particular traditional culture which is a saga of loss and decay under a complete process of digression, displacement and dislocation. Through *Midnight's Children* (1981) and *The Moor's Last Sigh*

(1995), Rushdie conveys his personal as well as the collective ethos of the third world in general, starting from the days of peace to crisis, struggle and freedom; with a dream of prosperity happiness and progress. There is deconstruction of the myth of an edenic past or future by presenting a counter-realism: first the shattering of the "myth of freedom" and then of "secularism," which was supposed to be the strength of the nation. Rushdie presents a blank universe around, with no feasible security. For this, Rushdie has made a good blend of private individual lives and public events by fictionalizing the history.

In *Midnight's Children*, Saleem Sinai, the narrator-protagonist, narrates the events of loss and dispossession that become a part of his as well as the nation's life. What follows is an intertwined history of the nation with his personal history, which he remembers. Sushila Singh remarks: "*Midnight's Children* is also a story about the past of its writer's nostalgic glance back from another country from which he has migrated."[7] Rushdie muses, "Writers in my position, exiles or emigrants or expatriates, are hunted by an urge to look back even at the risk of being mutated into pillars of salt. But if we do look back, we do so in the knowledge—which gives rise to profound uncertainties—that our physical alienation from India almost inevitably means that we will, in short, create fictions, not actual cities or villages but invisible, one's imaginary homelands, Indias of the mind." Rushdie evokes the old city of Bombay where he was born and spent his childhood with uncanny insight.

In the novel, Saleem Sinai, dying in a pickle factory in Bombay, becomes a narrator-cum-witness of an age gained and lost. He becomes a universal witness-cum-victim to the dispossession and displacement in the post-Independence scenario. Saleem admits of his fragmented and scattered identity: "I had been mysteriously handcuffed to history, my destinies indissolubly chained to those of my country."[8] Rushdie's urge finds a fictional alter-ego in Saleem. Anuradha Dingwaney states:

> Indeed, in the marketing and in the reviews of *Midnight's Children*, readers with Rushdie's tacit approval, have assumed that Saleem's life corresponds not just with that of his nation, but also

> with that of his creator: "Saleem and Salman are after all one," notes Rushdie, "if you look back etymologically, kinds of versions of the same name . . . so there are clear affinities made . . . he the same age as me more or less . . . he grows up in my house, he goes to my school, some of the things that happened to me happen in more interesting form to him.[9]

There is an obvious revisit and there comes the peeling of the history of its important layers to find out a lost identity, a home of one's own. The search in the fiction starts with one generation and deterioratingly passed on to the other travelling through the struggle for Independence, the partition of India, the communal riots, language riots, short time of prosperity under Nehru and topsy-turvy deterioration during the rule of Indira Gandhi. The fiction however, conveys the fact that freedom movement in India was "not merely a political struggle but also an all-pervasive experience that became a part of the life of almost all sensitive and enlightened Indians."[10]

Saleem Sinai throws a focused light to give the glimpses of the particular time of the history. History and biography comes in a fictionalized way but in fragments. All the fragments represent major historical events of some six decades and three generations of Saleem's clan which is symbolic of India. The events like xenophobic Jallianwala Bag massacre, Gandhian movements, Quit India movement, the freedom at midnight and after, form the chronological base of the novel. By doing so, Rushdie has made his quest for the home possible by reliving in those times of which he was not a part, as he has been in exile. He cannot forget that his roots are in India:

> As for me I, too, like all migrants, am a fantasist. I build imaginary countries and try to impose them on the ones that exist. I, too, face the problem of history: what to retain, what to dump, how to hold on to what memory insists on relinquishing, how to deal with change and to come back to "roots" idea, I should say that I haven't managed to shake myself free of it completely.[11]

It's because of this that he talks of dispossession and displacement in the sense of a migrant. Saleem feels no way of having a home or coming back to normal. He claims "a place centre of things" to find out a way if "I am to end up meaning . . . above all things, I fear absurdity" and the meaning is to come from the story which is to be told with "intertwined lives events miracles places rumours" as Saleem has "been a swallower of lives: and to know me just the one of me, you'll have to swallow the lot as well." (238-39) And the meaning that comes out is of a forgone prosperity where power becomes a means to culpritize the mankind. The condition, if one observes, has not changed even now. Saleem becomes a mirror to the postcolonial dispossession and displacement with an unending eternal attachment for home and the search continues. The notion which comes out is that freedom or Independence in the continent consciously or unconsciously has continued the same colonial estrangement and disparity in the shape of riots, poverty, assassination, and disintegration on the basis of race and caste as well as political aggression. To all this, Saleem Sinai becomes a witness-cum-victim. Saleem and the other midnight's children, who (born at or after the hour of Independence) possessed miraculous powers and hope for a bright future, receive frustration, dishope and despair. Saleem gets nothing else than a vast, unending multiplicity.

Through Saleem's story, Rushdie conveys the genuine reality of the subcontinent with basic postulates of orthodoxy and perversion, combining together to show the weak, corrupt political system, where there is no guarantee for a hope, which makes the midnight's children "to be both masters and victims of their times." They have "to forsake privacy and be sucked into the annihilating whirlpool of the multitudes and to be unable to live or die in peace." (463)

If *Midnight's Children* doesn't allow a space to settle into the land with just an imaginary, illusionary attachment, *The Moor's Last Sigh* (1995) is a tragic lament bringing nowhereness and annihilation with an unending unrest and frustration. It comes as Rushdie's post-*The Satanic Verses* disappointment in various ways. Rushdie's quest with full resentment and protesting voice searches down with Moraes Zogoiby, the protagonist, the history and culture which is to be assumed as his own. He conveys the breaking of a myth of cultural harmony and Nehru's secularism with a straight forward jab on the Hindu fundamentalism after he blasts the shame and shamelessness of Islamic fundamentalism in *Shame* and *The Satanic Verses* by bringing out the dilemma of credulous orthodoxy in a leaderless country. *The Moor's Last Sigh* comes as a saga of an eternal loss. David Myers says: "*The Moor's Last Sigh* is a renunciation of institutional religion and heroisation in spite of postmodernist jokes of the independent, secular artist. It is therefore, indirectly a justification of Salman Rushdie's own artistic cases, as his harsh, satiric vision of the world's sectarian evil earned him powerful enemies ranging from Mrs. Gandhi to Imams of Islam. Finally *The Moor's Last Sigh* is a tragic plea from beyond despair for the tolerance of multiculturalism in a world that is rent by ethnic and sectarian hatred and war."[12]

The novel is about the catastrophic events that took place in India. After *Midnight's Children*, this is a return to India of Rushdie but for a short while, it continues the voyage of Rushdie from where he stops in *Midnight's Children*. It completes the cycle of Rushdie's novels about the Indian sub-continent, particularly India, as Anuradha Dingwaney says:

> In a September 1995 interview, he notes that "The cycle of novels *Midnight's Children*, *Shame*, *The Satanic Verses* and *The Moor's Last Sigh*—that records his response to an age in history that bean in 1947 . . . is now complete." He implies he does not expect, therefore "a return to the subcontinent as his primary subject . . . of this exile lies *The Moor's Last Sigh*, which a number of readers, in fact read as a novel for leave-taking, last sigh in the Moor's words, for a lost world, a fear for its passing." (316-17)

The 'sigh' comes for the breaking of myth of freedom and secularism. Bombay to a great extent is India for Rushdie because of its secular, hybrid and cosmopolitan nature. In the novel Bombay (now Mumbai) becomes the wasteland of apocalyptic disorder conveying the demonic world of inhumanity. "Bombay," according to Moraes Zogoiby, the Moor "was central where all rivers flowed into its human sea" with which the "founding myth of the nation faded" and "what transpired was rooted in Bombay."

What comes out was "a tragedy . . . a national tragedy on a grand scale" and the consequence of it was that "the city quaked and collided, Bombay blew apart."[13]

Through the story of Catholics, and Jews of Cochin, Rushdie provides a base for the multicultural diversity of India which he brings to Bombay where it gets destroyed under factionalism and growing religious orthodoxy (pointed towards Shiv Sena). For this Rachel Trousdale says: "The Shiv Sena is a very useful enemy for Rushdie. It encapsulates many things he hates: religious fanaticism, intolerance, belief in cultural purity and violence. The fact that its leader, Bal Thackeray, is an educated and articulate man only makes it a better target. The Shiv Sena's communal politics, which first appear in *Midnight's Children*, become dominant theme in *The Moor's Last Sigh* and are counterweight, the opposing dream, to all of Rushdie's visions of his Ideal India."

Rushdie brings the orthodox politics in the novel through Raman Fielding nicknamed as Mainduck (based on the character of Bal Thackeray). With him and Mr. Abraham Zogoiby (father of the Moor) it has but become a game of power and control. It's the irrationality of the age with the issues like Babri Mosque in Ayodhya which "fell and plans for a mighty Ram temple on the God's alleged birthplace were executed." (351) Rushdie found a "battering Ram" coming into existence (363). It seems more like *The Wasteland* of T.S. Eliot and "The Second Coming" of W.B. Yeats; a topsy-turvy, perverted world where occurred "a national tragedy on a grand scale." (371) At the end, Moraes felt a blast inside out. He loses his family and the nation too. The Moor feels: "Catastrophe has become the city's habit, and we were all its users, its Zombies, its undead." (374) He goes into exile to Benengali in Spain in quest of his roots (his identity)—the paintings of his mother—stolen by Vasco Miranda (another painter, who'd worked and learnt the art of painting from the Moor's mother, Aurora Zogoiby), but what he gets is death.

The heaven of Bombay has been lost. The Moor feels: "It is no longer my Bombay, no longer special, no longer the city of mixed-up, mongrel joy. Something had ended [The world?] and what remained, I didn't know." (376) There was nothing to hold him there anymore and hence he turns his face off. David Myers observes: "There is little doubt that Rushdie means his work to be taken as an allegory of the fall of India, and specifically Bombay, from multicultural tolerance to fanatical sectarianism. More covertly, one can feel Rushdie's own tragic, recent history reverberating in the losses and defeats of his protagonist . . . we can feel Salman Rushdie's own fall from world-celebrated author to persecuted pariah in hiding from Islamic threats." (81-82)

The novel ends in tragic despair: the Moor laying down "upon this graven stone . . . and close my eyes, according to our family's old practice of falling asleep in the times of trouble, and hope to awaken, renewed and joyful in better time." (434) It seems to have got viral infection of dispossession and displacement with the end of cultural relativism. What comes out of the novel is degeneration and betrayal, "A Moor's tale, complete with sound and fury." (4)

What is observed from both the novels is Rushdie's allegorical representation of the upheavals beneath the fantasy. There is a sheer representation of repression, loss and disruption. It deconstructs all the existing notions of freedom, prosperity and righteousness. The characters who become symbolic representation of the culture also become the victims of it. There is no place to settle or return and hence the only scope left is to escape—to go into exile, which Rushdie, in reality has done.

The saga of dispossession and displacement thus continues. Rushdie, on the whole, doesn't find a space to come back to. Nothing is redeemed. India still exists as an imaginary homeland for Rushdie. There remains a continuous flight for him without finding a home to settle down. Even then he is totally Indian in his sensibility and style by making use of oral tradition of storytelling in his fiction, which is still prevalent in India. It has made him to take India as his subject again in *Shalimar the Clown* (2005). This can be traced as his conscious or unconscious desire to be one with the subcontinent (which is least possible in his case). His condition and choice does not allow him to do so.

On the whole, there is a sense of nowhereness in case of Rushdie and his novels just being identified with fragmenting multicultural identity. Otherwise what is found is "A self without walls." (288) The characters, as mouthpieces of Rushdie, have been observed to be in a trap of nowhereness. The quest for a home remains open with a continuous sense of dispossession and displacement. In Rushdie's case it comes out as fictive autobiography demonstrating his love and loss of India. He, in reality, remains homeless.

NOTES

1. Chelva Kanaganayakam, "Fabulating the Real," *Counter-Realism and Indo-Anglian Fiction* (Canada: Wilfred Laurier Univ. Press, 2002), p. 144.
2. Magic Realism: A technique in contemporary postcolonial fiction which frequently portrays the imaginary, the improbable or fantastic in a realistic rational manner. Margaret Drabbble, ed., *The Oxford Companion to English Literature* (U.K.: OUP, 2000), p. 629.
3. Kumkum Sangari, "Interview with Salman Rushdie," *The Book Review*, vol. 3, no. 5 (March-April 1984), p. 25.
4. Ian Hamilton, "The First Life of Salman Rushdie," *The New Yorker*, 25.12.95 and 1.1.96. 6 Aug. 2005 <.http: //www.flyingfish. rg.uk/article/rushdie/ price. Htm> 96.
5. Salman Rushdie, "In God we Trust," *Imaginary Homelands* (London: Granta, 1991), p. 385.
6. Jean-Pierre Durix, "Towards Hybrid Aesthetics," *Mimesis, Genres and Post-Colonial Discourse: Deconstructing Magic Realism* (London: Macmillan, 1998), p. ix.
7. Sushila Singh, " Salman Rushdie's Novels: From Fantasy to Reality," *The Commonwealth Review*, vol. 1 (1989), p. 116.
8. Rushdie, *Midnight's Children* (London: Vintage, 1995), p. 9.
9. Anuradha Dingwaney, "Salman Rushdie," Arvind Krishna Mehrotra, ed., *An Illustrated History of Indian Literature in English* (Delhi: Permanent Black, 2003), p. 308.
10. Shyam M. Asnani, "The Socio-Political Scene of the 1930s: Its Impact on the Indo-English Novel," *Commonwealth Quarterly* (Dec. 1981), p. 81.
11. Salman Rushdie, *Shame* (London: Vintage, 1995), pp. 87-88.

12. David Myers, "A Tragic Lament beyond Postmodernist Parody: Multicultural Art's Protest against Bigoted Fundamentalism in Salman Rushdie's *The Moor's Last Sigh*," ed. R.K. Dhawan, *Writers of the Indian Diaspora* (New Delhi: Prestige, 2001), p. 86.
13. Salman Rushdie, *The Moor's Last Sigh* (London: Jonathancape, 1995), pp. 350, 351, 352 and 371.
14. Rachel Trousdale, "City of Mongrel Joy: Bombay and the Shiv Sena in *Midnight's Children* and *The Moor's Last Sigh*," *The Journal of Commonwealth Literature* (May 2004), p. 104.

Wit and Humour: Indian Life and Indian English Fiction

RAMESH K. SRIVASTAVA

The basic purpose of comic elements is to provoke or evoke laughter. In the modern times, when the joint families are disintegrating and gossiping sessions have become endangered activities bordering on extinction, when intense working hours are steadily encroaching upon brief periods of relaxation, when mental activities are taking over physical ones, and when nights are no longer synonymous with cool slumber, neurological disorders are becoming the common ailments of the day. In such times, literature, movies, television shows and serials, public lectures and public presentations, marriage and birthday parties, and other such common activities of life with liberal inputs of comic elements are being widely welcome. Rollicking comedies, ironic, satiric, and comic poetry, recitation sessions of humorous poetry (*Hasya Kavi Sammelans*), jokes, laughing shows, idiotic behaviour, funny replies and witty repartees which tease, tickle and provoke laughter are becoming popular to give relief to the tension-ridden human beings in the modern world.

In the past, writers of tragedies and epic poetry considered introduction of comic elements in literature as an unwelcome activity close to farce and buffoonery not worth taking a serious note. Hence while highest eulogies were piled on the darkest tragedies and serious epics, wit and humour in the writings of poets, dramatists, novelists and essayists failed to find a respectable place in literature.

Gradually, more and more people of the world came to a slow realization that man is the only creature who experiences an emotion and laughs over it, and that wit and humour are as important in life and literature as are the serious issues. As researches are continuing in the therapeutic value of humour, and as cases of irremediable diseases being cured everyday through humour are coming to light, more and more people are beginning to testify that wit and humour are very essential for human beings in order to keep them in good health and cheer.

Indians, too, must have been aware of this fact because many kings and rulers in the past used to have the court jesters. Tenali Raman and Birbal are often named both for their intelligence and sense of humour. In marriages, Indians used to have *mirasees* and jesters who with their rhythmic beating of broom-like, hollow, battered bamboo staff would spin the funniest jokes, incidents, caricatures and exaggerated virtues or vices to regale the guests on the arrival or departure times of marriage parties. One laughed at the oddities, idiosyncrasies, and absurdities of imaginary characters, activities or manners narrated by them. The jesters attached to the rulers, jokers in circuses, *Maha-moorakh Sammelans (*assembly of greatest fools) and parodies also provided a lot of humour to divert the people at least momentarily from tension. Now laughing clubs have been formed in most cities where guffaws of loud laughter can be heard. A well-known Yoga specialist emphasizes laughter while demonstrating certain exercises, recommending that laughter can be used as a stress-management technique, particularly for the depressed. Some private hospitals are contemplating setting up humour-therapy departments.

Norman Cousins, onetime editor of *The Saturday Review*, cured himself of an irremediable disease by indulging in free laughter by watching Charlie Chaplin movies and extremely funny comedies, knowing well that humour and positive emotions play a significant role in medical treatment. Humour is a sort of defense-mechanism, an inner safety valve, a blocking agent which, like a bullet-proof jacket, "may help protect you against the ravages of negative emotions that assault you in disease" (Qtd. J. Singh 1989: 8). Subsequent researches have established a close relationship between humour, health and long life. Laughter, in the opinion of Cousins, is an "internal jogging" which alleviates depression and prevents heart-attacks. Aruna Chandraraju writes that "humour therapy is a treatment technique that uses the power of smiles and laughter to help heal" (4). The writer goes on to point out that in the United States and Europe, special rooms have been assigned in the hospitals and ambulatory-care centres which have ample of materials to help patients laugh. Movies, audio and video tapes, games, puzzles and comics are provided to patients of different age-groups. One U.S. hospital uses even a "laughmobile" to serve bedridden patients. The element of unexpectedness accompanying humour helps in creating something new, something sparklingly fresh which tickles the imagination of a person and provokes him to laughter.

By intervening in the normal activities, wit and humour promote health; they eject a person from a pit of gloom to cheerfulness through an appreciation of a playful discovery or expression of the absurdity or incongruity of life's situations. Such a diversion promotes healthy feelings and becomes a complementary treatment of mental, physical or spiritual illness. Laughter helps in increased breathing which means increased oxygen intake. It also exercises muscles and organs all of which stimulate the circulatory system. Aruna Chandraraju believes that "laughter releases endorphins or special neurotransmitter substances in the brain, which help control pain. . . . There is evidence that the chemicals that run our body and brain are the same ones involved in emotions. And that the body's healing mechanism responds positively to positive emotions like laughter and negatively to stress and unhappiness" (4).

Dr. C.R. Chandrasekhar, Professor of Psychiatry, and Deputy Superintendent, NIMANS, Bangalore, says: "Laughter helps because it replaces the debilitating negative emotions with positive ones. It takes their mind off the disease. It is especially effective in reducing the distress of the mentally disturbed, depression patients and those with psychosomatic disorders" (Qtd. Chandraraju: 4).

Some people have survived and succeeded in their tragic lives despite their serious handicaps by transforming themselves through humour to an advantageous position. But for humour, they would have died of heart attacks or might have committed suicide. James Thurber of *The New Yorker* had lost his left eye from an arrow when he was a boy of seven. In compensation, as his biographer Charles H. Holmes wrote, Thurber "cultivated his already crowded fantasy life, and developed his skills as a story teller and a comic mimic" (Qtd. Palakeel 36). Abraham Lincoln was a miserable and melancholy man but at the same time he could enjoy crazy nonsensical humour with gay abandon. For B.G. Tandon, laughter with Lincoln was "a safety device to drain out the tensions that overflowed his mind" (55). It camouflaged the pain that corroded his heart.

Of course, it is also true that there is good humour and ill humour, and whereas the former cures, the latter may worsen the situation. While cultivation of good humour and positive attitude to life are desirable, caustic jokes and witty pinpricks which hurt a person and breed negative feelings must be avoided.

II

The terms wit and humour are often confused and occasionally used interchangeably. Wit carries an element of surprise, throws light, and hence appeals to intelligence. At one time, wit was synonymous with intelligence or understanding, but later on began to be associated with humour. Humour is often scattered whereas wit shows brilliance. One stresses sympathetic emotions while the other one appeals to reason. For William Hazlitt, humour is the description of the ludicrous as it is in itself whereas wit is the expression of it by comparing or contrasting it with something else.

Wit implies a skilfully-worded phrase or sentence, somewhat pungent, like a bit of green chilly, which may evoke laughter but can carry a sting, with a momentary or lingering after-effect. It seizes an incident or a thought and by giving a sudden twist or turn presents it as something new and unexpected which gives pleasure. Related to repartees, it is an intelligent response to someone's words or statement. A repartee, like wit, can also be humorous. Humour provokes laughter through what is funny and amusing. For James Thurber, humorous is when an expected "future is replaced with an unexpected future. The more unexpected, the more humorous." Humour is based on the peculiarities or eccentricities of a person so that people enjoy a hearty, good-natured laugh at someone's whims and oddities.

Humour could be of many types. Grouche Marx, the American comedian, said, "There are all kinds of humour. Some is derisive, some sympathetic, and some merely whimsical. That is just what makes comedy so much harder to create than serious drama; people laugh in many different ways and they cry in only one." The best of humour is one which is directed at one's own self. Abraham Lincoln could joke about himself as naturally as about others. Often he joked about his own poor personality. Lincoln developed a keen love of jest with tragic sense of life.

It is not easy to enumerate the terms which fall within the broad area of the comic. To some extent: wit, repartees, humour, satire, sarcasm, banter, ribaldry, lampoons, irony, exaggeration, mimicry, caricature, cartoons, funny images, jokes, analogies between dissimilar things, distortions, oddities, idiosyncrasies, eccentricities, peculiarities, imaginary fears, incongruities, ridiculousness, verbal fencing, clumsy behaviour and manners, peculiar situations, absurdities, violation of accepted order of things, ticklishness, juxtaposition of two surprising situations, characters, cynicism, the sardonic word play, rhetorical expressions and verbal display, among others. In theatre, it is generated through undertones, overtones and oblique references bordering on sexual sleaziness. Verbal humour can result from a situation, a character or the language. Some may elicit just a smile or a chuckle or even less but what unites them is the presence of comic elements in different degrees and occasions. Caricature is usually a representation of a person in which some of his traits are exaggerated for comic effect.

III

Comic elements play an important role not only in popular magazines, periodicals and newspapers but also in literature in order to keep the readers in good humour. By periodic doses of funny news items, writings in lighter vein, cartoons and even jokes, the editors and writers punctuate the serious reading material to keep the readers away from unrelieved boredom.

In literature, some writers consciously introduce humour to entertain readers in order to save them from the tiresomeness of the serious reading material though the analysis of comic elements is often resented by them. Mark Twain in the beginning of *The Adventures of Huckleberry Finn* declared that the analysts of humour in his novel could be prosecuted. Robert Benchley commented: "there seems to be no lengths to which humorless people will not go to analyze humour" (Qtd. J. Singh, 1979: 17). Khushwant Singh wrote: "to analyze laughter is like dissecting a frog. You may see its entrails and whatever else it has inside, but you kill the frog in the process. You should just accept laughter as a phenomenon that releases tension and makes you feel lighter and happier" (1990: 5). The analysis of humour in a creative work is meant to enhance the reader's pleasure, not to kill it in the process.

One reason for discouraging analysis of humour could be because the appeal of humour is both personal and universal. In the first category, humour may evoke laughter for one person, but may not do the same for the other. A person falling down on the road may be a matter of laughter for one person but it could be an embarrassing or even a tragic event for the other. On the other hand, a funny situation or a joke could hurl the whole audience into vigorous laughter. Humour is a response which varies from person to person. A minor oddity or idiosyncrasy may provoke a person with cheerful temperament to laughter but a joke may fall flat and ineffective on a chronically serious person. The latter may find no humour at all in some of the examples from literary works I have given, because what evoked laughter in me may not cause even a chuckle among others. Whereas humour is fairly dominant in R.K. Narayan, Khushwant Singh and Arundhati Roy, it is quite dormant, almost apparently non-existent in Raja Rao, Mulk Raj Anand, Kamala Markandaya, Bhabani Bhattacharya, Anita Desai, and many more. The reason is not far to seek. The crude comic material in everyday life appeals to one and all, but when transformed into something subtle and sophisticated in the hands of a great artist, such as Henry James, it escapes the eyes of the common reader.

Shiv K. Kumar attributes the absence of humour in Indian literature to the Hindu religion and its beliefs because of the temperamental preoccupation of people with the life before birth or life after death, without seeking joy in the present. Ramesh K. Srivastava has the same view about deficiency of humour among Indians which he attributes to "the cumulative result of our ancient ideal of renunciation, our serious classics, our veneration of the ascetics and mendicants, and now the insatiable hunger for money as also the political fashions of indulging in circumlocutory and non-committal talks. . . . In general, India seems to be under perpetual puritan atmosphere where people have left the habit of enjoying life" (1992: 3). Hence, to quote Shiv K. Kumar, "a playwright, poet or novelist who generates laughter, however tenuous, is considered second rate—for tragedy is to us a lofty genre, ennobling and uplifting." Kumar himself believes that "humorous writing demands greater creative ingenuity than serious writing, since to sustain humour over a long narrative is often a formidable task." Stephen Leacock also realized that ordinary people rate humour rather low by underestimating the writer's difficulty of creating humour which is "hard, meritorious and dignified" (287-88). However, one cannot but disagree with Kumar when he categorically denies the existence of humour in Indian literature by saying that with a few exceptions, our literatures "are woefully devoid of any genuine humour. It's mostly satire which has been described as the cracking of thorns under the feet, not genial humour which is like the gentle sunshine on a placid sea." Kumar's remarks, if confined to the Indian writing in English, could have been to a limited extent justified. But when he encompasses all Indian literatures, which imply literatures in all Indian languages, he woefully shows his limited knowledge. Even in Indian writing in English, one can find abundance of humour, both crude and sophisticated, in the works of R.K. Narayan, Khushwant Singh, Nissim Ezekiel,

Bhabani Bhattacharya, Manohar Malgonkar and Arundhati Roy, among others.

IV

Raja Rao in his novel *Kanthapura* has taken care to inject, at least in a subdued form, a tone of pleasantry which makes the reading of the novel lively and even occasionally funny. The repetition of words by the village people, their use of epithets and compound names, their hyperbolic similes and metaphors, their colourful or ironical statements with undercurrent of pleasantness, their ignorance and misunderstanding assertively paraded as convictions, their descriptions of places and people laced with myths, fables and anecdotes, and their habit of using personified terms for objects of nature—all of them point out to the life and manners of village people which have been reflected well in the style of Achakka—the illiterate narrator of *Kanthapura,* but which to the city people may appear strange, peculiar, outlandish, quixotic and even downright comical. Thus on being excommunicated, a shocked Narsamma had a "tear big as a thumb." Waterfall Venkamma did not want to tie her "daughter to the neck of a pariah-mixer," that is, Moorthy (*Kanthapura* 52) whom she warns of giving "a jolly fine marriage-welcome with my broomstick." (53) Bhatta talks of grown up girls in the cities "fit enough to be mothers of two or three children, going to the Universities? And they talk to this boy and that boy; and what they do amongst themselves, heaven alone knows. And one too, I heard, went and married a Mohomedan. Really, aunt, that is horrible." (38-39) The serpent having disappeared from the Sahib's drawer becomes a Maharaja who must have "gone on his nuptial ceremony." (69-70) In rural dialogues, Raja Rao has reproduced the pauses, the repetitions, the fragmentary sentences, the circumlocutory ways peppered with his comic touches which bring the village pleasantly alive and kicking in the novel's pages.

Mulk Raj Anand's *Untouchable* is the story of a sweeper boy Bakha whose tale of suffering is so grim that hardly a moment of happiness could be found, but Anand has successfully fused in the novel a subdued sense of humour. He manages it by introducing oddities associated with swearwords, by describing Bakha's clumsy imitation of white sahib's manners, and through the literal translations of vernacular dialogues as well as through a few caricatures. Some of the swearwords and abuses which Lakha uses against his son Bakha, such as, "son of a pig," "illegally begotten" or a pig, a dog, a swine, appear as jokes because in these swearwords, Lakha virtually abuses himself in the sense that if Bakha were to be a pig, his father too must belong to the same biological category. While aping the white sahib, Bakha with his clumsily-imitated manners appears funny and humorous. In his ill-fitting clothes—an overcoat, an old jacket, and over-sized shoes, he looked like a comical figure or a three-dimensional cartoon, who unwittingly provokes fun and humour. Anand caricatures some of the characters to throw in an element of humour in the novel as also to make fun of the hypocritical Hindu priests and the ignorant-yet-zealous Christian missionaries respectively through Pandit Kalinath and Colonel Hutchinson. Instead of explaining to Bakha the nature of Jesus Christ, Col. Hutchinson goes on singing rhythmically. When Mrs. Hutchinson frowns on her husband for being with an untouchable, Bakha runs away "as if the Colonel's wife were a witch, following him with raised arms and crooked feet." (148)

Anand's use of English in dialogues is occasionally clumsy, ungrammatical and funny, carrying words of native language, distorted English words, and literal translations of Hindi or Punjabi dialogues. Thus sentences in English translations, such as, "He died over her" (35) for "*Wah us par mar gaya*" and "Why do you eat my head?" (36) for "*Mera sir kyon khate ho?*" might pass the test of authenticity of the literally translated dialogues but cause ripples of laughter for oddities in their meanings and implications.

Kamala Markandaya's *Nectar in a Sieve* has the dominant atmosphere of grimness but the novelist has fused an occasional note of mild, countryside humour with some rural jokes and similes. Kennington, who had treated Rukmani for her infertility, visits the latter and the conversation between them is delightful:

> "You *are* my benefactor," I [Rukmani] said stoutly. "Have I not five sons to prove it?"
>
> "Am I to blame for your excesses?" said he, grimacing, but his eyes were alight with laughter, no doubt at my crestfallen face.
>
> "Come with me," I said, recovering myself. "You shall see them, excesses or not." (36)

Here the humour is quite mild evoking merely a smile, but one has to remember that in an Indian village of the early twentieth century, the conversation between a foreign male and an illiterate Indian rural female could not have been more open.

Puli is an orphan child who, though having mere fingerless stumps for hands, is clever and witty enough to tackle Nathan and Rukmani. The innocent queries of Sacrabani—the illegitimate son of Ira—appear somewhat funny on surface but hide underneath the tragic part of his life because he, being a bastard, has no father. He asks his mother:

> "Mother, have I got a father?"
> "Yes, dear, of course."
> "Where is he?"
> "Not here, my son; he is away."
> "Why does he never come to see us?"
> "He will when he can."
> "But why not now?"
> "Because he cannot. You will understand when you are older."
> "How old?"
> "I don't know myself." (129-30)

The dialogues of the two children—Puli and Sacrabani—provide a weak spark or two of mild humour in a novel which is full of pathos.

In R.K. Narayan's *The Man-Eater of Malgudi,* the mythic and the comic modes are fused together to introduce some delightful elements in an otherwise grim tale. Whether in characterization, in dialogues or in the delineation of children's activities, Narayan displays his matchless gift of discovering something odd in what is ordinary, quaint and queer in what is natural and familiar, and quixotic, prismatic and outlandish in what is bland, banal and colourless; but in all of them, the end-result is always funny and humorous. Nataraj's feverish imagination in the novel conjures up visions which may be terrifying initially but turn out to be unfounded and hence funny. He imagines Vasu abducting him for a ransom of fifty thousand rupees, of destroying his family or of picking him up "between his thumb and first finger and put me down where he pleased." (40) And when every evidence was being sealed to investigate Vasu's murder, Nataraj fears that under orders of the police, he himself might be placed in a sack as some sort of evidence and sealed up for a possible future use. In the use of wit, both Vasu and Nataraj are excellent. Vasu's views about marriage are radical, funny but no less witty: "I don't know why people marry at all. If you like a woman, have her by all means. You don't have to own a coffee estate because you like a cup of coffee now and then." (33-34) On the ragman's complaint about old, waste papers being brown, Nataraj questions, "Did you think I would buy white paper by the ream and sell it to you by weight?" (23)

The activities of Narayan's eccentric characters as well as those of children are equally good in provoking humour. When Nataraj and Muthu encounter the difficulty of making the ill elephant Kumar get up, a child requests them to get a frog in order to make the elephant get up. Somewhat puzzled, they ask him how would he do it with a frog, the child replies, "When a frog is put under an elephant, it'll jump, and elephant will jump with it." (97) There is also in the novel an entire gallery of eccentric characters and their activities—the mono-syllabic poet, the Nehru-baiting journalist, the Adjournment lawyer, and the slowest bus driver who would apply "the brake when a piece of paper drifted across." (44-45) The best part is that most of these funny activities are innocent and do not harm any one even while they provoke a lot of fun and humour for readers.

Whereas R.K. Narayan was basically an entertainer with no sense of commitment to any other cause, Bhabani Bhattacharya was a social realist, and a predominant comic tone might have injured the seriousness of his objective. Bhattacharya's *He Who Rides a Tiger* is a grand joke played by Kalo on the society in order to take revenge. Bhattacharya's humour emerges, to quote

Srivastava, "from his play upon or with words, his comparisons and contrasts, epigrams and paradoxes, from his dealing with incongruities of characters, situations and behaviour, and from sheer exaggerations and light-hearted pleasantries" (1982:121). Kalo talks of the hidden desire of most people to fool themselves as well as the world by naming their children in an attractive way, even if their personalities happen to be diametrically opposite to the given names. Thus, a physically weak person could be named Veer Bahadur or Yudh Veer ("Warrior King" or "Brave in Battle"). A girl with a very dark complexion could be called Bijali Bai ("Lightning Streak") or Saroj Mala ("Lotus Wreath"). Occasionally, Bhabani Bhattacharya also introduces shrewd and dark humour fused with irony and satire through Chandra Lekha and Kalo. His humour is both relative and absolute through his presentation of the difference between appearance and reality without being vulgar and crude.

Khushwant Singh has liberally fused wit and humour in his novels, short stories and journalistic writings. His sense of humour is rooted in the Punjabi soil, is full-blooded, vigorous and suited to the people of all ages. Like Anand and Bhattacharya, Khushwant Singh uses literal translations of Hindi or Punjabi dialogues into English to lend the flavour of native language but they occasionally appear odd, and become a source of fun and humour. Hence in *Train to Pakistan*, "*Apka shubh naam kya hai*" becomes "What honourable name does your honor bear" and "*Apka daulatkhana kidhar hai*" becomes "Where does your wealth reside." (78) In *Delhi*, Bhagmati says, "I would like to eat some fresh air." (37)

The habit of Indians using one noun together with a similar-sounding meaningless word in vernacular appears quite humorous in English. In Khushwant Singh's *Delhi,* a Custom Officer asks the narrator what items he had brought from abroad:

"Any whisky—shisky?"
"No."
"No tape-recorder?"
"No."
"Transistor—shranzistor?"

"No."
"Camera—shamera?"
"No."
"Watch-shatch?"
"No." (3-4)

The encounter has multi-layered implications which evoke laughter. Khushwant Singh's forte is the exaggeration of a trait, an idiosyncrasy, a peculiarity, which would get converted into fun and jollity. While describing the short duration of a devastating dust storm in *Train to Pakistan*, Singh writes: "All this happens in a few seconds. Before you can say *Chakravartiyarajgopalachari*, the gale is gone." (80) In *Delhi*, Khushwant Singh finds the name of a Muslim king "as long as the road from Rikabganj to Paharganj—His Majesty Abul Mazaffar Shahabuddin Mohammed Sahib-i-Qiran Sani, Shadow of God on earth, King of Kings, Monarch of the Universe, Emperor of Hindustan." (124) Khushwant Singh's brand of humour may not quite fit into the traditional mould of decency but it is a mixture of laughing material having buffoonery, political jibes, communication gaffes and social blunders.

Manohar Malgonkar considered himself to be an entertainer whose chief concern was to keep his readers delighted and in good humour. In *A Bend in the Ganges,* he uses the verbal imagery—mostly similes and metaphors—to evoke humour. The clouds overhead are compared to "heaps of enormous gray cabbages." (65) The Pandit had "a clean, luminous face, the colour of a polished lime, a short, beaky nose, a razor-slit for a month, and pale rounded eyes." (33) Tukaram, a rural bullock-cart driver, does not know the difference between goggles and spectacles as is evident in the following conversation:

"What's the matter with your eyes, Chhote-babu?" he [Tukaram] asked.

Gian did not like being addressed as Chhote-baba, the little boy. "Why, nothing," he told him.

"Then why the glasses?"

"They are for the sun," Hari explained.

> "Glasses at your age . . . not even married yet! Your grandmother can still thread a needle." (25)

Malgonkar presents here the rusticity and inviolable innocence of rural people which arouses giggles and laughter among the urban men. Some of the superstitions and orthodox ideas invite Malgonkar's criticism and become a source of irony, humour and satire. A Punjabi girl Bhupinder makes fun of the sacred thread of Gian Talwar:

> Oh, how sweet to be seeing a real sacred thread!" She squealed, and the ripples at fair flesh left out by her tight costume shook with her mirth. And the others all joined in her laughter, trying to surmount the awkwardness that had suddenly come over them. (15)

Malgonkar, at the same time, does not spare modern generation which flaunts new-fangled ideas as ill-fitting as orthodox ones in Indian society. Being a skilful artist and with the aim of making his novel eminently readable, Malgonkar transforms any base material of life into gold through witty dialogues, comic images, caricatures and an earthy brand of humour.

In Anita Desai's *Cry, the Peacock*, humour is fairly subdued because the novel deals with the incompatible and tense married life of Maya and Gautama. Even though the entire novel is tragic, there are places in the novel where Anita Desai seems to have added some comic touches, but they appear so far from spontaneous and natural, so much subdued and mild that one can hardly smile over them. Desai depicts some eccentricities and whimsicalities of the minor characters like the Lals and the Singhs who come close to being caricatured. Leila's husband looks like an animal whereas Pom's husband Kailash shows his eccentricity by always buying green saris for his wife. Pom compares herself to a mouse and her small house to a mouse hole. Her act of comparing herself "with a timid, crouching mouse in a hole" appeared so comical to Maya that she laughed aloud and teased Pom being "so well-fed, so sleek a mouse, with so bright a mouse-hole in which to hide from the cats." (61) Maya also refers to Gautama's clumsy manners and forgetfulness which inject a bit of humour in the novel. Some similes and metaphors are also odd and uncommon. There are several references to laughter in the novel but they do not imply fun or humour. Maya laughs even after Gautama's death because her temperament is childish and she is driven to laughter by certain trivial things. Therefore, her laughter appears cold, hollow and meaningless emanating rather from insanity than from fun and humour.

Even though the story of Arundhati Roy's *The God of Small Things* is so tragic, so teasing and so puzzling, there is an undercurrent of comic vein in it. One finds something pleasant and playful about Roy's use of language—the words and images, the changed spellings, italics—the kind of language which children understand as it makes sense to them in the first impression. The language becomes one of the playthings of the children and provides a lot of humour. Roy joins two or more words, such as, "Finethankyou" and "Mostunfortunate," coins neologisms, such as, "Meeters from the Met, and Greeters from the Gret," splits one word into two or three, such as, "Lay. Ter" and "Never. The. Less." Estha and Rahel marvel over words, play with them and toss them around. The unfamiliar long words assume for children different forms, spellings and meanings in accordance with their limited knowledge so that "Locus standi" becomes "Locusts Stand I," and "pronunciation" becomes "Prer NUN sea ayshun."

An important source of Arundhati Roy's humour is her characterization undertaken through comic images. Chacko looked "like an untidy, beatified porcupine." He had "an amused air about him, and a way of narrowing his eyes as though he was trying to read a faraway sign and had forgotten to bring his glasses. His ears stuck out on either side of his head like teapot handles." (241) Pappachi drew attention to his supposed neglect by his wife Mammachi by sewing buttons that were *not* missing on his shirt. Mammachi, being myopic, would keep the cheques touching her eyelashes, wheeling her eye from word to word. K.N.M. Pillai crossed his arms over his chest and "clasped his own armpits possessively, as though someone had asked to borrow them and he had just refused." (128) Occasionally, the geniality of Arundhati Roy's humour disappears and she resorts to hard-hitting, ironical and satirical expressions against male chauvinists, such as, Pappachi who made "an effort to be civil to the photographer while plotting to murder his wife." (51) The stinging edge of Roy's irony comes when Ammu recalls the fact that the slight glitter in her husband's eyes on the day of wedding was not love or prospect of carnal bliss but eight pegs of whisky. Arundhati Roy's comic imagination makes her puzzlingly tragic novel palatable to the reader.

Jhumpa Lahiri is a diasporic writer who in her *Interpreter of Maladies: Stories of Bengal, Boston and Beyond* gives a number of delightful short stories of immigrants or expatriate Indians about baffling cultural differences. She writes now and then with occasional flashes of comic touches in characterization, in description, in images—particularly similes—in witty remarks, in strange perceptions of children, as also through depiction of cultural dissimilarities. Comic elements have also been introduced in character sketches through the description of some of their oddities and eccentricities. Mr. Pirzada has seven daughters in Pakistan whose names begin with the letter A but which he fails to remember. Lahiri's descriptions are also occasionally marked by comic touches, often by a phrase or an extended simile. Monkeys sat along the branches of trees in Orissa while their long gray tails "dangled like a series of ropes among the leaves." (47) Mrs. Das arranged her sunglasses "on top of her head like a tiara" (50) while her combing brush "resembled an oval bed of nails." (54) Occasionally, a few comic strokes of her pen make the fictional characters or their features quite interesting. Bibi Haldar is "better than coals." (168) The brief images in their casual forms present short yet sharp vignettes which remain so inextricably woven in the reader's memory that one chuckles in lonely hours as they invade the consciousness. The mischievous activities of children, their funny games, casual conversation and queries, and their understandings and misunderstandings create humorous situations. A seven-year-old boy Robin told Miranda, "You're sexy" because he thought the word "sexy" meant someone he did not know, and went on to explain "That's what my father did. He sat next to someone he didn't know, someone sexy, and now he loves her instead of my mother." (107-8) Many examples of witty expressions can be found in dialogues. While buying fish, Mrs. Sen asks if they were fresh and the salesman replies, "Any fresher and they'd answer that question themselves." (127) Jhumpa Lahiri makes her short stories extremely interesting by the fusion of appropriate photographic details and lighter elements of comedy.

There are many Indian novelists in English in whose works humour could have been traced, such as, Ruth Prawer Jhabvala, Nayantara Sahgal, Salman Rushdie, Vikram Seth, Shashi Deshpande, Amitav Ghosh, Manju Kapoor, and others, but in a short research paper, it could not have been done. Due to the same constraints, some of the Indian novelists translated into English, such as Munshi Prem Chand, Rabindranath Tagore, Sharat Chandra Chatterjee and U.R. Anantha Murthy, too, could not be taken up here, though they could be subsequently in a book-length study.

V

Humour in all its genial and sympathetic form is a great product of our civilization. It is not to be judged by the number of guffaws and laughter it evokes but by its quality which illumines and raises our literature to a high pedestal. For Stephen Leacock, good humour does not depend "upon a mere trick and quibble of words, or the odd and meaningless incongruities in things that strike us as 'funny.' Its basis lies in the deeper contrasts offered by life itself." (287-88)

There is hardly any area or activity of life in which wit and humour could not successfully be employed. Be it public or private life, official or personal work, business or commerce, games and sports, politics, legal or medical profession, preaching, teaching or research work, acting in theatre or in movies, travelling in the country or abroad—there is virtually no area in which wit and humour cannot be used to sweeten the activities of life. A lawyer's wit rather than his argument can be more effective in thrashing his adversary in the court. The witty yet judicious comments of a judge silence the court more effectively than do the repeated blows of his hammer. Politicians are known to revel in witty one-liners which become their election slogans. Broken relations can sometimes be mended by a delicate use of witty and comical words. Humour is extremely helpful in university teaching whether the subject be science, arts or literature. Srivastava writes: "By provoking a dull class to laughter, it enlivens the text, creates liveliness where there was dullness, and brings in a gust of fresh air to facilitate both teaching and understanding. A witty remark is quite elucidating. The tiring facts and figures retouched with wit and humour remain permanently embedded in the memory." But he warns against the excessive use, because in his view, "Wit and humour are to teaching what salt and pepper are to food; they must be used as much as add to the taste and not more" (1992: 3). Presidents of the U.S. have utilized humour to seek support and to minimize opposition to their elections by means of ready wit and humour. Indian politicians, too, have begun to hire comic poets to compose humorous rhymes and couplets in their honour. Sometimes, humorous responses help in facing challenging situations. Wit and humour are the sweetened pills of life which may not cure the chronic illnesses around but breed positive attitude, cheerful spirits, and help people bear all kinds of burdens and responsibilities in public and personal life.

Works Cited

Alisky, Marvin. "White House Wit: Presidential Humour to Sustain Policies from Lincoln to Reagan." *Presidential Studies Quarterly,* Spring 1990.

Anand, Mulk Raj. *Untouchable.* New Delhi: Arnold-Heinemann, 1981.

Chandraraju, Aruna. "Have a Laugh," *Hindustan Times Sunday Magazine.* May 15, 2005.

Desai, Anita. *Cry, the Peacock.* New Delhi: Orient Paperbacks, 1980.

Kumar, Shiv K. "Indian Literature Sans Wit and Humour," *Hindustan Times,* 8 March 1986.

Lahiri, Jhumpa. *Interpreter of Maladies: Stories of Bengal, Boston and Beyond.* New Delhi: Harper Collins, 1999.

Leacock, Stephen. *Laugh with Leacock.* Bombay: Jaico, 1957.

Malgonkar, Manohar. *A Bend in the Ganges.* New Delhi: Orient Paperbacks, 1964.

Markandaya, Kamala. *Nectar in a Sieve.* New York: The New American Library, 1954.

Narayan, R.K. *The Man-Eater of Malgudi.* Mysore: Indian Thought Publications, 1968.

Palakeel, Thomas. "Humorist for All Seasons," *Span,* Jan. 1983.

Rao, Raja. *Kanthapura.* ed. C.D. Narasimhaiah. Madras: Oxford University Press, 1978.

Singh, Jacquelin. "Behind the Mask of Comedy," *Span,* February 1979.

_____. "Jest for the Health of It," *Span,* September 1989.

Singh, Khushwant. *Delhi.* New Delhi: Penguin India, 1990.

_____. *Train to Pakistan.* Bombay: India Book House, 1967.

Srivastava, Ramesh K. "Bhattacharya's Prose Style," *Perspectives on Bhabani Bhattacharya*, ed. Ramesh K. Srivastava. Ghaziabad: Vimal, 1982.

_____. "What Is So Great in R.K. Narayan!" *Perspectives on R.K. Narayan*, ed. Atma Ram. Ghaziabad: Vimal, 1981.

_____. "Wit and Humour in University Teaching," *University News,* November 9, 1992.

Tandon, B.G. "Lincoln's Laughter," *Span,* April 2002.

What is Wrong with Novel and Why are They Saying Such Terrible Things against It?

GURUPDESH SINGH

For over a decade now, a big debate has been raging among both practitioners and commentators of novel that novel is nearly dead and irrelevant to the contemporary times, despite the slew of publications, chart toppers and enormous moolah that those concerned makes. Leading the debate is that irrepressible writer and maverick of our times V.S. Naipaul, who has repeatedly written and spoken in several interviews about the bleak future of this genre. In a recent interview given to Rachel Donadio (*The Irascible Prophet: V.S. Naipaul at Home,* New York Times, August 7, 2005), Naipaul again dwelt upon his acute awareness of novel's limitations, its inadequacy as a tool of understanding contemporary reality: "If you write a novel alone you sit and you weave a little narrative. And it's O.K., but it's of no account. If you are a romantic writer, you write novels about men and women falling in love etc., give a little narrative here and there. But again, it's of no account."

Naipaul does not consider it important to read made up stories, when the world is in deep crisis, the civilizations clash in the form of 9/11 catastrophe. He does not seem to be interested even in the details or consequences of the New York attack: "It has just been a spectacle, like a bank raid in a western film. They will be caught by the sheriff eventually." What is more important to him is the erosion of cultures, the religious intolerance and the imbalances in the postcolonial world. To understand and analyse this phenomenon, according to Naipaul, non-fiction is a much more powerful medium than fiction. Reality is so overwhelming and urgently upon us that we have to grapple with it directly without circumventing its force through the tricks of indirection and make-believe. "What I felt was, if you spend your life just writing fiction, you are going to falsify your material and the fictional form was going to force you to do things with the material, to dramatise it in a certain way. I thought non-fiction gave one a chance to explore the world, the other world, the world that one didn't know fully." In a world of global conflicts and invisible adversaries, it was equally important to understand the 'other' besides your own world. Probably, that is the reason Naipaul expended so much time being amongst different societies, religions and people and writing those insightful travelogues. "I thought if I didn't have this resource of non-fiction, I would have dried up perhaps. I'd have come to the end of my material."

But Naipaul's prose we know is no less than a narrative. "I ask simple questions and somehow make a narrative of that discovery," he says. The power of his non-fiction is deeply rooted in the attitudes of a storyteller, his keen observation, his minute attentiveness to individuals, their lives, struggles, triumphs and all those things that make our societies. However, referring to Conrad, Naipaul tells that the best part of *Heart of Darkness* is reportage, the fictional part is excessive and feeble. He likes Conrad because "he wished to look very, very hard at the world" and possibly had rid himself of the 'subtle corruptions of the novel or comedy of errors.' A direct reference to the 19th century where novel revelled in its novelty and flourished in the relative stability of times and the humorous and imaginative portrayal of its subjects. For Naipaul, the world since then has changed and grown bigger. He would like the novelist to leave the sitting room and travel abroad into the active, busy world. Only then he can reach the tragic vision that "the world cannot be contained in the novel."

In a separate essay published parallel to the interview (*Truth is Stronger than Fiction*, New York Review of Books, Aug.7, 2005), Donadio enumerates a list of authors who echo similar sentiments about novel. To sample, just read what Adrienne Miller, a novelist and the literary editor of Esquire has to say: "We're in dark cultural moment. I think people seem to feel more comfortable with non-fiction. The tragic theme here is that literary fiction has very limited cultural currency now. Fewer and fewer people seem to believe fiction is still essential for our emotional and intellectual survival." She also gives examples from international magazines which have decided to cut down on the publication of fiction. The point Donaldio is trying to make is that "novel isn't dead; it just isn't as central to the culture as it was." If we have Harry Potter fantasies selling in millions, it is only to escape the world, not to get illuminated about it. The novel has ceased to perform its function as a mirror or lamp to the society.

In an earlier interview given to Ray Suarez on Online Newshour (March 3, 2000) Naipaul says, "I got more and more convinced that, in this century, we are just carrying out and repeating the programs that were laid down by the great novelists in the last century, when novel was new. And I think that, therefore, a lot of the novel being written in our own time, howsoever intelligent and amusing, does not have any lasting power. They do not have that tension, that convincingness of what is absolutely new. They are novels written by people who have too many models, and possibly the same thing is true of cinema, which is a fair comparison. The first fifty years of the cinema were absolutely great years. Original minds were at work establishing the way to tell a story. And what is happening now is a copying, a pastiche-ing of what was done by great men." Naipaul apparently is missing innovation in the form and content of the contemporary novel. He gets a feeling of déjà vu every time he reads a modern novel and sees in it intertextual layers of the older novel. In fact, he dislikes to call it novel, because there is no novelty left in it.

At the heart of these statements is the suspicion that novel has failed in most of its established roles. If it was a source of entertainment, then it is too time-consuming and expensive by the present standards. People do not have time to spend long hours to pour on a fictional story, especially when you have television, movies, play station or even iPod to compete with. One can barely squeeze out any time for reading in the face of so many entertainment options. If fantasy or science fiction or romance is your diversion then let it be as these hardly qualify for the serious literary novel that critics fear is dying or is dead already. Naipaul anyway is baffled as to the importance of reading invented stories. "I don't see reading as an act of drugging oneself with a narrative. I don't need that" (*Reading and Writing*, New York Review of Books, Feb 18, 1999). The pleasures of reading a novel have been subjugated to its larger purpose of social utility.

If the great literary form of novel lies in its plot, character and events, then it sure has outlived its life. Naipaul believes that most important works of literature were written in the 19th century when the art of narration and fiction making was perfected by such masters as Dickens and Tolstoy having acute sense of social understanding. So each age rethinks and reinvents appropriate forms for itself. "Before the novel in Europe there was the essay, the narrative poem, theatre, the epic poem—all considered the principal forms on various times. There is no longer any need to consider the novel the principal form" (*ibid.*). Jason Cowley (*New Statesman*, Feb. 5, 1999) could not agree more with Naipaul as he experiences the constricting effect of form on his own writing in the "feeling of enervation that comes from working in borrowed forms, from the failure to liberate yourself from the pre-existing structures; at times you can hear the mechanical clunk and grind of your imagination as you move the action forward." The traditional narrative form ensures familiarity, order, artificial shape, resolution, omniscience—all those things that one fails to find in life. Naipaul realized early in his career that this fiction of make-believe could not take him long, so he diversified in travel and psychological realism. In the process of his search for new forms, he intermingled autobiography, social enquiry, reportage, documentary to "render the shifting complexity of the half-formed countries of the decolonized world" (*ibid.*). If fiction is understood as vehicle of imagination, of weaving a web of riveting plots and character, then Naipaul says he has reached the end of imagination. "But the person who, as it were, converts experience into imaginative adventure, he can only do a limited amount of work" (Ray Suarez).

Most of the critics of novel also agree with Naipaul that art forms have a limited tenure. Andrew Marr (*Fact or Fiction?*, *The Observer*, May 27, 2001) writes that novel, like symphony, ballet and representational painting, has a life cycle of invention, full expression and formal decay. Although people may still enjoy novel, but its great work, the time of discovery is over and done and cannot be reopened. In agreement with Naipaul, he writes: "The hundreds of novel craft workers, who have industriously and carefully learned the lessons of plotting and character, of where to be lush and where to be terse, are turning out modern replicas of thinking machines developed to their full a century ago." Ian Jack (*The 'Death' of the Novel*, Granta, May 30, 2001) trying to diagnose the cause of the death of novel, writes in more dramatic terms, "Its work was over, its purpose had gone, it was exhausted. Gentlemen: the novel has had a long time. Cervantes, Sterne, Austen, Melville, Tolstoy, Bellow. Wonderful years when it showed people the human condition as nothing else could. But no matter how much surgery we gave it—its life wasn't infinitely renewable. Gentlemen, quite simply the novel has died of old age."

As suggested above, the art form of novel is closely linked to its purpose and literary function. So most of the admonishers of novel when they stand for Naipaul essentially refer to the great social or realist novel, whose time they think is over. They agree that this function of the novel as an instrument of change has been rather well taken up by other competing media like television, investigative journalism, non-fiction books and even social movies, which can convey the social message in far less time and probably more graphic terms. Tom Wolfe declared long back that fiction couldn't reflect the accelerating grimace of contemporary reality. Naipaul says, "There was a time when fiction provided discoveries about the nature of society, about states, which gave those works of fiction a validity over and above the narrative element." But now, he says, the world cannot be contained in the novel. The novel today, as such, makes no claim to extend the boundaries of how we understand the world. It is no longer a way of understanding the world freshly.

If contemporary reality seems beyond the reach of novel, it is possibly because the new generation of writers are "suspicious of contemporary politics and the ability of language to represent reality" (Michael Bryson, *The Death of the [Canadian] Novel, The Danforth Review*, January 2001). Many critics under the influence of postmodernism think if the novel is dead it is because reality is dead. It has taken a multivalent shape and is practically unknowable. But Bill Buford (*The End of the English Novel*, Granta, 2001) is not much disturbed by such premonitions. He agrees: "postmodernism has inevitably become the reckless collusion of the new and the useless: it smells of literary leftovers, with thoughts like food, not quite digested." Yet he sees a great change happening in today's novel, "What it means to tell, to write, to narrate, to make up is changing, and it is a change significant enough to be distinguished from the aesthetic concerns which have dominated the last eighty years." He invites the writers to recognize the 'particular brutal emptiness' of the twentieth century. But as of now, the current fiction has a tendency of both 'arriving and departing at once.'

Naipaul, on the other hand, as we know, has been arguing for a long time that non-fiction is better suited to dealing with the big issues and capturing the complexities of today's world. In saying so, Naipaul is not justifying his own writings, but in a prophetic way announcing the arrival of non-fiction as a dominant genre of our times. In its expansive sweep, the genre has been changing its tenor radically from being flashy and sensational to highly reflective and stylistically promiscuous. According to Andrew Marr (2001) non-fiction writing is now "more ambition, more interesting, more dangerous than fiction—the tricks of the novel in rhythm, setting, authorial intervention and characterization have been better learned by new generation of historians and biographers than by the novelists." Donadio (2005) quoting Cullen Murphy, former Editor of *Atlantic Monthly* writes, "certain kinds of non-fiction writing have claimed some of the territory once claimed by fiction. Not because non-fiction writing has become 'fictional,' in the sense of taking liberties, but because certain traits that used to be standard in fiction like a strong sense of plot and memorable characters in the service of important and morally charged subject matter, are today as reliably found in narrative non-fiction as they are in literary fiction. Some might even say 'more reliably' found." The implication is if truth or facts can be packaged in a creative manner then why people would turn to fiction for understanding the world. No wonder then that the 9/11 Official Commission Report has sold more than a million copies. Non-fiction, anyway, is much quicker to take up the topical issue.

If non-fiction narrative shows ample signs of fictional strategies, then the reverse is true as much. Contemporary fiction has also directly included prose forms like newspaper reporting, journal writing, political discourse, history, philosophy in an ever thinning format of novel in works like *Sophie's World* and *Riot*, to quote just a couple of blatant examples. Shashi Tharoor's *Riot* particularly calls for a serious enquiry into the current state of novel. With a gossamer thin plot of a murder mystery, if Tharoor can present current Indian political crisis with reference to real issues, real people, real events, then how much of it can be really called a novel, as he prefers to do it. The formal ambivalence of this novel in fact speaks of the dilemma that Tharoor, like Naipaul, must have faced. The theme of the novel is more suited to the non-fictional mode than novel, but caught in the steel cage of a fictional form, he is desperate to devise an innovation that can do justice to his narrative compulsions. In a proxy statement, Lakshman, the protagonist, expresses the anguish of Tharoor: "I'd like to write a novel that doesn't read like a novel. Novels are too easy—they tell a story, in a linear narrative, from start to finish. They've done that for decades. Centuries perhaps. I'd do it differently." (135)

Naipaul was quick to realize those handicaps early in his working career, made true confessions about them and shifted to a form that allowed him more freedom and creative expression. In his August 7, 2005 interview, he told that he wrote *Half a Life* only to fulfill a publisher's contract and that *Magic Seeds* would be his last novel. In the recent past, we have also seen more and more Indian fiction writers taking up the alternative route of non-fiction to explore their world and give shape to their creative muse. Leading them is Arundhati Roy, who since her Booker Prize-winner has produced two major volumes of prose (and no novel). Shashi Tharoor himself is in the good company of such eminent fiction writers like Khushwant Singh and Shobha De, contributing a regular column to leading newpapers or producing exclusive books of essays.

Speaking about the laborious form that Roy's novel acquires due to its 'flabby plot' and 'overworked prose' (apart from other things), David Robson in the *Daily Telegraph* wrote, "Arundhati Roy's victory left me close to despair, if this is the novel of the year, then the novel is dead." (qtd. Lakshmi Gopalkrishnan Booker Snooker at *slate.msn. .com/id/1837*). One may not agree with the harsh criticism, but the message is clear. Novel with its contrived plots, fanciful characters and stylized diction is not able to sustain the cravings of a serious reader, who would like this world represented in more truthful, reliable and intimate terms.

To conclude, I would like to say that societies like India with plurality of cultures and a multitude of conflicting communities, histories, religions should listen to the following words of caution from Naipaul. Expressing his uncertainty on the usefulness of the novel form for India, Naipaul wrote, "But where, as in India, the past has been torn away, and history is unknown or unknowable or denied, I don't know whether the borrowed form of the novel can deliver more than a partial truth, a dim lighted window in a general darkness" (1999).

Contributors

Jagdish Batra	Hindu College, Sonepat
Santosh K. Bhatia	Guru Nanak Dev University, Amritsar
Ravi Bhushan	Govt. College, Nalwa (Hisar)
Subhash Chander	Research Scholar, Jammu University
P.K. Dey	Burdwan University, West Bengal
Sarika Goyal	D.A.V. College, Abohar
Seema Jain	Kanya Mahavidyalaya, Jalandhar
Sushil Kansal	S.D. College, Ambala Cantt.
Tejinder Kaur	Punjabi University, Patiala
Adarsh Khanna	Hansraj Mahila Mahavidyalaya, Jalandhar
Asha Khurana	M.D.S.D. Girls College, Ambala City
K.K. Khurana	D.A.V. College, Ambala City
Sanjeev Kumar	Govt. College, Ambala Cantt.
Jaspreet Mander	Punjabi University, Patiala
Swaraj Raj	Government Mohindra College, Patiala
Alka Sharma	S.D. College (Lahore), Ambala Cantt.
Pankaj Sharma	Research Scholar, Jammu University
Roshan Lal Sharma	Government College, Solan
S.K. Sharma	Kurukshetra University, Kurukshetra
Gurupdesh Singh	Guru Nanak Dev University, Amritsar
Ramesh K. Srivastava	Bundelkhand University, Jhansi
Vineeta	C.I.S.K.M.V. Dhand-Dadwana, Kaithal
Karan Singh Yadav	Govt. College, Ateli, Mahendragarh